Contemporary Belarus

Between democracy and dictatorship

Edited by
Elena A. Korosteleva,
Colin W. Lawson and
Rosalind J. Marsh

Routledge
Taylor & Francis Group
LONDON AND NEW YORK

First published 2003 by Routledge

2 Park Square, Milton Park, Abingdon, Oxfordshire OX14 4RN
711 Third Avenue, New York, NY 10017

Routledge is an imprint of the Taylor & Francis Group, an informa business

First issued in paperback 2018

Transferred to Digital Printing 2006

Typeset in Times by
Florence Production Ltd, Stoodleigh, Devon

British Library Cataloguing in Publication Data
A catalogue record for this book is available from the British Library

Library of Congress Cataloging in Publication Data
A catalog record for this book has been requested

ISBN 978-0-700-71613-5 (hbk)
ISBN 978-0-367-02689-9 (pbk)

Contemporary Belarus

Belarus is unique among the states of the former Soviet bloc, in that after twelve years of 'transition', the country remains 'stalled' and backward-oriented. Political and economic changes are characterised by half-measures, and recently a new suppression of dissent has been introduced; the country balances between the prospect of democracy and a retreat to authoritarianism. These developments contrast starkly with the many democratic changes in neighbouring states and suggest a possible alternative path for future development in Eastern Europe.

This book provides a thorough overview of current developments in Belarus. It looks at historical, political, economic and social changes, and at international relations, especially those with Russia and the European Union. It addresses a broader theoretical discussion to define the type of democracy, if any, that exists in Belarus, exploring the prospects for further democratisation.

Elena A. Korosteleva is the British Academy Postdoctoral Research Fellow at the Department of Politics, University of Glasgow, and is Research Network Coordinator for an INTAS project (99–00245) on 'The Comparative Analysis of Charismatic Political Leadership in Russia, Belarus and Ukraine'.

Colin W. Lawson is Reader in Economics at the University of Bath. He did his undergraduate and postgraduate training at the London School of Economics and has written extensively on the economics and political economy of transition, particularly in relation to Central and Eastern Europe.

Rosalind J. Marsh is Professor of Russian Studies, University of Bath, and Vice-President (formerly President) of the British Association for Slavonic and East European Studies (BASEES). She has written widely on Soviet and post-Soviet politics and culture, women in post-Soviet states, and European feminism.

Contents

Tables

Notes on contributors

Olga Belova-Gille is a PhD student at Science Po Paris (France) and a visiting scholar at the Yale Center for International and Area Studies, Yale University (USA). Her research interests include political elites and their influence on the nature of political systems in the post-Soviet countries such as Russia, Ukraine and Belarus. Her e-mail address is olgagille@aol.com.

Aliaksandr N. Danilov is Professor of Sociology at the Department of Sociology, Belarusian State University (BSU) in Minsk. He is also a member of the Belarusian Academy of Science, and principal editor for the specialist journal *Sociology* (BSU). He is author of more than 150 publications, including six monographs in Russian and Belarusian. His research interests include theory and methodology of sociology. His e-mail address is Isr@bsu.by.

Teresa Dumasy was Senior Research Analyst for Ukraine, Belarus and Moldova at the Foreign and Commonwealth Office, London, from 1998 to 2000. A language graduate, she later studied at the University of Cambridge, England, where she received a Masters in International Relations and a PhD in History. Her academic research included studies of Russian–Ukrainian relations following Ukrainian independence and Soviet foreign policy and the Hungarian uprising of 1956. She has lived and travelled in Eastern and Central Europe. Currently working at the British Embassy in Paris, she deals, in particular, with policy towards Africa and international aid and development issues. Her e-mail address is teresa.dumasy@freesbee.fr. or tdamasy@paris.mail.fco.gov.uk for urgent messages.

Christian W. Haerpfer is visiting Research Professor in Comparative Politics in the Centre for the Study of Public Policy (CSPP) at the University of Strathclyde, Glasgow (UK), and Director of the Centre for Strategic Development (CSD) at the Institute for Advanced Studies, Vienna (Austria). He teaches Political Science Research Methods in the Department of Politics at the University of Vienna and he is Scientific

Director of IHS-Burgenland at the Austrian–Hungarian border. He was visiting Professor in Comparative Politics at the Central European University in Prague (Czech Republic) and Research Fellow at the University of Essex in Colchester (UK) and the European University Institute in Florence (Italy). Christian Haerpfer is an academic consultant to the European Bank for Reconstruction and Development (EBRD) in London (UK), the European Commission in Brussels (Belgium) and the World Bank in New York (USA). His e-mail address is haerpfer@ihs.ac.at.

Elena A. Korosteleva received her Doctoral Degree at the Department of European Studies, University of Bath, and is Research Network Co-ordinator for an INTAS project (99–00245) on 'The Comparative Analysis of Charismatic Political Leadership in Russia, Belarus and Ukraine'. She is a Candidate of Social Science (Political Sociology), Belarusian State University. She has recently been awarded a Post-Doctoral Fellowship by the British Academy to be taken at the Department of Politics, University of Glasgow, 2001–4. She has published articles and chapters in books on the development of political parties in Eastern Europe. Her e-mail address is E.A.Korosteleva@socsci.gla.ac.uk (website http://www.gla.ac.uk/departments/politics/staff/korosteleva-polglase.htm).

Julia Korosteleva is a PhD student at the Department of Economics and International Development, University of Bath. On her graduation from the Minsk State Economic University, Belarus, in 1997, she became an employee of the JSSB 'Belarusbank' in Minsk. Soon after, Julia was promoted to the position of head of the Foreign Economic Development Division at the JSSB. In 2000 she was awarded an Overseas Research and Departmental Scholarship to undertake postgraduate research in the economic policy-making of Belarus *vis-à-vis* other small newly emerged states of Central and Eastern Europe. Her main research interests include transition financial systems in Central and Eastern Europe. Her e-mail address is ecpjak@bath.ac.uk.

Denis Krivosheev is currently completing his PhD on post-cold war British security policy at the Department of Government, University of Manchester. He studied philosophy and international relations at the Belarusian State University in Minsk, and received an MA (Econ.) in international relations at the University of Manchester in 1997. Denis Krivosheev was an intern at the Belarusian Ministry of Foreign Affairs in 1996, and has since worked for various NGOs, including Amnesty International. He is a regular speaker on the issue of Belarusian foreign policy and has published on the issue of security politics. His e-mail address is dkrivosheev@hotmail.com.

Colin W. Lawson is Reader in Economics in the Department of Economics and International Development at the University of Bath. After studying at the London School of Economics under Peter Wiles he moved to Bath, and has also held visiting posts at Harvard, Wisconsin and Manchester. He is a specialist in the economics of transition, and has also written on development economics, international trade and public economics. He has written on Albania, and the Czech and Slovak Republics, as well as on Belarus. His e-mail address is C.W.Lawson@bath.ac.uk (website http://www.bath.ac.uk/~hsscwl).

Nadezhda Lisovskaia is a PhD student at the Department of Government, University of Manchester. She received professional experience at the Ministry of Foreign Affairs and the Centre for the Analysis of World Economic Problems, Belarus. She obtained a Master's Degree at the University of Manchester. She has presented papers at conferences (BASEES, PSA) and published articles on economic issues of post-socialist transitions and the politics of international trade in Belarus, Russia and the UK. Her main interests include international political economy, transition, globalisation and the World Trade Organisation, international trade and finance. Her e-mail address is nlisovskaya@hotmail.com or anastasia_nesvetailova@hotmail.com.

David R. Marples is Professor of Russian and East European History at the University of Alberta, and Director of the Stasiuk Program on Contemporary Ukraine at the Canadian Institute of Ukrainian Studies. He is a Vice-President of the Association for the Study of Nationalities (New York) and the Associate Editor of *Canadian Slavonic Papers*. He is the author of eight books, including two on the Chernobyl disaster, and more recently, *Lenin's Revolution: Russia 1917–1921* (London: Wesley, Addison and Longman, 2000) and *Belarus: A Denationalized Nation* (Amsterdam: Harwood Academic Publishers, 1999). In 1999 he was awarded the Faculty of Arts Research Prize for Full Professors by the University of Alberta. He has published recent articles in *The Harriman Review*, *Nationalities Papers*, *Post-Soviet Geography and Economics*, and *Vermont Law Review*. He has served as a consultant on both Ukraine and Belarus on a regular basis to the US Department of State, External Affairs Canada, and the Senate Foreign Relations Committee, Government of Canada. His research interests lie in Belarus, Ukraine, and Russia, and he can be reached by e-mail at david.marples@ualberta.ca.

Rosalind J. Marsh is Professor of Russian Studies, University of Bath, and Vice-President (formerly President) of the British Association for Slavonic and East European Studies (BASEES). She previously held posts at the Queen's University of Belfast and at the University of Exeter, where she was Director of the Centre for Russian, Soviet and

East European Studies from 1989 to 1991. She is the author of *Soviet Fiction since Stalin: Science, Politics and Literature* (London and Sydney: Croom Helm, 1986), *Images of Dictatorship: Stalin in Literature* (London and New York: Routledge, 1989), and *History and Literature in Contemporary Russia* (London: Macmillan, 1995); and has edited four books on women in Russia and Ukraine, Russian women's culture and European feminism. She has written widely on Soviet and post-Soviet politics and culture, and her research interests include the role of the intelligentsia in the former USSR. Her e-mail address is R.J.Marsh@Bath.ac.uk.

Anastasia Nesvetailova is a PhD student at the Department of International Politics, University of Wales, Aberystwyth. She obtained her Master's Degree in International Political Economy with Distinction from the Department of Government, Manchester University. Her academic interests include the political economy of finance; capitalist formations; and the social structures of capital. In her postgraduate research she also focuses on the political economy of money and finance in the USSR and its successor states; the societal organisation of the post-Soviet states; and the relationship with western politico-economic elites and groups. Her e-mail address is Aan00@aber.ac.uk.

David G. Rotman is Professor of Sociology at the Department of Sociology, Belarusian State University. He is Director of the Centre for Social and Political Research, BSU, and involved in various international projects, including New Democracies Barometer (R. Rose and C. Haerpfer), research of electoral behaviour (H.D. Klingemann), COPERNICUS (C. Wallace, Austria), and INTAS (99–00245). He has more than 150 publications, including seven monographs. His major research interests include electoral behaviour, sociology of politics and youth issues. His e-mail address is Rotman@bsu.by.

Vital Silitski is Reader in Political Economy, European Humanities University, Minsk, Belarus. He received a Doctoral Degree in Political Science at Rutgers University, USA. His research interests include democratisation and authoritarianism in post-communist states; the politics of economic reform in Central and Eastern Europe and the former USSR; and the political economy of EU enlargement and its impact on the non-accession countries of Eastern Europe. He is a visiting Fellow at Central European University, Budapest. His e-mail address is brother_in_arms@yahoo.com.

Jan Zaprudnik is a graduate of the Catholic University of Louvain, Belgium (1954), and holds a Doctoral Degree in history from New York University (1969). He worked for Radio Liberty's Belarusian Service. Dr Zaprudnik has also taught the history of Russia and the Soviet Union at Queen's College of the City University of New York, and the history and politics of Belarus at the Harriman Institute of Columbia University. His books include *Belarus: At a Crossroads in History* (Westview Press, 1993) and *Historical Dictionary of Belarus* (Scarecrow Press, 1998). He has also made numerous contributions to journals and books on Belarus, Russia and other post-Soviet states. Jan Zaprudnik has visited his homeland regularly since 1991, keeping in touch with Belarus's world of politics, culture and scholarship. His e-mail address is Janzap@aol.com.

Acknowledgements

Financial support from INTAS (99–00245) and the British Academy (SG-31102) created a unique opportunity for successful collaboration with scholars from Moscow State University, Kiev Academy of Sciences, and especially the Belarusian State University in Minsk. This provided empirical grounds for the research conclusions in this book, based on the findings of the two-year project 'The Comparative Analysis of Charismatic Leadership in Russia, Belarus and Ukraine: its emergence, mobilisation and sustainability'.

We are also grateful to the European Research Institute at the University of Bath and its director Alan Butt Philip for funding the conference 'Belarus: the Forgotten Heart of Europe?' in February 2000, at which earlier versions of many of the chapters in the volume were presented. We should like to thank all the participants in the conference, who helped to make the occasion so successful and to stimulate debate and further reflection on many issues discussed herein.

The advice of Stephen White and Michael Kaser has been particularly helpful in preparing this volume.

Note on translation and transliteration

The majority of proper names have been given in their Belarusian form. Unless otherwise stated, all translations are by the contributors or editors. Belarusian, Russian and Ukrainian names have been transliterated in the text using Library of Congress transliteration (without diacritics), with the exception of some commonly occurring names such as Yeltsin and Minsk.

1 Introduction

Paradoxes of democratisation in post-communist Belarus

Elena A. Korosteleva, Colin W. Lawson and Rosalind J. Marsh

Until very recently, Belarus has received relatively little attention from western scholars and policy-makers. However, the political and economic development of Belarus since the fall of communism is eminently worthy of further investigation. First, Belarus, situated in the centre of the European continent, bordered by Russia, Ukraine, Lithuania, Latvia and Poland, occupies an important geostrategic position, and as the European Union and NATO enlarge, it could have a vital influence on the stability of Europe. Second, Belarus deserves to be better known to the world community because by the beginning of the twenty-first century it appears to be in full retreat from democracy and ruled by an increasingly repressive leadership. Since the rise to power of President Lukashenka in 1994, the country's constitution has been arbitrarily changed; elections have not been free and fair; parliament and the independent media have been suppressed; opposition leaders have unaccountably disappeared, been arrested or exiled; the authorities have increasingly relied on the security services (the KGB has not even been renamed); and there have been constant violations of human and civil rights. Third, post-communist Belarus provides an interesting case study because of its singular path of political and economic transition. Unlike many other post-communist states, it has defied all expectations and failed to move either in the direction of nationalism or towards democracy and a free market. This book aims to suggest, on the basis of an analysis of the hybrid post-communist regime in Belarus, that such contradictory developments need to be taken into account by general theorists of transition and the process of democratisation. Further, it will pose the question: is Belarus, after the fall of Miloševich in Serbia, the last dictatorship in Europe? Or have the preconditions for a democracy already been laid?

Several valuable studies of the history and politics of Belarus have appeared in English since the mid- and late 1990s, including some by contributors to the present volume.[1] David R. Marples has analysed Belarus's political development up to 1996–7, arguing that Belarus is largely 'a denationalized nation' – nationalism and anti-Russian feeling did not provide a new ideology or organising principle able to fill the vacuum left by the collapse of the USSR, as it did in Ukraine, the Baltic States and many other states of the CIS.[2] Kathleen Mihalisko has explored Belarus's exceptional development in the context of other post-communist transitions, emphasising factors that inherently favour and oppose democratic progress.[3] Garnett and Legvold have focused on Belarus's international situation, analysing its crucial importance for European security,[4] and White and Rose have produced a useful comparative survey of public opinion in Belarus, Russia and Ukraine in the year 2000.[5] The aim of the present volume is to update previous research, evaluating recent trends and the prospects for democratisation at the beginning of the twenty-first century.

It was in order to satisfy the perceived need to increase public and scholarly knowledge about Belarus that the first conference on post-communist Belarus in the UK was held at the University of Bath in February 2000. This book is based on revised and updated versions of papers given at the conference. The introduction will discuss the current political and economic situation in Belarus up to 2001, situating its development in the context of other 'third-wave' transitions, particularly in the states of the former USSR, before proceeding to summarise the main arguments of the book.

Third wave transitions[6]

The last decades of the twentieth century have witnessed the birth of many *new* regimes. Most countries in Latin America and almost all states in Central and Eastern Europe have begun remarkable transformations from semi-closed economies towards a free market; and from dictatorial-style regimes towards liberal democratic polities. Many political scholars emphasise the *sui generis* nature of the new regimes, primarily associated with (i) the high complexity of the transitional tasks[7] and (ii) the incomplete and non-progressive institutionalisation of the system. Scholars agree that many new regimes fit the minimal criteria of a polyarchy,[8] having adopted the practice of elections and certain democratic liberties. Nevertheless, inwardly they have appeared to demonstrate a different mode of development. Third-wave democracies are often cited as 'democracies by default', 'semi-democracies' or even 'façade democracies'.[9] This essentially implies little system change, populist politics, the lowering of public expectations of what could be achieved through political action, and consequently, low-level participation and delegated leadership in an 'alegal' environment, that is to say, a system that is not protected by its own constitution. Regimes of this type are, paradoxically, sustainable, and characterised by various degrees of non-institutionalisation, under-representation and non-intensive political competition. This suggests that a continuing enquiry into theories of transition and the process of democratisation should be undertaken.

Post-Soviet states, of which Belarus is one, have appeared to embark on a more complex transition to a democratic polity than any others in the European region. Historically, these countries were strongholds of socialism, and simultaneously, the initiators of transition. Culturally and structurally, they suffered most from inherited legacies and unresolved conflicts. Their present development has led to economic stagnation and impending system collapse, as well as the lingering threat of 'red' (or 'red–brown') dictatorship, mass alienated politics, extreme social divisions, and growing international isolation. The latter is particularly alarming for the Commonwealth of Independent States (CIS). The dual enlargement of the European Union and NATO eastwards, as well as the incorporation of more successful Central and East European countries (CEECs) into a global capitalist market, means that the states of the former Soviet Union feel increasingly isolated from the 'new' Europe. This isolation is not only geographical, but also isolation outside a newly built political and economic 'Schengen Wall'. This sense of exclusion, especially among the borderland countries like Belarus, Ukraine and Moldova, has begun to be manifested in an emerging conflict of identities – such as a pro-European versus a pro-Slavic Russian identity – and in an understanding of the limited opportunities that might be available to the ruling elite in this structurally constrained environment.[10] The situation has been aggravated by Russia strengthening its control over the borderland countries, primarily through demanding repayment of debts and limiting energy supplies to the dependent CIS states.

Belarus is a good candidate for analysis because it is an exemplar of the difficulties associated with third-wave transition and the CIS in particular. Its transition to democracy has been slow and disruptive. In 2001, Belarus was in its eleventh year of 'transition' from the *old* to the *new* regime, and, nevertheless, its democratic progress remains unsound, economic restructuring has not been initiated, parties remain weak and powerless, and the prospect of dictatorship is looming. Indeed, contemporary Belarus has arrived at a crossroads of transition: what lies ahead is either an irrevocable path to democracy or a slide backwards to dictatorship.

An overview of Belarus

The Republic of Belarus formally declared independence from the former Soviet system on 25 August 1991 and became – for only the second time in its history (a short-lived National Republic having been established in 1918) – an independent sovereign state. However, its path to democracy appears to be a long and unsuccessful *detour*. Its first parliamentary elections in March–April 1990 resulted in a short-term success for the democrats, who established the first 'Democratic Club' with nearly one-third of its deputies gaining seats in parliament. However, the communist majority prevailed and continued a course of counter-reform similar to that of the pre-*perestroika* period. In 1992 the nationalists initiated a call for new parliamentary elections which was widely supported by the electorate, but contemptuously ignored by the old-fashioned parliament. The latter was replaced only in 1995 by a new multi-party legislature after the first relatively competitive elections. However, while changing its external appearance, parliament internally remained unchanged. There was still a relative majority of non-partisan (48 per cent) and Left-oriented deputies (22 per cent communists and 17 per cent agrarians), and very few others. Its democratic tenure was brief and in most respects ended with the introduction of the presidency in 1994. The first President of the Republic of Belarus, Aliaksandr Lukashenka, dissolved the parliament in 1996, following an alteration to the 1994 constitution. Nevertheless, parliament continued to meet and was still recognised by all major international authorities on the basis of the 1994 constitution. President Lukashenka's term of office should have expired in July 1999; however, he did not accept this, and accordingly altered the constitution by referendum, allowing himself two more years in power. Consequently, parliamentary elections took place in autumn 2000, but none of the existing opposition parties expressed a desire to participate in them, and thus did not attempt to negotiate with the authorities through democratic means. At present the country is living through the aftermath of the 2001 presidential election, during which it proved difficult, if not impossible, for the opposition to challenge President Lukashenka, who remains the only credible leader in the contemporary Belarusian political arena.

Historically, Belarus possessed the structural foundation on which democracy could have been built, but this appeared to be insufficient for national consolidation. This foundation included a relatively stable economy,[11] significant intellectual capital, existing political divisions, an emerging opposition, and eager voters. However, structural and institutional factors[12] – as well as the decisive intervention of the 'elite factor' – have delayed democratisation. Notably, political parties – the basis of a strong democratic system – have failed twice to gain office and to sustain the momentum for change: first, in the 1995 parliament and second, as a result of their failure to win votes and seats in the 2000 parliamentary elections. Petty disputes, lack of co-operation and arguments between and within the parties led to a pessimistic prognosis about their future potential. Because of their continuing inability to win seats in parliament, parties have become increasingly disregarded by the electors, who would rather enjoy short-term benefits from the state than believe in parties' long-term promises. The populist President Aliaksandr Lukashenka, with his appointed loyal administration and system of clienteles, continues to control the 'representative' institutions of parliament, as well as the Constitutional Court, the mass media and the state bureaucracy. Paradoxically, the regime in Belarus remains sustainable, as in many other post-Soviet democracies, with the power balance heavily weighted towards the presidency and away from the legislature.

Paradoxes of contemporary policy-making in Belarus

Belarus displays a good example of a façade regime in which democratic 'scaffolding' conceals a dictatorial style of polity building. For example, outwardly Belarus seems to be a stable economy characterised by optimistic transition indexes[13] and economic growth. Inwardly, however, it presents a case of impending economic and political crises with no policy for reform. Externally, Belarus 'fits' the criteria of a developing polyarchy, as it has an institutionalised practice of elections and has nominally guaranteed constitutional liberties to its citizenry. Internally, the legal and bureaucratic systems fail to protect and promote individual human rights, and there are many informal mechanisms that allow the government to manipulate public opinion to its own advantage. Finally, there is an impression of an active political society. This is associated with a stable number of national political parties with crystallised ideological profiles, a multiplicity of non-governmental organisations (NGOs) and the consolidation of trade unions. However, this does not necessarily lead to the conclusion that they all possess equal opportunities to gain access to the decision-making arena. Since the alteration of the 1994 constitution this has been the sole prerogative of the incumbent President and his government, and subsequently Belarus has been ruled under a system of superpresidentialism.[14]

The economy

Owing to its geopolitical location and economic position, Belarus has been faced with a more complex transition than that of Central and East European countries (CEECs). On the one hand, Belarus has always been dependent on Russia's natural resources, and hence, its foreign policy-making. On the other hand, with its orientation to the East, and the involvement of CEECs in a transnational framework of co-operation,[15] the position of Belarus and many other CIS countries in the international arena is rapidly attaining the position of a self-contained regime situated beyond Europe's new 'Iron Curtain'.[16] As Light notes, 'There is an increasing belief in the outsider states that being "between" is not just a physical reality, but implies having to choose between Russia and the West.'[17] A feeling of exclusion has also been reinforced by the gradual economic progress of the CEECs, in contrast to the performance of the CIS states which have been lagging far behind in their development, despite the shared legacies of the Soviet past.

Belarus can be formally described as a regime moving towards 'democracy' as a state counterposed to its totalitarian past. Nevertheless, it still preserves many features of the command economy with central planning and limited privatisation. As Stephen White notes, the 'move to democracy' in Belarus, as in the case of many other CIS states, is a term which has to be carefully applied within the area: despite their façade features, some countries 'fall short of democratic practice' and 'go beyond a competitive struggle for the popular vote'.[18]

Belarus, like many other CIS regimes, has not yet seriously considered the wholesale restructuring of its economic system. The relatively enthusiastic initiation of reforms at the outset of transition seems to have stalled towards the end of the decade, and after the 1998 financial crisis in Russia, Belarus went into continuing recession. The average index of transitional progress in the new European democracies varies from 2.3 in the CIS, 2.7 in the Balkan countries, 3.2 in the Baltic countries, to the highest 3.5 score in East Central Europe on a 0–5 scale, with 4.3 being the highest score achieved by any one country.[19] However, as some scholars note, the averaging of disparate data that produces these scores is probably flattering to the CIS states.[20]

Belarus demonstrates a certain level of economic development.[21] The republic has been classified as a lower middle-income country by the World Bank.[22] Nevertheless, even if some of the transition indicators in Belarus presently demonstrate no economic decline, there are grounds to question the sustainability of its growth and development in the future. Belarus's cumulative level of direct foreign investment *per capita* has been rated as 'the lowest of its former centrally planned neighbours'.[23] In addition, its private sector contribution to GDP was 20 per cent, compared with 70 per cent in Russia, 55 per cent in Ukraine, and 45 per cent in Moldova. Belarus has not progressed far in any of the main transition indicators, including (i) macro-economic stabilisation; (ii) private sector development; (iii) liberalisation of prices and trade; (iv) enterprise reform; and (v) development of financial institutions. Hence, analysis of Belarus's problematic economic progress in transition will not only be revealing but also illustrative of the CIS development as a whole. This is undertaken by Colin Lawson, Anastasia Nesvetailova, and Nadezhda Lisovskaia in conjunction with Julia Korosteleva in the economic chapters of this book.

Institutional and structural environments

At the outset of reforms Belarus formally possessed certain characteristics of a pluralistic society: a structure favouring political debate and opposition, and representative institutions voted for periodically. Such a society, nevertheless, did not take shape, due to incongruous interactions between structures, institutions and individual actors. It has turned out that legacies and inherited structures, reinforced by institutional developments, have created an unfavourable environment for further democratic system consolidation in Belarus. At the same time, the low ideological profile of parties and other interest organisations, their inability to capitulate on voters' preferences and their limited organisational and financial capacities explain why the system remains fragile and dominated by presidential decision-making.

Unlike other newly emerged states, Belarus had a limited pre-authoritarian experience, which did not aid the development of institutional and participatory skills for independent existence and policy-making. In addition, the authoritarian legacies of a Moscow-centred system, an inactive civil society, a mixed population demographics, a lack of natural resources and a strategic geopolitical position predetermined Belarus's role *within* the operation of the CIS. Nevertheless, the resources and incentives did exist in Belarus to stimulate an independent and democratic path of development; and comparative analysis provides evidence of the concealed power of political/social conflicts that could have led to the emergence of opposition forces and mass mobilisation.[24] Paradoxically, neither the conflicts, nor opposition elite bargaining inspired political forces to follow the path of democratisation. The process of building democracy in Belarus has taken an alternative route.

The alteration of Belarus's transitional path did not occur only because of either Lukashenka's excellent manoeuvring skills or the incompetent strategies of his opponents, including their lack of preparation, their absence of internal unity, and the petty wars they fought with each other. There were also structural factors, such as opportunities for the old-guard elites, censorship, and public adherence to a strong leadership, that promoted non-democratic political change.

Structural legacies, especially a weak state, fully exploited by the *nomenklatura,* ineffective law, a system of patronage, and structural dependence on Russia remain the principal obstacles to party system institutionalisation. These have also been reinforced by the public's traditionalist adherence to a strong leadership, a moderate nationalist stance and a pining for Soviet-era stability, which have been skilfully exploited by Lukashenka in referenda. In addition, pre-existing but subtle political divides, of which the main ones are the dichotomies between the centre and the periphery, and between European and Russian identity, have had both positive and negative effects on the consolidation of the opposition.

A new regime in Belarus was structurally driven to amalgamate the properties of the socialist state. New developments were bound to occur in a situation dominated by former structures and a pervasive agency, that is, the *nomenklatura*. The whole situation had opened up a window of opportunity for the rise of a Lukashenka-type of politician and for the formation of a paradoxically sustainable regime based on a combination of strong leadership and a truncated representation of public interests – a delegative type of polyarchy. This presupposes unlimited authority for the popularly elected leader, juxtaposed with limited representation and a low level of citizenship.[25] Despite its democratic façade, this type of regime may lead to a dictatorship, when not reinforced by functional representative institutions.

Institutional factors also have an inverse effect on the process of democratisation. First of all, in Belarus the strong presidency was supported by all political forces – by the democratic opposition, in an attempt to avoid inertia in decision-making; and by the Communist old guard in order to secure their position in a changing society. Nevertheless, this 'move' from a 'semi-parliamentary' to a presidential regime, with Lukashenka's accession to power, appeared to be fatal for the fragile democracy in the republic.

Lukashenka used various levers to concentrate power in his hands and avoid consensual policy-making. For example, by amending the constitution in 1996 Lukashenka has not only changed the arrangements of governance, but with popular consent he has also shifted power away from the legislature and formed a regime of supreme presidential authority. The implication of this restructuring was the alteration of the course of democratisation, which could no longer be called 'representative'. Stretching a point, Belarus's transitional façade can be defined as a 'delegative' type of democracy; however, the balance between this democracy and imminent dictatorship is very fragile. The autumn 2000 parliamentary elections could have 'saved' the situation from the looming prospect of dictatorship if the opposition parties had participated in the campaign. This, however, did not occur, and the country presently finds itself on a path remote from democracy.

Lukashenka has proved that it is quite possible to overrule institutional limits and to tailor the constitution to the tailor's needs, if personal ambitions and available resources permit. In order to achieve such stunning results, one must play 'the game' as forcefully and devotedly as the President does, following the principle of 'winner-takes-all' or 'all or nothing'. Belarus is presently characterised by a malleable parliament, weak parties and an all-permissive electorate. Behind this façade there appear to be not only agents, but also an agency that permits unlimited public tolerance of political will power and demagoguery, and allows structural loopholes for these outrageous political moves.

A paradoxical electorate

Public opinion in Belarus is also highly ambivalent. On the one hand, the Belarusian electorate distinctly favours strong leadership and the populist promises of the incumbent President and authoritarian leader Aliaksandr Lukashenka. His public rating has not changed over the last three years and has remained consistently around 41 to 45 per cent on average, whereas the rating of other political actors has significantly declined. On the other hand, the electors show positive and stable attitudes to further democratisation, resistance to the idea of dictatorship and no desire to retreat back to the USSR. These contradictions may be conditioned by many factors, which will be explored in the following chapters of the book.

The prominence of existing political conflicts and their under-representation in the public sphere determine the degree of controversy and division in society. On the one hand, public opinion favours the issues of independence, nation-building, the inevitability of radical economic reforms, and on the other hand, reunion with Russia, social security and immediate state benefits. It is literally split in two. Nevertheless, the existing political actors represent people's needs inadequately, since the opposition parties are not in public office to make policies; and the pro-government parties unanimously express the official discourse dictated by the President. These factors obviously lower the degree of representation of public interests, which subsequently causes high levels of volatility and public distrust of parties. Parties are perceived therefore as not being capable of winning office, and the population becomes increasingly unresponsive towards their appeals.

Consequently, this increases people's approval of the presidential authority, despite the fact that the people in principle are strongly against dictatorial governance and would theoretically opt for democracy. In addition, Aliaksandr Lukashenka's strong personality is a contributory factor in his success. He is charismatic, simple, a fast learner, and has the political will for change. This distinguishes him from the rest of the political milieu composed of 'faceless' parties, over fifteen hundred NGOs, numerous trade unions, a puppet parliament, and an inaccessible government.

In their earnest desire for social change, Belarusian voters are torn between supporting their preferred political parties, which in a normal democracy would promise some direct or at least indirect representation for them, and the President, whose monopolisation of power means that only he can satisfy their demands. Thus voters often vote against their party preferences, for a President who at least can deliver to them some material resources. It is interesting to note that the electorates of the President and the anti-system parties considerably overlap, and this forms an environment for vote-switching along the 'president – anti-president' divide. In other words, contemporary voters demonstrate rational 'flexibility' in their voting behaviour, which allows them to pursue their own short-term interests despite their ideological motivations and personal beliefs – and this is the major paradox of contemporary voters in the new regimes.

Politics and culture of Belarus

Since this book is based on conference papers, there is no unanimity of approach among the contributors on domestic or foreign policy. Rather than try to impose a spurious unity on the chapters which follow, we have preferred to let them speak for themselves. There is, however, a broad measure of agreement among the contributors on three key features of post-communist Belarus: the relative absence of nationalist sentiment; the failure of the opposition; and the popularity of President Lukashenka.

National identity

Several contributors, notably David Marples, Vital Silitski and Jan Zaprudnik, suggest that without sufficient nationalist feeling, it is difficult to create a cohesive modern state. In Chapter 2, Marples traces the lack of nationalism in Belarus back to the country's communist and pre-communist history. In particular, he argues that Belarus's Brezhnev-era experience under the leadership of Piotr Masherau (1965–80), who was mysteriously killed in a car accident, played an important part in defining Belarus's post-communist political development, since many Belarusians have accepted the myth that this period represented a 'golden age' of economic and cultural development, free from corruption. He suggests that historically, Belarus has little experience as either an independent nation or a democratic state, and that after the collapse of communism there was insufficient nationalist sentiment to give the people any incentive to participate actively in democratic politics. Similarly, in Chapter 3 Vital Silitski, focusing on the legacy of the last ten years, condemns xenophobic ethnic nationalism, but points to the continuing need for a sense of Belarusian identity based on inclusive, democratic principles which would further the consolidation of the state.

There is, however, some scholarly dispute both within and outside this volume about whether Belarus does in fact possess a national tradition that could be readily revived in the twenty-first century. Belarusian historians frequently refer back to the Republic of Lithuania, Rus and Samogitia in the fourteenth to sixteenth centuries, the national revival in the first decade of the twentieth century based around the journal *Nasha niva* (founded in 1905), and the Belarusian National Republic of 1918 which preceded the establishment of the Belorussian Soviet Socialist Republic. However, with the great losses sustained by Belarus in the Second World War (25 per cent of the population), the purging of native Belarusian cadres under Stalin and the wholesale Russification introduced by the Soviet regime, by the time of the collapse of communism in 1991 there was only a small proportion of the population of Belarus who spoke their native language.[26] After the short-lived national revival of 1991–4, it was thus relatively easy for Lukashenka to reverse the decision of 1990 to make Belarusian the sole official language of the country, to open negotiations on union with Russia and to reintroduce the symbols of the Soviet era.

In Chapter 8 Jan Zaprudnik, while acknowledging these obstacles to the development of Belarusian national identity under Lukashenka's presidency, nevertheless argues that there is a difference between linguistic and political Russification, and that the Russian language may be as great a force for democratisation as Belarusian. He concludes quite optimistically that there are indications that national self-awareness was increasing in the 1990s in culture, religion, historical scholarship and education, and especially among the younger generation. He does, however, concede that the development of a sense of national identity slowed down after the referendum of 1995 and still remained comparatively weak by 2000. In Zaprudnik's view, it is essential for Belarusian political statehood to be maintained and for the West to support the democratic political opposition and the NGOs in Belarus.[27]

A similar conclusion is reached in the chapters by Denis Krivosheev and Teresa Dumasy which focus on Belarus's foreign policy, especially the relations between Belarus and the West. In Chapter 12, Krivosheev explores both the domestic and external influences on Belarus's foreign policy since the 1990s, showing that Belarus, largely ostracised by the West, has retreated into a problematic 'union' with Russia which is likely to involve increasing political, economic and military dependence on its powerful neighbour, and that Lukashenka has also been driven to establish relations with 'rogue states' such as Iraq, Iran, Libya, Cuba and China. In Chapter 13, Dumasy concentrates on Belarus's relations with the European Union, pointing out that the western powers have largely abandoned Belarus, the only East-Central European country not to be accepted into the Council of Europe, although in her view they would be well advised to try to continue exerting influence on the Lukashenka regime. Clearly, Belarus, as a hostile frontline state bordering on an enlarging NATO, could, in combination with an increasingly assertive, nationalist Russia under Putin, pose continuing problems for the western democracies. Both contributors argue that it is short-sighted of western policy-makers to ignore Belarus or regard it as simply an extension of Russia, but perceive little likelihood of change in Belarus's foreign policy while Lukashenka remains President. However, one possible scenario is that, although union with Russia may offer Belarus some benefits from an economic point of view, it is improbable that President Putin (unlike the weaker Yeltsin) will allow Lukashenka to become dominant in the Union.[28] If, as seems likely, Putin's election has weakened Lukashenka's influence, he may wish to assert greater autonomy for Belarus in the future.

President and opposition

Many contributors analyse the close connection between the weakness of the Belarusian opposition and the election of the virtually unknown collective farm director Aliaksandr Lukashenka as President of Belarus in 1994. Silitski stresses the opportunities opened up by the liberalisation of Belarusian society in the early 1990s which enabled an 'outsider' to defeat the existing political elite. Both Silitski and Rotman and Danilov in Chapter 7 demonstrate that the opposition is itself largely to blame for its fragmentation and unpopularity, and trace in detail the mistaken and self-defeating tactics adopted initially by the nationalist Belarusian Popular Front (BNF), then by the democratic opposition in parliament, which lost the confidence of the voters. The failure of the alternative presidential elections organised by the opposition parties in May 1999 and their boycott of the 2000 parliamentary elections which weakened their links with the electorate illustrate their continuing disunity and low public appeal.

Several chapters trace Lukashenka's unexpected rise to power, emphasising that he first came to public attention as head of the parliamentary anti-corruption commission in June 1993, which enabled him to vilify other presidential candidates such as Pazniak and Shushkevich. His charismatic approach and populist platform enabled him to appeal to the masses of ordinary voters as a fighter for justice with clean hands; and subsequently to play on widespread pro-communist and pro-Russian feelings, especially among the older generation.

The intelligentsia has not played such a significant part in Belarusian politics as in Russia, and is now largely suppressed, divided and exiled. Unlike Russia and the Baltic States, Belarus had no highly developed dissident movement during the Brezhnev era, and was relatively slow to respond to Gorbachev's *glasnost,* with the result that there was no widespread intellectual opposition to communism by 1991. Some democratic opposition had arisen in the aftermath of the Chernobyl disaster of 1986, and the revelations of 1988 about the mass graves of victims of Stalinism in the Kurapaty forest near Minsk. However, in the Soviet period democratic opposition never reached the same proportions as in Russia and Ukraine, even though the population of Belarus had been subjected to over 70 per cent of the radiation from Chernobyl.[29]

The most prominent Belarusian writer, Vasil Bykau, famous since the 1960s for his frank writing about the Second World War, and in the post-communist period for his works dealing with issues of Belarusian national identity, has played a civic role as 'conscience of the nation' somewhat akin to that of Solzhenitsyn in Russia. Bykau founded the group 'Martyrology of Belarus' in 1988 and entered the Supreme Soviet as a People's Deputy of the USSR in 1989. In the 1990s he was vocal in his opposition to Lukashenka, but was eventually forced into exile in the West. He nevertheless still displays considerable civic courage in bringing human rights abuses in Belarus and the potential extinction of the Belarusian language to public attention.[30] Bykau is too talented a figure for the government to be able to suppress his voice completely, but his works are now published in Belarus only in small print runs.[31] However, Lukashenka still appears to regard Bykau as a threat, since he has vilified him personally and encouraged his aides to defame him on television.[32]

It is no secret that many members of the intelligentsia oppose Lukashenka's policies. In February 2000, the President tried to woo Belarusian writers by inviting them to a reception, but Bykau and two other prominent Belarusian writers, Sviatlana Aleksievich and Rygor Baradulin, did not even reply, and shortly before the meeting, the president of the Writers' Union, Uladzimir Niakliaeu, suddenly emigrated to Poland.[33] It has, however, to be admitted that by the beginning of the twenty-first century the intellectual opposition within Belarus has proved largely ineffective. An 'independence congress' of Belarusian intellectuals called in August 2000 to discuss the state of the nation was able to propose little more than 'slogans about the rebirth of the nation',[34] and the main opposition to Lukashenka now appears to be confined to the Russian media, the Internet, and prominent Belarusians exiled abroad. The political opposition within Belarus has weakened too, since, as Elena Korosteleva shows in Chapter 5, many political parties have compromised with the presidential power, taking advantage of government funding. Nevertheless, as Rotman and Danilov's analysis suggests, a potential opposition of the future could be composed of young people, those with a higher education, and those living in the capital and the main regional centres.

Stability of the current system

Another major theme of this book is an investigation of the factors which make the current presidential power in Belarus relatively stable *vis-à-vis* the opposition. In Chapter 4, Olga Belova emphasises the influence of the attitudes and strategies of the Belarusian elites on the country's political culture. She demonstrates that the elite in post-independence Belarus initially came from the same groups as during the communist era: old party bureaucrats who had supported the conservative coup against Gorbachev in August 1991 and wanted to preserve their power, members of the technocracy and the security services. Since the mid-1990s, the composition of the Belarusian elite has narrowed further: Lukashenka has promoted close associates in the Mahileu (Mogilev) region who helped him win the election, some with little expertise or experience, and reshuffles them periodically in order to prevent anyone offering a challenge to his supremacy. Since 1997, she argues, the main credential for recruitment to the political elite has been complete loyalty to Lukashenka, which leads to extreme conformism and the unlikelihood of a change of power.

Elena Korosteleva provides a detailed analysis of the party structure in Belarus from 1990 to 2000, suggesting that a system with a large number of parties with weak ties to a fickle electorate has proved harmful to democratic development. The instability of party formation and crystallisation in Belarus has led to a high level of electoral volatility and favoured the strengthening of the presidential power at the expense of the legislature. In general, political parties, the basis of any genuinely democratic system, have become increasingly less influential in Belarus in the period 1990–2001. The pro-government parties are totally dependent on state resources, have accommodated themselves to the presidential power and have no need to appeal to the voters, while the opposition parties appear divided and incapable of winning power. Thus the Belarusian electorate exercises rational choice by preferring a strong president who, they think, can provide them with immediate benefits and lead them out of crisis.

Democracy or dictatorship?

There is some difference of opinion between the contributors about whether Belarus has any potential for democratic development in the future. Several contributors, notably Korosteleva, Belova and Krivosheev, emphasise the preconditions for democracy which have been established in post-communist Belarus: a constitution, presidential and parliamentary elections, and a multi-party system. Further significant evidence about Belarus's democratic potential is provided in Chapter 6 by Christian Haerpfer, who analyses the political behaviour and attitudes of the Belarusian electorate in the period 1992–2000 in comparison with those in six other post-Soviet states. He finds that in 2000, 47 per cent of citizens of Belarus expressed support for their government – a pattern of electoral support similar to that in Estonia, Latvia and the Balkans, but different from that in Russia and Ukraine. There appears, however, to be even more support in Belarus for democratic institutions such as the parliament, even though it has been declining gradually from over 60 per cent in 1996 to over 50 per cent in 2000. Using data from the New Democracies Barometer, an international survey project which he directed, Haerpfer also makes the astonishing discovery that support for a strong leader in Belarus dropped dramatically by 53 percentage points between 1992 and 2000, and that, contrary to popular opinion and media speculation, Belarus has the second most democratic electorate within the former Soviet Union after Estonia. Consequently, Belarus and Estonia are the only CIS states that can be classed as 'emerging democracies' at the level of mass politics. Haerpfer concludes that there appears to be a 'Belarusian paradox' – the contrast between a partially democratic mass public and an authoritarian political system – similar to that in the former Yugoslavia under Miloševich. Lest we imagine that an imminent change of power might occur, he reminds us that in 2000, 59 per cent of the Belarusian electorate remained neutral or non-democratic. As Rotman and Danilov's analysis also shows, in 2001 President Lukashenka still enjoyed a high level of trust, and democratic ideas are far more popular than democratic leaders in Belarus.

Other contributors lay greater stress on the authoritarian elements prevalent in contemporary Belarusian politics and society. Marples and Silitski focus on Lukashenka's ability to manipulate democratic institutions: the introduction of referenda enabling him to strengthen the power of the executive (1995) and to prolong his term in office (1996); the dissolution of an elected parliament and its replacement with a hand-picked legislature; the dissolution of the Constitutional Court; the violation of the democratic constitution; the manipulation of voting procedures; and the assertion of control over the media. The most disturbing feature of Lukashenka's authoritarian regime has been the widespread abuse of human rights, notably the disappearance, arrest or expulsion of opposition leaders[35] and the brutal suppression of demonstrations by OMON (special police) troops.[36] Lukashenka has not even been averse to using force against parliamentary deputies from the BNF who protested against his constitutional coup of 1996. His statements and actions have become increasingly erratic and unpredictable, typical of an authoritarian ruler: for example, the admiration he expressed for Hitler in 1995,[37] his decision to hound foreign diplomats out of their residences in 1998, and his absurd suggestion in 2001 that elections could be decided by a sporting contest.[38] Ironically, Lukashenka is the first elected President in Belarusian history, but his unlimited presidential power is closer to the style of leadership in the post-communist republics of Central Asia than to that in the new democracies of East-Central Europe.

Is Belarus in 2001 an authoritarian system, or a fully fledged dictatorship? The consensus of this volume is that it is not a total dictatorship, since it retains some aspects of a democratic state, but that it could be described as an 'elected dictatorship', or, in Silitski's words, a state possessing 'preconditions without democracy'. Currently Lukashenka's presidency and the prevailing 'Party of Power' appear relatively stable, and in 2001 there was still no single credible alternative candidate to stand against him. Rotman and Danilov suggest, on the basis of opinion poll evidence, that Lukashenka's popularity among voters over sixty and those living in the countryside enabled him to win the presidential election of 9 September 2001 at the first ballot.

Economic prospects and the economy of Belarus

The economy of Belarus is unusual in that it is one of the least transformed in the former Soviet bloc. While the early post-Soviet years saw some significant market-oriented changes, the election of Aliaksandr Lukashenka in July 1994 marked the beginning of the end of the reform period. By 1996 change had virtually ceased, and indeed appeared to go into reverse in some subsequent years. This experience raises some key questions about the economy of Belarus, and its future prospects. For example, how much central planning has been retained? What would happen if transition were to be resumed? If an opposition party or coalition of parties were to come to power, what policy changes could we expect? If there is no change in power, what will happen in the proposed economic union with Russia? Our three economics or political economy chapters provide evidence and arguments on these issues.

In Chapter 8 Colin Lawson explores the process of transition, and tries to assess the future path of the economy if a serious attempt at reform were to be made. He finds that although some of the institutions of central planning have been removed, many of the policies of that system have not been significantly altered. Most importantly, the current ruling elite, who grew up in the old system, show no sign of wanting to run a market system. The state sector is clearly favoured over the private sector, and there is a marked preference for direct intervention when a problem arises. Because the current hybrid system of economic management – part market and part plan – is the result of a political choice, we cannot say that the transition has failed. More accurately, it has not been tried. It is argued that although the current market–administrative mix has failed to deliver sustained significant growth, that reflects more the internal contradictions in the current system than any fundamental failure of the market model.

The current economic system suffers from soft budget constraints, non-market credit allocation, ubiquitous political and administrative intervention and significant barriers to the development of private firms. But while there may be minor moves to re-establish Soviet policies, for example the 2001 decision to mobilise students to help with the harvest, it does not seem likely there will be a full-scale reconstruction of the planning institutions. For example, in June 2001 the World Bank gave its first loan approval to Belarus since 1994. The loan – to improve heating and lighting systems in schools, hospitals, and other social welfare facilities – could be granted because Belarus liberalised its exchange rate in 2000.[39] Lawson argues that behind the rhetoric and indeed reality of state intervention there is sometimes a more pragmatic approach to economic management.

The question of what would happen if there were to be a serious attempt at transition is tackled using cross-section regression models of transition indicators on economic growth. It is shown that while in the longer run there is good evidence for a positive link between transition and growth, in the short run there would be output losses. This means that there may be few short-run political gains to reversing the present economic policies. As for so many early post-communist governments, there would be a need for politicians either to take a longer view, or to accept that they would likely not be re-elected. This would be the poisoned political legacy of Lukashenka.

In Chapter 9 Julia Korosteleva and Nadezhda Lisovskaia examine what might happen if there were to be a change in government, by comparing and contrasting the policies of the political parties. The government position is contrasted with the five main opposition parties: the Party of Communists of Belarus, the Belarusian Social-Democratic Party 'Hramada', the Belarusian Popular Front, the United Civic Party and the Belarusian Republican Party. They focus on the four main areas of economic policy: fiscal policy, monetary and foreign exchange policy, investment policy, and structural policy – which encompasses privatisation and price policy.

The policies of the Party of Communists of Belarus and those of the Belarusian Communist Party differ significantly only in that the former backs Lukashenka, while the latter opposes him. Their economic policies are essentially similar, and both call for a return to full central planning. Both parties are also committed to recreating the Soviet Union, and as a step towards this, to economic union with Russia. Obviously this creates a contradiction. As long as Russia refuses to reinstate central planning, then the proposed economic union, and specifically the monetary union, where the Russian rouble will be in sole use from 2005, is inconsistent with Belarus having full central planning.

Korosteleva and Lisovskaia provide an explanation for the development of government economic policy, and an analysis of the dominant role of the state and the subordinate role of the market in the economy. They note that because the government has used some of the policies of central planning, and has largely ignored market devices to influence outcomes, the market elements that exist sometimes do so within relatively unfettered conditions. For example, customs duties have been relatively low, and as far as foreign producers are concerned VAT and excise duty regulations have been relatively liberal. Against the background of the government's preference for state intervention it is interesting to note that while the opposition parties are very critical of official policy, most of them also envisage a very considerable role for the state.

Anastasia Nesvetailova echoes this last point when she argues in Chapter 10 that much of the population still exhibits Sovietism in their mentality, and that this accounts for their identification with Russia and their support for union with it. She provides a detailed analysis of the political economy of the pro-union movement, and concludes that apart from mentality, there are some cogent economic arguments in its favour. Belarus is not well endowed with natural resources, and it would benefit considerably by access to cheap Russian raw materials and fuels. Russia is also offering a significant economic aid package to cushion Belarus during the changeover period. Russia clearly benefits by securing direct access for her pipelines into Western Europe and by gaining a closer link to a reliable ally. But as the European Union has found, monetary union produces pressures for fiscal coordination, and that in turn will probably lead to pressure for even closer policy links. It is not likely that monetary union will be the end point of the process, either for the European Union or for the proposed Belarus–Russia Union. Nesvetailova argues that limiting the latter union to the economic sphere is a compromise between economic gain and loss of political sovereignty. Whether that compromise proves to be stable remains to be seen.

In conclusion, this work aims to offer the reader an introduction to Belarus by way of analysis and polemical discussion of where Belarus has come from and where it is currently in contemporary Europe. It raises awareness of Belarus's problematic development – a country often referred to as a 'black hole' on the map of Europe, or a 'Soviet-era theme park'; however, Belarus should not be viewed in either of these manners. Although overlooked by researchers, analysts and the media in the past decade in favour of more volatile countries in central and south eastern Europe, Belarus has remained a strategically important European nation both geographically and politically. Belarus's future may remain unspecified at present; however, as history so rightly reminds us Belarus will undoubtedly become a focus of attention again.

Notes

1 J. Zaprudnik, *Belarus: At a Crossroads in History* (Boulder, CO: Westview Press, 1993).
2 D.R. Marples, *Belarus: A denationalized nation* (Amsterdam: Harwood, 1999).
3 K. Mihalisko, 'Belarus: Retreat to Authoritarianism', in K. Dawisha and B. Parrott (eds), *Democratic Changes and Authoritarian Reactions in Russia, Belarus, and Moldova* (Cambridge: Cambridge University Press, 1997), pp. 223–81.
4 S.W. Garnett and R. Legvold (eds), *Belarus at the Crossroads* (Washington, DC: Carnegie Endowment for International Peace, 1999).
5 S. White and R. Rose, *Nationality and Public Opinion in Belarus and Ukraine* (Glasgow: Centre for the Study of Public Policy, University of Strathclyde, 2001).
6 There has been much debate among scholars about whether it is more appropriate to use the term 'transition' or 'transformation' to define the range of post-communist regimes. In this book, the word 'transition' is used simply to designate the political changes which have occurred after the fall of a communist regime, not to imply any inevitable development towards a full democratic system or a market economy. See the discussion by Christian Haerpfer in Chapter 6 below.
7 This includes democratisation, state and market – 'the triple transition', as described by C. Offe, 'Capitalism by democratic design? Facing the triple transition in East Central Europe', *Social Research*, Vol. 58, No. 4 (1991): 865–92.
8 Dahl interprets polyarchies as 'polities characterised by some degree of stability in representation and leadership: but they are not yet democracies'. See R. Dahl, *Polyarchy: Participation and Opposition* (New Haven and London: Yale University Press, 1971), pp. 8–10.
9 L. Whitehead, 'The alternatives to "liberal democracy": a Latin American perspective', *Political Studies*, Vol. XL (1992), Special Issue: 146–59; S. Mainwaring, *Rethinking Party Systems in the Third Wave of Democratization: The Case of Brazil* (Stanford: Stanford University Press, 1999); G. O'Donnell, P. Schmitter and L. Whitehead, *Transitions from Authoritarian Rule* (Baltimore: The Johns Hopkins University Press, 1986), 4 vols; S. White, 'Russia, elections, democracy', *Government and Opposition*, Vol. 35, No. 3 (2000): 302–24.
10 This will inevitably be a painful choice. If the ruling elite's orientation is towards a wider Europe, a country has to embark on lengthy and unpopular reforms, which are non-profitable and costly in the short term. If it is a pro-Russian choice, it will imply short-term economic sustainability with the inevitable prospect of pending system collapse. The situation is such that the CIS are essentially centred on Russia, both structurally and economically, and may not have much freedom to make their own choice.
11 This will be analysed in Chapters 9–11 below.
12 Such structural factors include the persistence of the 'Soviet' power elite and their total control over the decision-making process, the lack of electoral practice and an outdated electoral code, the pending economic crisis with a limited reform programme, a strong presidency giving precedence to decree over law, mass media owned and controlled by the state, and the non-independence of judicial and legislative bodies from the state. The 'elite factor' includes a lack of organisational unity among the opposition, and their ill-articulated ideological and programmatic profiles, as well as Lukashenka's unprecedented impact,

and political interference from Moscow in the decision-making process in Belarus.

13 See Elena Korosteleva's discussion in Chapter 5 and the detailed statistics in the Appendix.

14 For further details, see E. Korosteleva, 'Explaining Party System Development in Post-Communist Belarus', unpublished PhD thesis (University of Bath, 2001).

15 There is a wide range of economic, political and military strategic policies that the EU and NATO offer to sustain stability in the regions with their expansion eastwards: from Partnership for Peace, Partnership and Co-operation Agreements and common strategies to modest programmes of cross-border co-operation and aid.

16 The theme of 'outsiders' is presently being developed by M. Light, J. Löwenhardt and S. White, under the ESRC research project (L213252007) entitled 'The Outsiders: Russia, Ukraine, Belarus, Moldova and the New Europe'. For details, see M. Light, J. Löwenhardt and S. White, 'A wider Europe: the view from Moscow and Kiev' (1999); S. White, 'Belarus, Moldova and Ukraine: Looking East or looking West?' (2001); J. Löwenhardt, 'Two forgotten countries: Belarus and Moldova'; M. Light, 'Ukraine: Between Russia and the West' (2001), papers presented for BASEES Conference, 7–9 April 2001.

17 Light, 'Ukraine: Between Russia and the West'.

18 S. White, 'Russia, elections, democracy', p. 322.

19 European Bank for Reconstruction and Development (EBRD), *Transition Report 1999: Ten Years of Transition* (London: EBRD, 1999), p. 24.

20 There is a strong argument that transition indicators are not really located on an equal interval scale. It is in fact more difficult to move from level 2 to level 3 than it was to get from level 1 to level 2. For this reason the CIS states are further back along the path than their average score would indicate. See Chapter 9 below.

21 It is worth mentioning that Belarus has an average score for many developments in the CIS. In accordance with the EBRD's indicators, the transition is about 39 per cent complete for the CIS as a whole, and 15 per cent complete for Belarus. Belarus's score for transition progress is 1.5 compared to a CIS average of 2.3. During 1997–8 the CIS received $27.6b in direct foreign investment, of which Belarus accounted for $444m; in *per capita* terms Belarus's $44 compares to a CIS average of $69. The corruption index for Belarus reaches 3.4 (58th), as against 2.6 (75th) for Moldova and Ukraine. For more details, see EBRD, *Transition Report* (1999); Colin Lawson, Chapter 9 below.

22 *World Bank Development Report* (London, 1996).

23 *Economic Trends Quarterly*, January–March Report (2000).

24 See E.A. Korosteleva, 'Political Cleavages and Voting Behaviour in Belarus 1991–1998: an Evaluation of the "Freezing Hypothesis"', unpublished MA thesis (University of Manchester, 1998).

25 G. O'Donnell, 'On the state, democratization and some conceptual problems: a Latin American view with glances at some post-communist countries', *World Development*, Vol. 21, No. 8 (1993): 1355–70.

26 In the 1989 Soviet census a majority of ethnic Belarusians (80 per cent) declared Belarusian to be their native language, but sociological studies have established that it is spoken mainly within the family, and in rural areas.

27 International contacts have operated productively at a local level: for example, the relations between the Mendip Borough Council in the south-west of England and the Belarusian city of Svetlogorsk. For details see 'Steps to inclusivity', TACIS City Twinning Project (http://www.tacisinfo.ru/), retrieved 11 November 2000.

28 On the uneasy relations between Putin and Lukashenka, see S. Anisko, *Segodnia*, 20 September 2000, p. 4. According to opinion polls, if the post of President

of Belarus and Russia had existed, by April 2000 31.1 per cent of Belarusians would have supported Putin, compared to 22.3 per cent who would have supported Lukashenka: Iu. Andreev and I. Maksimov, *Vremia novostei*, 28 June 2000, p. 2.

29 See the moving documentary work by the Belarusian writer Sviatlana Aleksievich, *Chernobyl'skaia molitva* (Moscow: Otlozh'e, 1997).

30 Bykau referred to Lukashenka as a 'dictator' and spoke of the 'unnoticed catastrophe' of the decline of the Belarusian language and culture at the anniversary meeting of the Organisation for Security and Co-operation in Europe, Tampere, Finland (July 2000).

31 See S. Karpekhova, *Izvestiia*, 26 March 1998, p. 6. Many of Bykau's views on Belarusian democracy and independence are collected in Iu. Zaloska, *Dyialohi z Vasiliom Bykavym* (Minsk: Mastatskaia litaratura, 1995). On Bykau's literary work, see A. McMillin, *Belarusian Literature in the 1950s and 1960s: Release and Renewal* (Cologne: Böhlau, 1999), pp. 205–30.

32 N. Galko, *Nezavisimaia gazeta*, 23 February 2000, p. 5.

33 Ibid. Those who did attend apparently demanded the immediate dismissal of the government official in charge of literature, Deputy Prime Minister Uladzimir Zamiatalin.

34 P. Burak, *Obshchaia gazeta*, 3–9 August 2000, p. 5.

35 See, for example, A. Neverovskii and B. Volkhonskii, *Kommersant,* 1 April 1999, p. 4.

36 See, for example, N. Galko, *Nezavisimaia gazeta*, 19 October 1999, pp. 1, 5; A. Neverovskii, *Kommersant*, 28 March 2000, p. 11.

37 Reported in *Izvestiia*, 28 November 1995.

38 *Radio Free Europe/Radio Liberty Newsline*, Part 2, 29 June 2001. http://www.rferl.org/newsline/ retrieved 29 August 2001.

39 *Radio Free Europe/Radio Liberty Newsline*, Part 2, 7 June 2001.

2 History and politics in post-Soviet Belarus

The foundations

David R. Marples

Introduction

In common with its neighbours Ukraine and Moldova, Belarus was relatively ill prepared for independence in 1991. In March of that year, over 82.7 per cent of the population supported the preservation of the USSR as a federation of sovereign states.[1] Its political leadership was taken by surprise by the events in Moscow, and adopted independence formally on 25 August. No referendum was ever held on the question of independence (in contrast to Ukraine) and there was not even a clearly defined structure of leadership. For some time authority was divided between the Speaker of the parliament and the Prime Minister. The process of nation building had barely begun, and even the development of the state language and culture were in their infancy. Belarusian had been declared the state language only in 1990, not enough time for such a move to have a significant impact in schools, higher educational institutions, government, or business. These factors were to exert a major influence on politics during the early years of the independent state.

Belarus did play an important role in the ending of the Soviet Union, however, as the host of the December 1991 meeting between its parliamentary Speaker Stanislau Shushkevich, Ukrainian President Leonid Kravchuk, and Russian President Boris Yeltsin, which effectively established the Commonwealth of Independent States (CIS) and in the process deprived Soviet leader Mikhail Gorbachev of any further meaningful role in political life. On Belarus, then, and Shushkevich in particular, was heaped blame for the collapse of the Soviet Union by communists, pro-Soviet activists, and those who regretted the sudden change of fortunes.[2]

Historians have tried to remedy this apparent 'lack of history'. Two historians of the late nineteenth and early twentieth centuries – Dovnar-Zapol'skii[3] and Ihnatouski[4] – have presented skilful outlines of a specifically Belarusian heritage from the East Slavic states. However, in the Soviet period, historians blurred such distinctions and treated Belarus as part of an East Slavic whole. Today, historians argue as to the origins of the republic and the role of ethnic Belarusians in the Grand Duchy of

Lithuania, one of the largest states of medieval Europe, prior to the Union of Lublin of 1569, which united the ruling houses of Poland and Lithuania. After falling under Russian rule in 1795, Belarusian territories were subjected to strong Russian influences, and national aspirations developed slowly. Nonetheless, the turn of the century saw a period of unprecedented cultural development, particularly after the revolution of 1905.[5] By the time of the revolutions of 1917, there was a small but prominent group of intellectuals prepared to espouse the cause of a Belarusian state as an autonomous entity within the Russian Empire.

However, despite a history that reaches back a thousand years, it is the Soviet period of rule that is the focus of most contention among both historians and political leaders. Soviet rule was ambivalent in more than one sense. It saw the establishment of the Belarusian Soviet Socialist Republic (BSSR), which by September 1939 had reunited most ethnically Belarusian territories within its borders. Concomitantly, negotiations between the Soviet and Lithuanian governments resulted in the transfer of Vilna and its environs from Soviet-occupied western Belarus to Lithuania.[6] Vilna has a history as a cultural centre for many groups, including Belarusians, Jews, Poles, and Lithuanians. For Belarusians, the loss of Vilna – it can hardly be termed a genuine loss since it had not been under Belarusian control – signified that there was no major cultural focus for Belarusians other than the city of Minsk.

Stalin's leadership brought the virtual elimination of the intellectual elite, purges, and mass executions in places such as the Kurapaty forest north of Minsk (to be discussed further below).[7] In the post-war period, while the republic became both urbanised and under the influence of the Russian language and culture, it also saw the leadership of Piotr Masherau (1965–80), one of the least corrupt of communist leaders, and still the subject of veneration in some circles of Belarus today (as will be discussed below). In this same period, the living standards of Belarusians were significantly higher than the Soviet average. Thus many Belarusians have retained affection, or at least nostalgia, for the Soviet past.

What one might call the nationalist history of the twentieth century, on the other hand, is riddled with controversy. Belarus declared independence briefly on 25 March 1918 after the collapse of the Russian Empire and under German military occupation. The Germans prohibited all activities of the government of the Belarusian People's Republic (BNR) and its Rada from early April onward. The Berlin government had reached agreement with Soviet Russia, and thus would not recognise the BNR without Russian consent. Among a number of anti-Soviet organisations, a Belarusian Central Rada (BTsR) was recreated on 21 December 1943 under German auspices and the leadership of R. Astrauski. The collaborationist nature of this regime is cited regularly by the Lukashenka administration, which has linked the BNR and the BTsR with the Belarusian Popular Front (BNF) as representative of the worst aspects of

Belarusian national existence. The issue is a complex one, but official propaganda has been quite successful in convincing the public that such a link exists. A similar paradox surrounds the Masherau period.

The paradox of the Masherau period

From 1965 to 1980, Piotr Masherau was the First Party Secretary of the Central Committee of the Communist Party of Belarus (CC CPB), a second successive leader from the wartime Partisan movement,[8] but one who was to have a lasting and pervasive influence on political developments. Under Masherau's leadership, Belarus fared well economically *vis-à-vis* the other Soviet republics. Moreover, the period coincided with Brezhnev's leadership of the USSR and, after 1975, a period of increasing corruption and stagnation in the party hierarchy. That Masherau was free from this sort of corruption is evident from all sources; what is less clear is how far he distanced himself from the events in Moscow. Following his tragic death in a freak automobile accident,[9] Masherau became something of a martyr in Belarus and there is no question that the general public widely mourned his death. Subsequently, accounts of the Masherau years have varied. Some portray him as a virtual oppositionist struggling against the party leadership in Moscow, whereas others see him as an orthodox communist, who rarely wavered from the party line. These analyses are significant in an assessment of the state of national consciousness at the time of independence and thus we will examine them both briefly.

The portrayal of Masherau as an oppositionist, who advanced Belarus's interests over those of the USSR as a whole, owes much to one of his biographers, Slavamir Antanovich. According to Antanovich, Masherau was a virtual ascetic who kept close ties with 'common people' and who regularly visited stores and markets in Minsk. His relations with Brezhnev were cordial prior to the Soviet leader's visit to Belarus, after which Brezhnev 'realised how independent Masherau was'. In the 1970s their relationship cooled. Masherau, as a result, never ascended beyond the level of Candidate Member to the Politburo of the Central Committee of the Communist Party of the Soviet Union (CC CPSU) and he had particular conflicts with chief ideologist Mikhail Suslov, but he survived because Brezhnev, a weak figure, disliked conflicts.[10] In 1975, Brezhnev became seriously ill and suffered 'clinical death'. Thereafter sycophantic followers surrounded him and many of his closest colleagues, such as A.N. Kosygin, were unable to gain access to him and had to rely on telephone conversations.

In Antanovich's view, the situation for Masherau soon deteriorated further. Brezhnev's attitude toward Masherau became uneven. Sometimes they went hunting together, on other occasions he was pushed aside. The biographer leaves no doubt that Brezhnev's most prominent colleagues, including the future Soviet leader Konstantin Chernenko, treated Belarus badly. However, two incidents in particular lay the foundation for the theory of the USSR–Belarus 'rift'. The first pertains to the awarding of the title of Hero City to Minsk for its wartime exploits. Minsk received the award in 1974, but there was then a four-year delay before the Soviet leaders bestowed the 'golden star'. Why was there such a delay? Did it indicate that Masherau was out of favour? Certainly the delay had little to do with the actual exploits of Minsk during the war. Second, in 1980, several Soviet leaders went to Alma-Ata to commemorate the sixtieth anniversary of the Kazakhstan Soviet Socialist Republic. According to Antanovich, after Masherau's speech, Brezhnev made a 'grimace of complete displeasure' and averted his face, a gesture that was duly noted by the public watching the general news programme 'Vremia'.[11] As a result of Brezhnev's dissatisfaction, this view implies, Masherau's sudden death a few weeks later should not have been a surprise. One should append to this perspective the comment that the view depicts Masherau as an orthodox communist struggling against the perversions of the centre, a true Leninist, incorruptible and determined. The view equates Belarusian economic success with adherence to Leninist principles rather than to some unorthodox experimentation with a different path.

Malafeeu, the then First Party Secretary of the CC of the Communist Party of Belarus (CPB), adopts a similar view, in which he perceives the Masherau period as one in which the Communist Party of Belarus boldly sought new paths without guidance from above, but hardly in conflict with the CC CPSU. The 1970s were thus a time for the development of Belarusian education, science, and culture.[12] Writing on the seventieth anniversary of Masherau's birth, two historians, Iu. Smirnov and A. Lebedev, comment that with the fraternal aid of Russians and other peoples of the USSR, new cities and settlements arose in Belarus in Masherau's time, along with huge modern industrial and agricultural enterprises that increased the material riches of the republic. Masherau ruled 'not by the arguments of power, but by the power of arguments, by the force of logic'. He belongs 'to the heroic generation of Bolsheviks'.[13] One can find similar uncritical remarks about the former leader upon each major anniversary of his birth. In truth they tell us little about a leader whose presence still looms over the Belarusian political landscape. They contribute to the myth of Masherau, which, like the partly mythical exploits of the partisans, largely defines the limitations of political change in the post-Soviet republic.[14]

Where does reality lie? Masherau's career is not dissimilar to that of his contemporary Petro Shelest in Ukraine. He appears to have been an orthodox and principled communist, but not one who was prepared to differ widely from the official line propagated in Moscow. Like any regional leader, Masherau was dependent upon having significant support in the shape of one or more mentors in Moscow. In Masherau's case, the mentor was Mazurau, his predecessor in Belarus. According to a western observer, Mazurau, in turn, was a protégé of Aleksei Kosygin. When Kosygin's fortunes began to wane therefore, the impact reverberated not only in the

Politburo in Moscow, but also in the republics. By 1976, according to this view, Brezhnev had begun to advance the career of N.A. Tikhonov, who was given the same title of First Deputy Premier that Mazurau held. By 7 November 1977, Mazurau's photograph at official ceremonies had been blacked out. In this way, Belarus first lost its spokesperson in the Kremlin, but second, Masherau no longer had a sponsor in Moscow.[15] Thus whether Masherau was a reformer or not at home may have been largely immaterial and there were several changes in the provincial party administrations in Belarus that suggested Masherau's future was limited. Politically, there seems no doubting that Masherau was a hardliner on foreign policy, an opponent of any kind of rapprochement or détente with the West (also similar to Shelest, removed from office in 1972). However, the sudden and unexpected death of Masherau in October 1980 appeared to coincide with his increasing distance from the Brezhnev leadership and fostered suspicions that the car crash was no accident and that he was a political victim of a Soviet regime that had 'gone soft' on the West.[16]

If one were to make a survey of republican and regional party leaders of the late Soviet period, the result would not be very edifying. Masherau stands out as one of the more committed leaders of the past as a Soviet wartime hero. His popularity was highest in rural regions and among factory workers rather than among the intellectual elite, and there is currently in Belarus no attempt to analyse his time in power critically by historians. His period has fostered an aura of leadership that has been exploited skilfully by the Lukashenka administration. The post-Masherau communist leaders have been lesser figures: Nikalai Sliun'kou, for example, was preoccupied by the enormous problems engendered by the Chernobyl disaster and prior to Lukashenka there was a virtual vacuum of power at the top (see below). Thus when the Belarusian public turns to the past, it often can see no further than the hero-figure of Masherau. Indeed it would be surprising otherwise given the pervasive influence of the 'Great Patriotic War' and the monuments to that war that are evident in every settlement and town. The supporters of an independent state, or those seeking to promote state-building processes have always had to deal with the Masherau factor, an era that is often regarded as a kind of 'golden age' of economic and cultural development rather than what it was: a period of resolute communist orthodoxy guided by a staunch communist, albeit one who appeared to be unmarked by the corruption that surrounded the leadership in Moscow.

The Gorbachev period: a tumultuous interlude

The period 1985–91 saw dramatic changes in Belarus, catalysed for the most part by events in Moscow. The most significant were a campaign of partial de-Stalinisation, which echoed Gorbachev's rehabilitation of Stalin's victims; the effects of the 1986 disaster at Chernobyl, which affected Belarus with more high-level fallout than any other part of the USSR; and significant cultural developments that culminated in the decree declaring Belarusian to be the state language of the republic in 1990. All these events promoted the development of a non-communist political movement, the Belarusian Popular Front (BNF), without having a significant impact on the structures of power or the mindset of the general population. When Belarus declared independence on 25 August 1991, it did so without adequate preparation and in response to events outside the republic. Though it was considered necessary to outlaw the Communist Party, which dominated the Supreme Soviet, its members still remained in place and held about 85 per cent of the seats in the legislature. Only with the decision to elect a president, as mandated by the constitution of 1994 did the political situation change dramatically in Belarus. Remarkably, the period of great changes did not foster the widespread disillusionment with the period of Soviet rule manifested elsewhere (Ukraine, for example) because the national movement lacked both the numbers and sufficient time to exert a significant influence on public perceptions.

The Chernobyl disaster affected about 80 per cent of Belarus with radioactive iodine fallout and severely contaminated about 20 per cent of the republic with more long-lasting radio-nuclides.[17] For three years, however, the population lacked information about the degree of contamination of the soil. Moreover, inquiries into Chernobyl and its effects took on political connotations from the outset as the Belarusian Popular Front under Zianon Pazniak assumed the leadership on the matter and accused the authorities of withholding information from the general public about the situation. Pazniak was also the investigator into a mass gravesite discovered at Kurapaty, in the northern outskirts of Minsk. Though overwhelming evidence (including that of 55 eyewitnesses) indicated that the NKVD were responsible for the executions in the period 1937–41, the authorities chose to give weight to the view that the German occupants had committed the atrocity after June 1941.[18] At the same time, the communist leaders mounted an extensive propaganda campaign to discredit Pazniak and the BNF, which was linked to collaboration with the Nazis during the war. This was largely successful over the long term, though in the late 1980s, the tacit support of the authorities in Moscow bolstered the anti-Stalinist line in the regions.[19] The outcome therefore was that the criticisms of many aspects of Soviet life were less acute in Belarus than elsewhere, and the authorities managed to attribute them to 'extreme fringe groups' rather than the sentiment of the general population.

By and large the processes of change moved more slowly in Belarus than in other Soviet republics of the European USSR. Yet there was still discernible progress because traditionally policies developed at the centre of the USSR received unquestioning acceptance at the republican level. Belarus thus began a process of cultural self-development. Along with the promotion of the Belarusian language – not widely spoken outside the villages, despite official statistics that cited the contrary – there was a cultural resurgence reminiscent of the more tolerant period of the 1920s. A language debate developed in the official media and there was renewed interest in the national history of Belarus, rather than the traditional version from the Soviet perspective. There was never, however, the demands for independence that occurred in western Ukraine. Change came slowly in Belarus. After the collapse of the putsch in Moscow of 19–21 August 1991, the Belarusian parliament hesitated to break away from the Soviet Union. On 25 August, it did so, on the grounds that the parliament was giving the status of constitutional law to the declaration of 'state sovereignty' of the BSSR.[20] This statement was significantly less than an outright declaration of independence. Belarus entered the independence era with several facets of the Soviet structure intact, including the most prominent politicians, the KGB (evidently unsullied by the actions of its counterpart in Moscow), and the communist elite (though with a new title, the Party of Communists of Belarus).

The independence period

The national idea has never been accepted among a majority of the population. This statement is reflected in the language situation: that is, the elevation of Russian to a state language in 1995 and effectively as the language of government and business, and in the politics of the present leadership of the country, which does not recognise any distinctive Belarusian traits. As a result of such policies, Belarusian politics have become polarised. In 1991 in Belarus (in contrast to Russia and Ukraine), there was never a working alliance between the communists or former communists on the one hand, and the nationalists of the Popular Front on the other. Belarus suffered from a distinct lack of middle ground in politics. To put it simply, those on the Left regarded independence as a betrayal of the causes for which Belarusians had fought in the past (particularly during the Great Patriotic War), whereas those on the Right regarded the former communist political leaders as obsolete and lacking in national consciousness.

The years 1991–3 are hardly remembered with great fondness by many residents of the republic. They were years of acute economic hardship and political infighting. The *ipso facto* leader of the country, parliamentary Speaker Stanislau Shushkevich, had to run the gauntlet of a recalcitrant parliament made up mainly of former communists, and the BNF, which saw him as too compliant and unwilling to embark on a more radical programme that would have oriented Belarus toward Europe and away from Russia. Thus in the first presidential elections of 1994, held shortly after the acceptance of Belarus's first constitution, Aliaksandr Lukashenka was perceived as an alternative to a period of economic stagnation and decline (associated misleadingly with Shushkevich, dismissed in January

1994), to the representative of the 'old regime' (Viacheslau Kebich), and to the candidate of the 'Russophobic' Popular Front (Zianon Pazniak). Above all, his position as chair of a commission on corruption may have been a decisive factor among a population bewildered by the new forces of the market, which they associated largely with criminal activities.

Nevertheless, the new President, a youthful 39, was also hardly alien to most voters. He portrayed himself as a man of the people,[21] he spoke their simple and non-convoluted language, he was (overtly at any rate) nostalgic about the Soviet past and ties with Russia, and he was hostile to nationalists of the Belarusian Popular Front and their ideals. He was in short a symptom of the sentiments of many Belarusians, particularly the elderly, those living in rural areas close to the Russian border, and the military, espousing political ideas and ideals that reflected their political past. The election of Lukashenka *per se* was neither startling nor illogical; indeed from the perspective of June–July 1994, many voters may have thought that they lacked choice. Further, the constitution of 1994 placed significant limitations on presidential powers, particularly through the Supreme Soviet and the Constitutional Court. These restrictions are illustrated by the number of presidential decrees turned down by the Court in the first months of Lukashenka's tenure. It appeared therefore that even if the new President failed to live up to expectations, there were limits that could be placed on his authority.

Subsequently, as is well known, there have been significant intrusions by the Presidential Administration into the democratic structure, most notably following the referenda of 1995 and 1996. The latter referendum granted the President the authority to dissolve parliament, create a new upper assembly, and to establish a revamped Constitutional Court. The parliament of the thirteenth session was thus dissolved (illegally in the eyes of the EU and most international observers) and a new assembly of 120 members (from the original 260) was formed. In late December, a 'new amended' version of the 1994 constitution was published. In reality it was a new constitution that gave powers to Lukashenka that are unmatched elsewhere in the former Soviet Union.[22] A period of consolidation of power developed into an authoritarian regime that controls most facets of political life. Most notorious examples have been control over the media,[23] harassment, punishment, and detention of opposition figures, and restrictions on demonstrations and public activities of all kinds by groups outside the purview of the government. In 1999, all political groups had to be reregistered, and words such as 'Belarusian' and 'popular' were removed from their titles. The BNF, for example, had to shorten its name to an acronym and at the time of writing had still not been officially registered as a legitimate party.[24] Will this situation change? Can Belarus develop as a state that would eventually be a candidate for membership of the European Union or at least become a civilised European state? Let us look at these questions in three sections: the presidency; the opposition; and foreign policy.

The presidency and the opposition

Unlike its neighbours, Russia and Ukraine, Belarus has had only one elected president. Like Boris Yeltsin in the Russian Federation, Lukashenka has taken steps well beyond the bounds of his mandate to retain and extend his authority. The changes he has made to the 1994 constitution signify that any president of Belarus will have significantly more authority than his counterparts either in France or the United States. The legal basis for such changes, in so far as it exists at all, lies in the national referendum of November 1996, held under conditions that restricted the voice of the opposition and included gross improprieties in the voting procedure. The president's office dominated the media, harassed all those espousing opposing views, and phrased referendum questions in a way to suggest what the answers should be. The President is known for his idiosyncrasies, his unpredictability, and for his verbosity.[25]

A prerequisite for the progress of a democratic path in Belarus is the lifting of all restrictions on freedom of assembly and publication, in addition to the necessity of equal access of all to the press, television, and radio prior to the parliamentary elections of 2000. The realities of political life in Belarus can be expressed in the following observations: a former Prime Minister in prison until recently (Mikhail Chyhir); the erstwhile leader of the largest opposition party a refugee from his own country (Zianon Pazniak); the leader of the Agrarian Party and Speaker of the Supreme Soviet of the thirteenth session in exile in Lithuania (Siamion Sharetski); while the former Minister of Internal Affairs (Iuryi Zakharenka) and Deputy Chair of the former parliament (Viktar Hanchar) have simply disappeared, their whereabouts unknown for several months.

In some respects the opposition has been its own worst enemy, particularly the Belarusian Popular Front, which has attempted to bring about changes in the political environment that were hardly warranted by the level of national consciousness in the country. Yet extremism at the highest levels has nurtured extreme responses. The division of the BNF into two wings is a case in point. The emergence of Vintsuk Viachorka as the Minsk-based leader has ended the BNF's official policy of non-compromise with other political parties. Viachorka is a nationalist but very much a European-style politician, fluent in several languages and a firm proponent of the democratic process.[26] Pazniak's influence within Belarus has dwindled and his new Christian Conservative Party is likely to remain on the periphery of the political spectrum.

Historically, Pazniak's leadership has been an important one. He, perhaps more than any other individual, has made residents of Belarus aware of many of the iniquities of the past. He has also provided a conception of Belarus that is markedly different from either the Soviet or current post-Soviet models. He has, however, been overtaken by events,[27] and at key times he has remained unwilling to make compromises. Above all, this dogmatic approach has shortened his political career.

Belarus's neighbours represent two possible paths to the future. In Russia in 1993 the President succeeded in consolidating his authority *vis-à-vis* the parliament by violent means. In Ukraine, on the other hand, the divisions in parliament in the recent past hindered significantly economic and political development, and fostered authoritarian tendencies within the Kuchma government and the Ukrainian parliament.[28] In 1999 in Belarus the opposition faced two serious dilemmas. First, the unofficial presidential elections of May 1999 ended in controversy and dispute, particularly regarding the methods of voting and the number of votes obtained, and the withdrawal from the race of Pazniak at a late stage. In particular, the employment by the organiser of these elections, Viktar Hanchar, of a pre-election voting system that saw ballot boxes carried around apartment buildings aroused the ire of Pazniak. And when Hanchar declared that over 50 per cent of the electorate had taken part in the elections, voters who had been unable to find ballot stations were unable to comprehend such a figure.[29]

Second, the efforts of the Organisation for Security and Co-operation in Europe Advisory and Monitoring Group in Belarus (OSCE AMGB) to develop a dialogue between the government and its opponents initially left the latter in a difficult situation, since it forced those who have been victimised by the regime to legitimise it merely by the act of entering discussions.[30] Should opposition leaders refuse to enter discussions they would be perceived as obdurate and hindering the process. In this respect, a commendable initiative by the OSCE AMGB benefited initially the government rather than the opposition (even though the latter could gain significantly in the long term). By late 2000, however, the OSCE presence had irritated the government sufficiently to demand its departure from Minsk.[31]

The OSCE AMGB initiative also affected the position of both the parliament of the thirteenth session (disbanded by Lukashenka in November 1996, but still widely recognised outside Belarus as the legitimate parliament) and its leader Siamion Sharetski, who fled from Belarus to Lithuania in July, believing that his arrest was imminent. Sharetski announced on 27 August 1999 that he was going to form an alternative government and organise elections,[32] but made it clear in an interview that such a government, in the view of the OSCE, would be unlikely to receive any recognition.[33] Ironically, Sharetski would only be following the mandates of the 1994 constitution, Articles 87, 104, and 105.[34] Lukashenka, on the other hand, may have extended his mandate as President by illegal means, but since he is clearly in the main position of authority in Minsk then he continues to receive recognition by foreign emissaries. These emissaries recognise that he has violated the constitution of 1994, but seek to maintain a dialogue that embraces all political forces in the country, of which the President remains the major one. The opposition and the harassed deputies of the thirteenth parliament therefore could hardly be blamed for regarding the western democracies as somewhat duplicitous. On the other hand, the OSCE has always emphasised that the government is required to make concessions towards more open media and provide a more tolerant environment (including the freeing of political prisoners) before any meaningful discussion can occur.

Foreign policy

For more than four years, Belarus's foreign policy has moved in the direction of Russia, with varying degrees of success and commitment. A Community and then a Union that appeared attractive to many Belarusians in 1996 and 1997 looked distinctly less attractive as the year 1999 came to a close. The proposed union between Russia, Belarus, and the remains of Yugoslavia – made in April 1999 at the height of the NATO bombing campaign when President Lukashenka visited Belgrade[35] – seems to have been merely a propaganda exercise; the prospects for Ukraine joining a Russia–Belarus Union are better, but largely dependent on the results of the late October presidential election in that country. Most Belarusians perceive the logic of close and friendly political and economic relations with the Russian Federation. It seems less likely that the majority favours such a one-dimensional foreign policy, particularly given the acute financial problems that have beset Russia over the past year. Yet integration of one form or another has constantly been part of the government agenda – no matter what the motives behind it and whether there has ever been a genuine desire to bring such an idea to fruition.[36] The confederation formed in December 1999 added to the process of gradual integration, particularly in the military-security field. Such a programme has provided an impression outside the country of a state with a 'death wish,' unwilling or unable to take its place among the family of nations,[37] an astonishing exception to the general rule of nations and nationalities pursuing national statehood from Dagestan to Quebec.

Clearly nation-building in Belarus cannot begin if official policy is to seek – or to be seen to seek – to merge the state with its larger neighbour. Thus the government of Belarus has increased markedly its power to rule the country while failing singly to identify the state that it controls. Lukashenka has no wish to relinquish the source of his power (though he may wish to occupy the larger stage of Russia), but inasmuch as he recognises the country at all, it is in the form of the old BSSR rather than the Republic of Belarus. This is reflected in matters such as the state flag and symbols in use since May 1995, and national holidays and commemorations that are Soviet rather than post-Soviet in origin,[38] and in the often overt hostility to western institutions and organisations, such as NATO and the IMF. The regime often indulges in 'Cold War rhetoric', even though its foreign policy has never been limited to relations with the former Soviet republics. As yet there has not been a foreign policy that distinguishes Belarus as a newly independent state, with its own unique interests and goals.

Conclusions

Belarus has survived for over nine years as an independent state. It has often been stressed that the country occupies an important geo-strategic position at the very centre of Europe. More important, however, is the question of its borders. To its north-west and west are states (Poland, Latvia, Lithuania) that have clearly taken on economic reforms and developed, albeit with varying degrees of success, as new democracies. To the south and east are countries (Ukraine, Russia) that have embarked on reforms, but have run into difficulties of both a political and an economic nature. They have not given up the struggle, but are facing questions potentially as serious as those faced by Belarus today. Belarus is a relatively homogeneous republic,[39] and it has a highly educated workforce. Its lack of natural resources might be considered an impediment but it is not an insuperable one for a modern state, as the example of Japan has shown. Thus in some respects, Belarus has significant advantages as a developing nation-state.

Its progress, however, has been determined increasingly by a narrow ruling group that is motivated more by nostalgia for the past than a desire to consolidate and improve both the lives of citizens and the place of Belarus in the world. In part, this process is a result of the pursuit of power by the President, using the KGB and the militia as his instruments, and the concomitant restriction of any source of authority in any other quarter of society. Such activity has extended beyond the realm of politics. Civic life, as it developed in the latter years of the Gorbachev administration, has ended in so far as politics and economics are concerned – though it continues in terms of cultural debates at a lower level and to some extent among university students. Moreover, all change in Belarus at present must come from the highest level of government; there is neither capacity nor facility for a grassroots movement to develop because the political conditions imposed do not allow for such a development. The average village resident or factory worker is as dependent on the state today as in the Soviet period. Indeed Belarus has even been cited in a travel book as the republic to visit if one wondered what life was like during the Soviet period!

Belarus is facing serious alternatives as it experiences the first year of a new century and there is nothing that is inevitable about the decisions to be made. Either it can take its place as a central European state that recognises human rights and a pluralistic political system (as stipulated in the 1994 constitution), or it can become a political and economic backwater, isolated from its neighbours through adherence to a state-controlled society and economy, with diminishing democratic and human rights, and with all power vested in its president. This latter alternative also entails the increasing impoverishment of its population with potentially devastating social consequences. The western democracies can facilitate change and a path of democratic reform first and foremost by recognising that whereas the opposition has clung fastidiously to the rules of law set forth in the constitution, the Presidential Administration has violated and continues to violate those laws at will. The early months of 2001 saw the opposition trying to unite on the question of a leader who would oppose Lukashenka in the September 2001 presidential elections. A resultant delay in making such a decision and subsequent failure of the opposition negated the election as a meaningful contest – assuming that democratic conditions might prevail. Instead Belarusians would continue to experience the demagogic and erratic rule of Aliaksandr Lukashenka, self-proclaimed 'Orthodox atheist' and 'President for life'.

Notes

1 E.L. Abetsedarskaia *et al.*, *Istoriia Belarusi* (Minsk: Ekoperspektiva, 1997), p. 294.
2 The National Library of Belarus in Minsk contains the stridently Leftist newspaper *My i Vremia*, which in the period 1992–3 missed no opportunity to denounce in articles and cartoons the 'traitors' who had eliminated the Soviet Union by signing the agreement at the Belavezha hunting lodge in western Belarus.
3 M.V. Dovnar-Zapol'skii (1867–1934), a historian and folklorist who published extensively on the social and economic history of Belarus and Lithuania, particularly on the sixteenth century.
4 U.M. Ihnatouski (1881–1931), a historian and political activist who became president of the Belarusian Academy of Sciences in 1928 (he later committed suicide). His best-known historical work is *Karotki narys histor'ii Belarusi* (Minsk, 1926).
5 The first legal newspaper was published in this period in Vilna (Vilnius), *Nasha dolia* (subsequently it appeared under the name *Nasha niva*). See, for example, U.M. Ihnatouski, *Karotki narys histor'ii Belarusi* (Minsk: Belarus, 1992), p. 173.
6 'K zakliucheniiu dogovora o peredache Litovskoi Respublike goroda Vil'no i Vilenskoi oblasti i vzaimopomoshchi mezhdu Sovetskim Soiuzom i Litvoi', *Sovetskaia Belorussiia*, 11 October 1939, p. 1.
7 In 1988, the archaeologist Zianon Pazniak rediscovered mass graves in the Kurapaty Forest, about 10 miles north of the centre of Minsk. His findings were highlighted in the newspaper *Literatura i mastatstva* (3 June 1988). For an account of the subsequent investigation and eventual government cover-up, see D.R. Marples, 'Kuropaty: An Investigation of a Stalinist Historical Controversy', *Slavic Review*, Vol. 53, No. 2 (Summer 1994): 560–70.
8 The first was Kiryl Mazurau, First Party Secretary of the CC CPB from 1956 to 1965, and then First Deputy Chairman of the Council of Ministers of the USSR in Moscow and a member of the ruling Politburo.
9 See, for example, N. Zenkovich, 'Ot Lenina do El'tsina', *Podvig*, No. 3 (1995): 101–12, for a description of the accident in which Masherau was killed.
10 S. Antonovich, 'Piotr Masherov: "Riadom" s Brezhnevym', *Respublika*, 24 September 1993, p. 7.

11 Antonovich, 'Piotr Masherov i Respublika', 28 September 1993, p. 7; and 29 September 1993, p. 11.
12 A. Malofeev, 'Mozhno li ne schitat'sia s istinoi?', *Sovetskaia Belorussiia*, 18 June 1991, p. 1.
13 Iu. Smirnov and A. Lebedev, 'Vsia zhizn' – sluzhenie narodu', *Sovetskaia Belorussiia*, 13 February 1988, p. 1.
14 In the parliamentary elections of October 2000, Natalia Masherauva, daughter of the former leader, was a comfortable winner over former Prime Minister Mikhail Chyhir.
15 A. Knight, 'Piotr Masherov and the Soviet Leadership: A Study in Kremlinology', *Survey*, Vol. 26, No. 1 (Winter 1982): 154–6.
16 Once again, Antonovich has been at the forefront of the debates centred on Masherau's death. See, for example, Slavomir Antonovich, 'Piotr Masherov: bylo li "politicheskoe ubiistvo"?', *Respublika*, 1 October 1993, pp. 22–4.
17 See D.R. Marples, 'Belarus: Ten Years After Chernobyl', *Post-Soviet Geography*, Vol. XXXVI, No. 8 (August 1995): 1–28.
18 Marples, 'Kuropaty', pp. 513–23.
19 Pazniak received only 13 per cent of the vote in the presidential elections of 1994. In 1996 he left Belarus and was awarded refugee status by the United States. The BNF later split into two branches, with the main party now led by Vintsuk Viachorka. One can conclude that the campaign to discredit Pazniak as a reputable and popular political leader was successful. He is no longer a major player in Belarusian political life.
20 Cited in I.N. Kuznetsov and V.G. Mazets, compilers, *Istoriia Belarusi v dokumentakh i materialakh* (Minsk: Amalfeia, 2000), p. 640.
21 He is particularly fond of sport, and is often seen wearing a hockey sweater and helmet.
22 See D.R. Marples, *Belarus: a denationalized nation* (Amsterdam: Harwood, 1999), pp. 96–9.
23 During the years of the Lukashenka administration, all the editors of the high circulation daily newspapers have been replaced with others sympathetic to the government or else prepared to serve as government mouthpieces. These include the highest circulation daily newspaper, the Russian-language *Sovetskaia Belorussiia* and the formerly independent parliamentary organ, *Narodnaia hazeta*. The BNF newspaper, S*vaboda*, was dissolved in 1998. Six newspapers propagate either an independent or an opposition line, the most prominent of which are *Narodnaia volia* and *Belorusskaia delovaia gazeta*.
24 Personal communication from Vintsuk Viachorka, chairman of the Belarusian Popular Front, 18 February 2000.
25 Perhaps the best illustration of the President's views is his October 1999 speech to the Russian Duma, in which his targets included the IMF and Madeleine Albright. For a complete text of this speech, see the following web page: http://www.charter97.org/Materials/m119.asp
26 See D.R. Marples and Iu.A. Shimko, 'Interview with Vintsuk Viachorka', *Belarusian Review,* Vol. 12, No. 1 (Spring 2000).
27 This became most evident during the unofficial presidential elections of May 1999, when Pazniak, increasingly out of touch with the situation in Belarus, sent fax after fax to Minsk, much to the irritation of his colleagues. See, for example, Iu. Dubina, 'Zenon Pozniak vyshel iz prezidentskoi gonki', *Belorusskaia gazeta*, 17 May 1999, p. 5.
28 See V. Zviglianich, 'Pre-election Ukraine: Kuchma's Administration in the Eyes of the Electorate', *Prism–Biweekly Report*, 30 August 1999: 15–18.
29 See U. Padhol and D.R. Marples, 'Belarus: The President and the Opposition', *The Harriman Review,* Vol. 12, No. 1 (September 1999): 11–18.

30 On 19 August, the opposition newspaper *Narodnaia volia* featured an article by Mikhail Podoliak, which implied that Ambassador Georg Wieck, head of the OSCE's Advisory and Monitoring Group in Belarus, had placed heavy pressure on the opposition to enter talks with the government. The title of the article, making reference to Ambassador Wieck, was 'The President's middleman'. Ambassador Wieck has vigorously denied the accusation. See International League of Human Rights (ILHR), *Belarus Update*, Special Issue, 1 September 1999.

31 This followed the OSCE's failure, along with the EU and PACE, to recognise the October 2000 parliamentary elections as legitimate.

32 Reuters, 27 August 1999.

33 See ILHR, *Belarus Update*. Incidentally, if such a government were formed, it would signify that there are three existing 'governments' of Belarus: the Lukashenka regime, the Sharetski government-in-exile, and the exiled government of the Belarusian National Republic, formed in 1918.

34 According to these articles, if the presidency becomes vacant or if the President is unable to continue his duties, all authority is to be transferred to the Chairman of the Supreme Soviet until a new President-elect is sworn in. According to Article 104, the President can be removed if he violates the constitution, provided that a minimum 70 deputies of the Supreme Soviet agree to it. If the office of President is vacant, the Chairman of the Supreme Soviet is obligated to call a new presidential election after a minimum of 30 days have elapsed, but before the expiry of 70 days.

35 The invitation to Yugoslavia to join the Russia–Belarus Union actually came from the Russian side, through the Speaker of the State Duma, Gennadii Seleznev, on 8 April. It was subsequently discussed by telephone between Boris Yeltsin and Aliaksandr Lukashenka on the following day. See *Belorusskaia delovaia gazeta*, 12 April 1999, p. 1.

36 Not only western observers have raised questions about the seriousness of the Union. The Ukrainian President was cited in *Izvestiia* on 10 November as declaring that the 'Slavic Union is nothing more than a political trick, an abstract theoretical construction that has no real basis or historical prospects'. See *Radio Free Europe/Radio Liberty Newsline*, 10 November 1999.

37 The British analyst Taras Kuzio thus writes of Belarus's '*de facto* return to the status of a Russian dominion'. T. Kuzio, *Ukraine under Kuchma: Political Reform, Economic Transformation and Security Policy in Independent Ukraine* (New York: St Martin's Press, 1997), p. 182.

38 The main national holiday is thus 3 July, the date in 1944 when Minsk was liberated from German occupation. See Astrid Sahm, 'Political Culture and National Symbols: Their Impact on the Belarusian Nation Building Process', *Nationalities Papers*, Vol. 27, No. 4 (December 1999): 649–60.

39 At the time of writing, the results of the new (February 1999) census were not known. According to the previous census of 1989, the population of 10.15 million was made up of Belarusians (77.9 per cent), Russians (13.2 per cent), Poles (4.1 per cent), Ukrainians (2.9 per cent), and Jews (1.1 per cent). State Committee of the Belorussian SSR for Statistics, *Narodnoe khoziaistvo Belorusskoi SSR v 1989g.* (Minsk: Belarus, 1990), p. 16.

3 Explaining post-communist authoritarianism in Belarus

Vital Silitski

Introduction

The aim of this chapter is to explain the trajectory of post-communist political development in Belarus. The country terminated its move towards democracy as a result of the November 1996 constitutional referendum, carried out, ironically, at the initiative of its first democratically elected President, Aliaksandr Lukashenka. A new version of the constitution entrusted the President with effective control over all the institutions of authority, including the judiciary, local governments, and even the legislature. Post-referendum Belarus fails to comply with minimal democratic criteria.[1] Thus, the right of the people to elect the government in free and fair elections has been infringed by the dissolution of an elected parliament and its replacement with a hand-picked legislature, and the concomitant political rights and civil liberties have become subject to systematic attacks by the government. The undemocratic nature of the Belarusian government has been recognised by the international community.[2] Unlike some of the countries in the former USSR (especially the Central Asian countries) that also witnessed the emergence of a system of 'unlimited presidential power',[3] Belarus did not experience a direct transition from the Soviet to a post-Soviet dictatorship. In between, the country went through a period of extensive political liberalisation,[4] which was reversed by an outsider whose very rise to power would not have been possible under the old system. An explanation of post-communist political development in Belarus should therefore account for the factors and events that have influenced its transformation in the last decade, rather than being exclusively focused on the legacies of the Soviet past or of even earlier historical periods.

The theoretical foundation for such an explanation may be found in the studies of third wave transitions, generally organised around the two competing approaches. The structure-oriented approach (SOA) is preoccupied with the social and economic prerequisites for democracy. Those include: living standards and level of inequality, degree of industrialisation, urbanisation, level of educational attainment, past experiences with market reforms and liberalisation in the past that has given rise to civil societies and private sectors.[5] Likewise, the rise of authoritarianism (especially in Latin America) has often been explained by specific features of social, economic, and political structures that laid down the foundations of authoritarian societies.[6] An alternative theoretical perspective that explains the process and the outcomes of the regime change is the process-oriented approach (POA). It assumes that 'the high degree of indeterminacy embedded in situations where unexpected events, insufficient information, hurried and audacious choices, confusion about motives and interests, plasticity and even indefiniteness of political identities as well as talents of specific individuals are frequently decisive in determining outcomes'.[7] It stresses the active role of human beings in determining the dynamic and shaping the outcomes of transformation. The key concept in the POA is 'crafting',[8] which can be understood as a consistent, purposeful set of actions undertaken in order to initiate the transformation (or destruction) of a political regime.

The few available studies of the failure of the democratic transition in Belarus have focused on the strength of civil society, indicators of socio-economic modernity, and institutional arrangements as factors that virtually predetermined Belarus's movement towards authoritarianism, regardless of the period of political changes. The argument has generally been constructed within the SOA approach.[9] The same spirit of predestination has imbued culture-related explanations, which have focused on the legacies of the Soviet era, such as a long period of Sovietisation and the destruction of the national identity.[10]

The application of SOA to explaining post-communist transformations is complicated by the fact that structures and legacies have often been inconclusive in determining the outcomes of transitions. This may be proven by the emergence of 'democracies without prerequisites',[11] which comply with minimal democratic criteria but fall short of being called substantive democracies.[12] Such regimes have survived and evolved even in an unfriendly socio-economic and cultural environment. In the case of Belarus, the focus on malign legacies often overlooks such factors as the high level of urbanisation and educational attainment in the society, the absence of serious ethnic or religious conflicts, the low degree of income inequality – all factors which are usually considered favourable to a country's prospects for establishing a democracy. Moreover, public attitudes at the beginning of the period of political change were not any more anti-democratic than they were in many other post-communist societies, many of which have undergone quite successful democratic transitions.[13] However, explaining trajectories of post-communist political transformation only by means of POA may also be problematic, for 'such approaches fail to address the factors that shape actors' political preferences, the conditions under which these preferences change, and even the identity of pivotal actors'.[14]

A combination of these two approaches may overcome the problems associated with a straightforward application of either of them. Structures and prerequisites may widen or narrow down the range of feasible political strategies for major political players, sometimes leaving both democracy and dictatorship as feasible outcomes of transformation. The strategies and choices of political players, their capacity to craft the outcomes of transition, may determine the ultimate direction of regime change. In the post-communist world, major dimensions of crafting may include (a) achieving internal unity among the democratic forces; (b) reaching consent on the fundamental rules of the game of a future democracy, especially between 'soft-liners' within the (post)-dictatorial government and 'moderates' within the opposition; (c) establishing mechanisms or institutions for society-elite communication though which the public can provide feedback on the elite's conduct; (d) building up social support for democratic changes and the formulation of a credible democratic alternative to the autocratic challenges to which the process of democratisation may be subjected.

Inherited economic and socio-demographic structures, political institutions, and legacies of 'sovietisation' and 'Russification' considerably affect Belarus's chances for a successful democratic transformation. Belarus could hardly emulate Poland or the Czech Republic, and it was not predestined to depart from its eastern Slavic neighbours, both of which emerged as 'minimal' democracies. An explanation of the rise of Lukashenka to power should include constraints and opportunities opened up with the processes of liberalisation of Belarusian society, which allowed an 'outsider' to enter the race for the presidency. It should also emphasise the ability of President Lukashenka to manipulate democratic institutions, as opposed to the self-defeating strategies pursued by his opponents. The latter were reflected in the internal disunity of the democratic forces; a confrontational style of relations between major political elites; the dominant role of 'hard-liners' and 'radicals' in Belarusian politics; and the inability of the opposition to produce, and propagate, a credible alternative to Lukashenka's populist platform. This line of behaviour resulted in the failure of the country's political elite to achieve consensus on the mutually acceptable rules of the game that would guarantee democratic development, the creation of an opportunity for the populist challenger to assume power, and the elite's inability to withstand Lukashenka's efforts to concentrate unlimited authority.

Independence and beyond: towards the politics of division

The Soviet system began opening up in Belarus in the late 1980s. The major mass democratic movement of the time, the Belarusian Popular Front (BNF) emerged in 1988 as a nationalist movement in a republic with a deeply damaged national identity. Its demands for independence and 'Belarusisation' appealed only to a tiny group of nationalist intellectuals. The BNF nevertheless managed to attract public support by combining the nationalist agenda with advocacy of issues that were important to the public and were able to win a broader voter. These included demands to disclose all the information about the consequences of the Chernobyl disaster and to reveal the truth about the scale of Stalin's repressions in the 1930s. The BNF initially united all the democrats and was open even to rank-and-file Communist Party members. Having elected only 25 MPs in the 360-strong Belarusian Supreme Soviet, the BNF helped to organise the 'Democratic Club', which was joined by more than 100 MPs. The *nomenklatura* had to make certain concessions to this bloc. Thus, it allowed democrat Stanislau Shushkevich to be elected as First Deputy Chairman of the parliament, and Viacheslau Kebich to be appointed as Prime Minister.

After the collapse of the hard-line putsch in Moscow in August 1991, the Communist Party was suspended, Shushkevich was appointed as Speaker of the parliament, national symbols were restored, and the independence of Belarus was proclaimed. The *nomenklatura*, however, retreated from party cabinets to the institutions of the executive power, and the Council of Ministers emerged as the top decision-making body in the country. Together with its supporters in the parliament, it began to be called 'the Party of Power', which was confronted by the BNF-led opposition. The failure of elite compromise was partly caused by the inability of the Party of Power to accept the changes that had taken place after 1991 and by its conservatism and the absence of soft-liners in its ranks who would have shared at least some values and aspirations with the opposition.[15] Still, within the Belarusian *nomenklatura* there was a considerable body of high-ranking soft-liners who later became prominent leaders of the anti-Lukashenka opposition. Among those were Miacheslau Hryb, a police general and successor of Shushkevich as Speaker of parliament, Piotr Krauchanka, Minister of Foreign Affairs, Siamion Domash, head of Hrodna regional administration, and Pavel Kazlouski, Minister of Defence. However, the opposition was not ready to compromise either. After the August 1991 events, the BNF flatly rejected any idea of working together with the *nomenklatura*. Instead, it concentrated its efforts on capturing power without building a broader political alliance. No serious and structured political force existed between the two camps. The country 'lacked a political movement that was not tied to the state administration or to the Communist Party, and at the same time could work with those bodies to promote their aims'.[16] There was also a lack of an effective leader who could bring together constructive elements from both sides to provide for reforms and a relatively smooth transition to democracy.

In the execution of its strategy, the BNF started in December 1991 a campaign to call a referendum on the dissolution of parliament. About

440,000 signatures in favour of the motion were collected. Resorting to technicalities, the parliamentary majority refused to authorise the vote on the grounds of violation of the procedures for collecting signatures. The defeat of the referendum initiative proved that the BNF had overestimated its public support and its capacity to defeat the Party of Power by itself, and proved that it had failed to grow beyond a narrow movement with weak roots in society. It also highlighted the deep split among the democrats. Thus, the motion to reject the referendum was actively supported by Shushkevich, who by that time began to side with the pro-government majority on many issues. To some extent, the inconsistency of his political behaviour reflected his status as a political outsider and democratic Speaker in a conservative parliament. The BNF never forgave Shushkevich for what it believed was his betrayal. The rivalry between Shushkevich and the BNF's leader Zianon Pazniak seriously weakened the whole democratic camp.

The rejection of the referendum petition gave rise to a hard-line reaction on behalf of the Party of Power. Within a few months, an independent TV station was closed, privatisation was suspended and the ban on the Communist Party was lifted. In March 1993, Kebich suggested that Belarus should create an economic union with other CIS states and abandon its neutral status in favour of joining the CIS military alliance. Shushkevich sharply objected and returned to the opposition. This generated an open confrontation between two leaders. It ended in January 1994 with the removal of Shushkevich as Speaker and his replacement by Hryb. The Party of Power was set to consolidate control over the country – provided that the rise of Lukashenka had never happened.

Filling the vacuum: Lukashenka's rise to power

A growing confrontation between an increasingly hard-line government and a radical opposition took place in an increasingly apathetic society. Deteriorating economic conditions caused an increase in public disaffection with the whole political elite. This prepared the ground for the advancement of a populist outsider, a role played by Lukashenka, then a rank-and-file MP.

In his first years in politics, Lukashenka had positioned himself as a democrat who had criticised the party leadership for its inability to pursue political and economic reforms.[17] Having been elected to the Belarusian parliament in 1990, Lukashenka was initially close to the BNF, even trying to initiate a split in the Belarusian Communist Party by forming a faction 'Communists of Belarus for Democracy' in the parliament. Having noticed the growing public dissatisfaction with the political changes since August 1991, Lukashenka quickly changed his position. He sided with the pro-government majority and became a vocal opponent of political and economic reforms. He supported Kebich's policy of establishing a military and monetary union with Russia. In summer 1993, he visited Moscow to demonstrate his support for the anti-Yeltsin opposition in the Russian parliament.

Lukashenka's political fortunes grew as his opponents underestimated his capabilities. When the power struggle neared its climax, competing camps attempted to take advantage of his scandalous behaviour and populist appeal. The exploration of the corruption issue brought Lukashenka to the forefront of Belarusian politics in 1993–4. Public attention to corruption in the government was in fact attracted by the efforts of the opposition-controlled media, which endlessly reported facts of public embezzlement in 1992–3. The opposition, however, surrendered the issue to its outspoken opponent when the parliament established the anti-corruption commission in June 1993. It was Shushkevich who nominated Lukashenka, by that time his most vocal critic, to the chairmanship of the committee. Many BNF MPs voted in favour of approving him, apparently counting on the fact that Lukashenka would discredit the *nomenklatura* with his allegations. Meanwhile, the pro-Kebich majority counted on Lukashenka's zeal to defame Shushkevich. Indeed, Shushkevich was accused of embezzlement in the anti-corruption committee's report, which was presented by Lukashenka on 14 December 1993. Immediately after the Speaker was replaced, Lukashenka retargeted his attacks on top government officials, including Kebich himself. The allegations attracted huge public attention. As the Belarusian economy started to crumble in the aftermath of the withdrawal of the Russian rouble in July 1993, his accusations provided a simple explanation of reasons for the country's decline. The government repudiated by closing down Lukashenka's committee, only to boost his popularity rating before the planned presidential elections.

Lukashenka's chances to succeed to power were reinforced with the adoption of the new constitution on 15 March 1994. The constitution established a presidential republic, replacing the parliamentary system that had existed since the declaration of independence. The change was implemented to secure the election of Kebich as President, and, in so doing, to strengthen the control over the country by the Party of Power. The vote was set for 24 June.

The introduction of a presidential republic sharply reduced the chances for a successful democratisation in Belarus. The problem was not the form of government as such, but the context in which it was introduced. The country had no strong tradition of local government and the regional authorities were politically and financially weak compared to the centre; there was only one central state TV station and one state publishing house where almost all central newspapers and magazines were printed. In these circumstances, only effective parliamentary control over the government could bridle the executive's efforts to concentrate power. A drastic reduction in the extent of this control, however, would be more appropriate to serve the growing political ambitions of Kebich. A strong presidency would provide a prospective winner of elections with the opportunity of ruling without achieving or respecting ‘contingent consent’[18] with his opponents on the fundamental rules governing the political process.

Yet, it was Lukashenka who benefited from the constitutional changes, as his increasing popularity was given a chance to materialise into victory in the presidential election. Belarusian analysts usually explain his success in the presidential elections of 1994 as public disappointment with economic and political reforms and nostalgia for the Soviet past.[19] The margin of Lukashenka’s victory, however, was no match for the strength of pro-communist and anti-reform attitudes among the public. In summer 1993, for example, 22 per cent of respondents said that they would vote in elections for a democratic candidate and 13 per cent for a communist one. The numbers changed to 17 per cent and 20 per cent respectively in spring 1994.[20] Still, the April 1994 polls showed that 17 per cent of the public wanted a leftist president, 12 per cent a rightist one, and about 57 per cent a centrist.[21] Nostalgic feelings and support for the communist platform in society were on the rise, but had not become overwhelming. The key to winning the presidential election was to capture the average voter, not mobilised by existing political forces. In the event, all contestants, with the exception of Lukashenka, failed to do so.

Both opposition candidates, Pazniak and Shushkevich, were let down by an underestimation of their chances of winning the elections in their own right, by the weakness and incompetence of the political organisations that supported their candidature, and by their inability to address the most important issues of the election campaign. Neither of them spread his appeal beyond the committed democratic electorate, which ended up being divided. Pazniak’s chances of winning office were further reduced by his adoption of a radical nationalist rhetoric, which put him into conflict with other democratic parties and politicians, who were often declared to be puppets of Moscow for not sharing the BNF’s national platform.[22] The attempt to imitate Popular Fronts in the Baltic States in a country with a weak sense of ethnic identity limited public support for the BNF to a small constituency of ethnically conscious voters. To make things worse, Pazniak’s xenophobic statements directed towards Russians and his attempts to put forward territorial claims on Russia in January 1994 further hurt the BNF and the whole democratic movement.[23] Official propaganda received an opportunity to portray him as a Nazi who would wage a conflict with Russia and would persecute his opponents once he came to power.[24]

National revival is an important dimension of democratisation in so far as it provides a basis for the consolidation of the state, without which no modern democracy seems to be possible. The weakness of ethnic nationalism should not preclude Belarus from forming a sense of identity based on other principles. For instance, the promotion of a civil form of national identity to accommodate the Russian-speaking (though not necessarily pro-Russian) majority, would have equated 'the demos of the nation' with 'the demos of the state'[25] and therefore increased the country's chances of establishing a stable democracy. Meanwhile, the promotion of a radical version of ethnic nationalism deepened the split of Belarusian society into ethnically conscious Belarusians and a Russian-speaking majority. The accentuation of this division by the BNF only helped Lukashenka to use Pazniak as a counter-image and to consolidate the pro-Russian vote.

Shushkevich's campaign was equally inefficient. His candidacy was supported by two smaller opposition parties, which could not provide him with a strong political base. Shushkevich's popularity had dwindled since his removal from the speakership.[26] Name recognition turned into a liability for him, as the public tended to blame him for the economic and political cataclysms since the declaration of independence. Shushkevich's election platform consisted of a lengthy lecture on economic and political reforms that found sympathy only with highly educated constituents in large cities, primarily in Minsk.

As for Kebich, his presidential campaign was ruined by his over-reliance on the Russian bail-out of the Belarus economy, which he was trying to secure before the elections. Monetary union was blocked by the liberals in the Russian government, who saw it as a threat to Russia's financial stability. Russia provided a certain support to Kebich[27] by extending cheap credits and selling fuel at discount prices, which, however, was far from being enough to save his one-issue campaign. Lukashenka, meanwhile, managed to neutralise Kebich's trump card by declaring that the agreement on monetary union did not take into account Belarusian national interests, and pledged to arrange a new deal that would be founded on the equality of the participants rather than allowing the absorption of the Belarusian financial system by the Russian one. He positioned himself as a better defender of Belarusian interests.

Lukashenka's own campaign was run in a highly efficient and energetic manner. The promises of eradicating corruption, bringing down inflation, and developing closer ties with Russia and other CIS states tackled the issues of foremost concern to the majority of voters, some of which the opposition failed to articulate. Having attracted public attention, Lukashenka managed to impose upon the electorate his own interpretation of the 'causes of all the evils' in the country. At the same time, while exploring hard-line rhetoric, Lukashenka managed to present himself as an alternative to both the government and the opposition, thus absorbing the support of uncommitted voters. His controversial statements left the public guessing about his true political agenda. Lukashenka was able to combine support for political union with Russia with advocacy for the country's sovereignty, criticism of market reforms with pledges to continue privatisation, and allegations of corruption among top officials with promises not to purge the state apparatus. This campaign strategy allowed Lukashenka to maximise public support, as the inconsistency of his election platform duplicated the confusion of public opinion.[28] Clumsy attempts by the official media to discredit Lukashenka only intensified public interest in his campaign. As for the opposition, it virtually refused to believe in the credibility of Lukashenka's challenge, and abstained from attacking him. At most, the democrats saw him as a vote-splitter who could diminish the electoral chances of Kebich (against whom the election campaigns of both democratic candidates were targeted).[29]

On 24 June, Lukashenka obtained 44.82 per cent of the votes, Kebich finished second with 17.33 per cent, Pazniak third with 12.82 per cent, and Shushkevich fourth with 9.91 per cent. In the second round of voting that took place on 10 July, Lukashenka won with 80.4 per cent of the vote.[30] The election ended a sequence of equally self-defeating actions by both the Party of Power and the opposition, who, willingly or not, created the opportunity for the rise of a populist outsider.

Slipping towards autocracy: from Lukashenka's inauguration to the November 1996 referendum

A brief period of reforms was initiated by new Prime Minister Mikhail Chyhir and National Bank chairman Stanislau Bahdankevich soon after Lukashenka's inauguration was over, after the President had faced the political liabilities associated with price liberalisation and the tightening of credit to state enterprises. Growing increasingly hard-line, Lukashenka initiated a referendum on whether to endow the president with the right to dissolve parliament, to approve closer ties with Russia, introduce Russian as the second official language, and replace the post-independence national symbols with Soviet-era ones. The referendum gave Lukashenka positive answers to all four questions.

Meanwhile, the fragmentation of the opposition continued before the May 1995 parliamentary elections. The BNF formed an alliance with four smaller nationalist parties. The liberals attempted to form a bloc called 'Civil Accord' that would unite the United Democratic Party (ODP), Party of People's Consent (PNS), and the Civic Party.[31] Pazniak branded the bloc leaders as agents of Moscow's influence in Belarus. Moreover, 'Civic Accord' broke down before its creation was finalised, and candidates from the three parties ran against each other as well as against BNF-supported candidates. As a result, the BNF and United Democrats failed to elect a single MP in the first round of elections, whereas the Social Democrats elected just one. Unlike the democrats, the communists and their allies (the Agrarian Party) did unite and gained about a half of the parliamentary seats. Yet, it was not clear whether the new parliament would be given a chance to convene at all, as Lukashenka sought to remove the last constraints on his authority by obstructing the parliamentary elections and calling upon his supporters to boycott the vote. As a result, in the first two rounds of voting, only 119 out of 260 deputies were elected.[32]

In spite of the obstruction by the President, the Supreme Soviet of the thirteenth convocation was elected on 10 December 1995. The democrats finally managed to learn from their defeats and united. A new political party, the United Civic Party (OGP), was created through the merger of the ODP and the Civic Party, and a district-sharing agreement was reached between the BNF and OGP to increase the chances of democrats getting elected to parliament. While the BNF once again failed to elect a single member to parliament, the OGP won a majority of constituencies in Minsk. In a Left-dominated parliament, 21 MPs of the OGP-organised 'Civic Action' group acted flexibly in order to have a chance to establish themselves as an influential force. The faction helped to elect the Speaker of the new parliament, an agrarian, Siamion Sharetski, over the communist candidate, and actively worked to draft pro-reform bills, which the Left-dominated parliament found possible to adopt. The parliament soon found itself in opposition to Lukashenka's attempts to concentrate power at the expense of the parliament and Constitutional Court. Remarkably, the opposition was joined by the communist faction, which found his aspiration to consolidate unlimited authority a threat to its own political position. Lukashenka was left with only 60 MPs from the pro-presidential 'Accord' faction.

Lukashenka replied to the growing independence of the parliament with another referendum initiative. The new vote was to be on a new version of the constitution that would transfer many of the parliament's functions (such as appointment of members of the Constitutional Court, the Central Election Commission, and even part of the newly created upper house of parliament) to the presidency, extend his term of office by two years, and, by breaking the system of checks and balances, eventually liquidate the remaining democratic institutions in the country. The Supreme Soviet tried to counter-attack Lukashenka by proposing its own version of the constitution, which would have limited the President's authority. Viktar Hanchar, having won a parliamentary seat, was appointed as head of the Central Election Commission. A consultative council of seven major opposition parties, from communists to nationalists, was established to combat Lukashenka's referendum.

A concerted action of the opposition in parliament and outside initially forced Lukashenka to make certain concessions. He agreed to reschedule the date of the referendum from 7 November to 24 November, and to put the alternative version of the constitution to the vote. Finally, the parliament received backing from the Constitutional Court, which ruled that the referendum could only be advisory, as the 1994 constitution did not provide for the adoption of a new basic law by referendum. Lukashenka responded to the Court ruling by a decree annulling its decision. He declared that the referendum had legal force, transferred responsibility for conducting the referendum from the Central Election Commission to local authorities, and reduced media coverage of the referendum to official propaganda. The voting started two weeks before the date, which was normally allowed only for itinerant voters. Hanchar prematurely declared his intention to invalidate the results of the referendum, thus provoking his removal on 13 November, administered by the riot police on the President's orders. The last attempt at resistance, an impeachment procedure against Lukashenka, was initiated. The case signed by 70 MPs was passed to the Constitutional Court.

The opposition ranks crumbled when the Constitutional Court meddled with the impeachment proceedings, apparently under pressure and blackmail from the presidential office. On 21 November, a high-ranking delegation of the Russian leadership, including the Prime Minister Viktor Chernomyrdin and the Speakers of both houses of the Federal Assembly arrived in Minsk to broker a compromise. A part of the opposition placed high hopes on the Russian intervention, as they believed the Russian democratic leadership would not allow a dictatorship to be established in Belarus. The readiness of Russia's political establishment to support its most loyal ally, regardless of his human rights record, was underestimated. The compromise brokered by Chernomyrdin anticipated that Lukashenka would agree on the referendum's advisory status in exchange for the parliament calling off the impeachment proceedings. A Constitutional Assembly would have to be formed by the President and the parliament on a parity basis after the vote to amend the constitution. Since Lukashenka would have controlled the majority in a hypothetical assembly (by directly appointing one half and having his supporters in the parliamentary half), the deal only postponed the constitutional changes initiated by Lukashenka, falling short of preventing them. However, Siamion Sharetski and Valeri Tikhinia, Chairman of the Constitutional Court, signed it, for reasons ranging from intimidation by Lukashenka to attempts to please the top Russian leaders with their goodwill. On 23 November, when parliament voted to ratify the compromise, pro-Lukashenka MPs voted it down. Using this as a pretext, the President accused the Supreme Soviet of obstructing the deal. On the voting day of 24 November, Lukashenka again declared the referendum results to be binding. Several MPs were forced to recall their signatures under the impeachment petition to the Constitutional Court. The latter found itself in a position of political stalemate and concluded the impeachment hearings on 25 November, after the vote had been counted. The official tally gave 70 per cent in favour of Lukashenka's constitution, which was signed on 27 November. On 28 November, the parliamentary chamber was shut down, the Constitutional Court was dissolved, and the House of Representatives composed of 110 members was appointed by Lukashenka's decree. The country lost its democratic constitution after the opposition failed to withstand the President's attack on it.

Conclusions: lessons from the past and implications for the future

Post-Soviet Belarus might not have had all the prerequisites for establishing a stable democracy, yet the possibility of 'democracy without prerequisites' was not altogether foreclosed. It was the country's political elite, which did not stand up to the task of crafting democracy. The turn to authoritarianism was facilitated by the self-destructive behaviour of the opposition, namely by its internal disunity, lack of pragmatism, shallow grassroots support and weak public appeal. This pattern of behaviour prevented it from taking advantage of the opportunities, and reacting adequately to the structural, institutional, and cultural constraints in which they operated. For example, the fact that ethnic nationalism was an efficient tool of mobilising public support in the Baltics did not make it as efficient in Belarus. The socio-economic structure of the Belarusian electorate required the opposition to accentuate a different set of political issues during the election campaigns. Unresolved contradictions between democratic parties might have created the basis for a healthy competition between parties in Central European countries where the authoritarian alternative had mostly vanished, rather than in Belarus, where democratisation had not been completed and the danger of a comeback by the hard-liners remained possible.

The changes, which have occurred in the political landscape, economic conditions and the international environment since November 1996 are a mixed blessing for the country's prospects for democratisation in the future. The consolidation of the system of personal authority has made problematic the possibility of an evolutionary path out of the existing situation. Having limited access to decision-making or influence on public opinion reduces the range of instruments available for the opposition to promote its political agenda. Economic problems caused by the systematic avoidance of market reforms have turned public opinion against Lukashenka and his policies. However, dissatisfaction with the government is of a rather passive nature, as only a tiny fraction of Belarusian society takes part in any kind of organised protest actions. The international isolation of Belarus has induced Lukashenka to seek a way out in political and economic union with Russia. The increasing political, economic, and military dependence of Belarus upon Russia coupled with disengagement from the West may make western pressure on Belarus ineffective. However, the recent liberalisation of economic policy in Russia and the shift towards a more pragmatic approach in Russia–Belarus relations by the government of President Vladimir Putin poses serious challenges for Belarus and threatens to undermine political stability in the country if the economy fails to adjust. Furthermore, the developing co-operation between Russia and the European Union may affect political and economic developments in Belarus, sandwiched between these two entities. The stability of the political regime masterminded by Lukashenka, hence, is far from guaranteed. The emerging opportunities for change, however, have to be utilised by the elites. For the cause of democracy to prevail, Belarus needs the proponents of democracy to unite, to be able to adjust to the changing environment, to learn, and to practise, the art of democratic craftsmanship. Post-referendum developments, however, prove that the democrats may still not be up to this task.

A major effort to unite the opposition was undertaken at the Congress of Democratic Forces convened in January 1999, which established an umbrella for the opposition, the Coordinating Council of Democratic Forces. However, the failure of the opposition-organised alternative presidential elections in May 1999 highlighted the persisting divides. The vote that might have turned into a straw poll determining the leader of a united opposition turned into a farce. Some of the campaign organisers undertook a series of actions that discredited the whole campaign in the eyes of the public. Thus, Hanchar, who headed the shadow election commission, allowed gross falsifications of the election results, having provided for dubious voting procedures and eventually over-reported the turnout.[33] Moreover, Pazniak, who ran against Chyhir, withdrew from the race in the last days before the completion of the vote in order to disrupt the elections and in so doing to prevent Chyhir from rising to political prominence.[34] As Pazniak's withdrawal was not supported by the BNF leadership, the emerging rift within the party led to a split in September 1999. After the majority of the BNF's congress disapproved of Pazniak's tactics and failed to re-elect him as leader, his loyalists defected to create a new party. The OGP, of which Hanchar was a member, was also close to a split over his tactics.

The events that followed the shadow elections gave room for some optimism. A group of young opposition leaders, known as 'the New Wave', came to the forefront after the autumn of 1999. This group managed to organise a series of mass protests known as 'The Hot Fall-1999' and 'The Hot Spring-2000', which drew thousands of participants and received a lot of international coverage due to the police crackdown. Bowing to mass protests and to pressure exerted by the West, Lukashenka agreed to negotiate the terms of the upcoming parliamentary and presidential elections with the opposition. The opposition's demands included liberalising the election code, extending the prerogatives of parliament, allowing opposition representatives to speak in the state media, and releasing prisoners of conscience.

The negotiations came to a stalemate as it became clear that Lukashenka would only partially honour the opposition's demands, falling short of satisfying the most crucial ones. The announcement of elections to the House of Representatives set for 15 October 2000 precipitated another division of the opposition into competing factions advocating different ways out of the political standstill. The major division line now lay between those who boycotted the elections (the BNF, OGP, Belarusian Social Democratic Assembly), and those who participated (the Belarusian Social Democratic Party, Belarusian Yabloko, and a number of politically active non-governmental organisations and prominent individuals, such as Chyhir and several former deputies of the Supreme Soviet); or between, respectively, radical and moderate camps. Besides personal ambitions, the split was caused by the opposition's lack of a common vision of the future of the country and of a common strategy for restoring democracy. Radicals refused any actions that might be interpreted as betrayal of the 1994 constitution and collaboration with the government, preferring extra-institutional forms of political activity and anticipating that sweeping political changes would take place soon. Moderates, sceptical about the short-term possibility of a radical change, chose to work within the system masterminded by Lukashenka. Mutual recriminations and suspicions among former allies mounted. The truth was that none of the proposed strategies would work if it had to be carried out by separate factions involved in partisan warfare. Although the radicals were satisfied with the low turnout at the elections, one could hardly observe any public enthusiasm for their campaign.[35] As for the moderates, their quest to establish a systemic opposition was blocked by the election authorities – they disqualified most of the independent parliamentary candidates even before the vote had been carried out. Those who were registered had to withstand dual pressure from the authorities and from the pro-boycott opposition, as its efforts were concentrated in the large cities, where democrats ran. As a result, only two opposition candidates were elected to the House of Representatives. The situation came close to threatening the very existence of the democratic opposition, on the one hand, by the opportunism of those who were prepared to accept the existing rules of the game and were satisfied with the partial concessions made by the regime; and, on the other, by the maximalism of those who abhorred each and every attempt at negotiation or compromise. The internal conflicts continued after the elections. Moderates were purged from the Co-ordinating Council of Democratic Forces, while several opposition figures announced their intention to run for the presidency even before any attempt to agree upon a single candidate had been made.

New divisions occurred in the context of a continuous relegation of the opposition to a parallel society. In this condition, the opportunities for influencing public opinion, let alone the social and political processes in the country, are strictly limited. Political parties remain small and undeveloped and the network of non-governmental organisations is still concentrated in the capital. The opposition's inability to break out of the parallel society (or its reluctance to do so under the pretext that this may be done only by joining the 'official' society, which may be interpreted as collaboration with the authorities) reduces its chances of building up grassroots support, of articulating an alternative to Lukashenka's authority, and of establishing itself as a credible political force. Ironically, the ideas advocated by the democratic leaders have become more popular than the democrats themselves.[36]

Hitherto, the opposition has not drawn lessons from its previous political defeats, once again preferring disunity and factionalism to co-operation and compromise. If this line of behaviour is not changed, the opposition may continue to forfeit the chances of bringing Belarus back on the path towards democracy. Changing socio-economic conditions, growing public support for democratic reforms, the rise of civil society, and the emergence of an external environment more favourable to the prospects of democratisation may not be converted into political changes. Such possible developments may lead to a new political situation that may be characterised as 'prerequisites without democracy'.

Notes

1 According to R. Dahl, *Dilemmas of Pluralist Democracy: Autonomy vs. Control* (New Haven and London: Yale University Press, 1982), pp. 11–12, these include: control of government decisions by elected officials; the right to elect government in frequent and fair elections; universal suffrage; and rights to self-expression, alternative sources of information, and to form public associations.

2 The Council of Europe deprived Belarus of observer status. Freedom House downgraded Belarus's political rights and civil liberties rating from 'partly free' in 1992–5 to 'not free' since 1996: http://www.freedomhouse.org/ratings/afghan.htm, accessed 10 December 2000. The US Department of State report on human rights practices states that President Lukashenka 'has consolidated power steadily in the executive branch through authoritarian means'. See http://www.state.gov/www/global/human_rights/1999_hrp_report/belarus.html, accessed 10 December 2000.

3 Term used by D.R. Marples, *Belarus: a denationalized nation* (Amsterdam: Harwood, 1999), p. xii.

4 According to G. O'Donnell and P. Schmitter, *Transitions from Authoritarian Rule: Tentative Conclusions about Democracies* (Baltimore: Johns Hopkins University Press, 1986), p. 7: 'By liberalization we mean the process of making effective certain rights that protect both individuals and social groups from arbitrary or illegal acts committed by the state or third parties.'

5 S. Haggard and R. Kaufman, *The Political Economy of Democratic Transitions* (Princeton: Princeton University Press, 1995); S. Huntington, *The Third Wave: Democratization in the Late Twentieth Century* (Norman: University of Oklahoma Press, 1991); D. Rueschemeyer, E. Huber Stephens and J. Stephens, *Capitalist Development and Democracy* (Chicago: University of Chicago Press, 1992).

6 See, for example: A. Hirschman, 'The Turn to Authoritarianism in Latin America and the Search for its Economic Determinants', in D. Collier (ed.), *New Authoritarianism in Latin America* (Princeton: Princeton University Press, 1979), pp. 61–98; R. Kaufman, 'Industrial Change and Authoritarian Rule in Latin America: A Concrete Review of a Bureaucratic–Authoritarian Model', in Collier, *New Authoritarianism*, pp. 165–254.

7 O'Donnell and Schmitter, *Transitions from Authoritarian Rule*, p. 5.

8 The term used by G. di Palma, *To Craft Democracies: An Essay on Democratic Transitions* (Berkeley: University of California Press, 1990).

9 V. Karbalevich, 'Put' Lukashenko k vlasti', in D. Furman (ed.), *Belorussiia i Rossiia: obshchestva i gosudarstva* (Moscow: Prava cheloveka, 1998), pp. 226–59; K Mihalisko, 'Belarus: retreat to authoritarianism', in K. Dawisha and B. Parrott (eds), *Democratic Changes and Authoritarian Reactions in Russia, Ukraine, Belarus, and Moldova* (Cambridge: Cambridge University Press, 1997), pp. 223–81.

10 Mihalisko, 'Belarus: retreat to authoritarianism', p. 224, claims: 'It is the lack of nationalism . . . that makes Lukashenka possible.' An equally strong argument could be made that it is nationalism that contributed to the emergence of the dictatorship of Miloševich.

11 Term used by S. Fish, 'Mongolia: Democracy Without Prerequisites', *Journal of Democracy*, Vol. 9, No. 3 (1998): 127–41.

12 Substantive democracies are understood here as those that correspond to Dahl's criteria for an 'ideal democratic process': Dahl, *Dilemmas of Pluralist Democracy*, p. 6.

13 See, for example, A. Fintfer and E. Mickiewicz, 'Redefining the Political System of the USSR: Mass Support for Political Change', *American Political Science Review*, Vol. 86, No. 4 (1992): 857–74.

14 Haggard and Kaufman, *Political Economy*, pp. 5–6.

15 See S. Connors, D. Gibson and M. Rhodes, 'Caution and Ambivalence Over Joining NATO', *Transition*, 11 August 1995: 42–6, for evidence of strong anti-western and anti-reform attitudes among the Belarusian elite.

16 Marples, *Belarus*, p. 65.

17 A. Lukashenko, 'Diktatura: belorusskii variant?', *Adkrytae Hramadstva*, 1 (1999): 37–40.

18 According to O'Donnell and Schmitter, *Transitions from Authoritarian Rule*, contingent consent consists of the winners' commitment to exercise political authority in a way that protects the right of the opposition to take office in future; and of the losers' determination to respect binding decisions made by the government in exchange for having this right.

19 See Karbalevich, 'Put' Lukashenko k vlasti'; Mihalisko, 'Belarus: retreat to authoritarianism'.

20 *Sovetskaia Belorussiia*, 10 March 1994.

21 *Sovetskaia Belorussiia*, 25 May 1994.

22 See, for example, 'Prodolzhenie "Proekta Chigiria"', *Belorusskaia delovaia gazeta*, 31 March 1999.

23 Z. Pazniak, 'O russkom imperializme i ego opasnosti', *Narodnaia hazeta*, 15–17 January 1994.

24 See L. Masliukova, 'Vlast' peremenilas'', *Sovetskaia Belorussiia*, 3 Febuary 1994.

25 Terms used by J. Linz and A. Stepan, *Problems of Democratic Transition and Consolidation: Southern Europe, South America and Post-Communist Europe* (Baltimore: Johns Hopkins University Press, 1996), p. 16.

26 Shushkevich's approval rating was 52 per cent in January 1992, 47 per cent in May 1992, and 33.6 per cent in January 1993, according to an opinion poll conducted by the sociological company 'Public Opinion'.

27 A. Sensatsionnyi, 'sensatsionnyi rezul'tat vyborov v Belorussii', *Izvestiia*, 26 June 1994.

28 Thus, respondents could return positive answers to mutually exclusive statements or suggestions, such as to strengthen independence and to achieve union with Russia, to build a market economy and to regulate prices, etc. See 'Zhizn' v nashe vremia', *IISPS News*, No. 4 (December 1999): 20–45.

29 'It happened that criticism during this struggle for votes did not go outside the trio Kebich–Pazniak–Shushkevich. The opinions of these candidates were widely

known, as were their weak and strong sides. Lukashenka, at the same time, stood aside from being criticised. Still, he spared no words against his opponents.' S. Owsiannik and J. Strielkowa, *Wladza a spoleczenstwo: Bialorus 1991–1998* (Warsaw: Rzeczpospolita, 1998), p. 95, translated from Polish by the author.

30 *Narodnaia Hazeta*, 11 December 1995: 2–3.

31 For full details about parties, see E. Korosteleva's table in Appendix to Chapter 5.

32 *Narodnaia Hazeta*, 28 November 1995.

33 Hanchar claimed that some 53 per cent of voters voted in the election administered through mobile election committees. Sociological surveys showed that only 5 per cent of adults admitted participating in these elections. See 'Vybory-99: prodolzhenie sleduet', *Belorusskaia delovaia gazeta*, 23 July 1999.

34 Pazniak claimed Chyhir's candidacy to be the outcome of a Russian plot to mastermind a puppet opposition leader who would maintain Belarus's loyalty to Moscow once he had come to power. See Iu. Dubina, 'Zianon Pozniak o planakh vozvrashcheniia na rodinu i rosiiskikh spetssluzhbakh', *Belorusskaia gazeta*, 15 March 1999.

35 According to independent opinion polls, only 6 per cent of the voters mentioned the boycott as a reason for their non-participation in the election. See 'Monitoring', *Belorusskaia delovaia gazeta*, 1 December 2000.

36 Support for a market economy grew from 52.1 per cent in June 1995 to 72.2 per cent in November 1999, and support for the creation of a union state between Russia and Belarus declined from 31.2 per cent in May 1996 to 21.8 per cent in November 1999. Whereas public support for Lukashenka consistently remained around the 40 per cent level, approval ratings for opposition leaders did not exceed 5 per cent. See 'Zhizn' v nashe vremia'.

4 Difficulties of elite formation in Belarus after 1991

Olga Belova-Gille

Introduction

At the beginning of the 1990s, most of the new independent states stemming from the disintegration of the USSR chose a democratic institutional design for their new political systems. Nevertheless, the political evolution of these countries differed considerably. By the end of the decade, authoritarian practices of power coexisted with democratic political institutions in some of these new countries. This was not surprising, because consolidated democracy is not the only possible outcome of transition from authoritarian rule. Even when established, democratic institutions may generate outcomes that cause some politically important forces to opt for authoritarianism.[1]

One of the most significant variables that can explain the differences of political development in the CIS countries is linked to the elite formation process. In many cases political actors' decisions and strategies have been more important for the construction of political systems (democratic as well as authoritarian) than economic and socio-cultural conditions. These strategies can be crucial for the development of political regimes, especially under conditions of instability during the transition period in post-communist countries with weak social structures and an absence of social groups with defined interests and fixed political allegiances. This is why the political elite continues to figure heavily in studies of communist breakdowns and the post-communist regimes, which have emerged in Eastern Europe.[2] It is therefore crucial to study the elite formation process in Belarus, in order to understand how it could influence the country's political development.

The members of the political elite can be defined as the people occupying top-level positions in Belarus's main political institutions[3] and capable of taking part in important decisions on a national level. The political elite is part of a larger political class, which comprises all political actors and, in particular, opposition politicians who are presently excluded from the main political institutions. This study focuses on the official political elite. Therefore, members of the political opposition in Belarus who were not represented in the executive institutions and who lost their representation in parliament after the constitutional crises in autumn 1996 will be excluded from this analysis.

Before directly addressing this subject, some preliminary remarks about the state of the Belarusian ruling elite under the communist regime are necessary. First, within the Belarusian ruling elite during this period there was neither hierarchical contestation, nor any political ambition to build an independent state and implement new policies. The perfect integration of the Belarusian elite into the Soviet power system prevented the emergence of a new political elite in Belarus as well as any possibility of rapid adaptation of the former elite majority to the ideas of national independence and democratic reform.

Second, until July 1994, the old conservative elite dominated the main political institutions of newly independent Belarus. The absence of political and economic reforms in this period reduced the possibility of elite renewal and favoured the elaboration of mechanisms for transferring the power of the former ruling elite to the new political institutions. These included the creation of the powerful presidential institution and the maintenance of a majoritarian electoral system for parliamentary elections.

Third, one of these mechanisms for the transfer of power led to a significant turnover within the national political elite from July 1994 to December 1996. The unexpected election of Aliaksandr Lukashenka was followed by the replacement of the majority of the top politicians within Belarusian political institutions during this period. A study of individual appointments to top-level positions allows us to define the main mechanisms of recruitment to the national political elite. Nevertheless, the importance of these changes was limited by the fact that the newly elected President chose to rebuild a hierarchical model of power in order to reinforce his personal authority. He proceeded to create patronage networks favouring recruitment on the basis of personal loyalty rather than professional competence.

Finally, the relative stability that has characterised the composition of the political elite since the beginning of 1997 provides an opportunity to analyse the Belarusian political elite in a more dynamic way, disclosing general trends related to political turnover. Our research will demonstrate that the category, which benefited from the rapid changes in the mid-1990s and attained the status of the national political elite, includes middle-level regional administrative managers and representatives of the security forces.

The Belarusian elite under the communist regime

In order to understand the process of political change in Belarus at the beginning of the 1990s, which involved changes of institutional design as well as the modification of the political elite, it is first necessary to review certain aspects of the previous political regime.

For the majority of the former Soviet republics the virtual non-existence of a national political elite became a crucial problem at the outset of transition in the late 1980s. Institutional design at republican level reproduced, in theory, the hierarchy of the main political institutions at the Union level, but in reality no important political decision could be made at regional levels without prior consent from above. The Central Committee of the Communist Party of Belarus (CPB) was a subsidiary of the Central Committee of the Communist Party of the Soviet Union (CPSU). Republican Supreme Soviet sessions were used simply to approve decisions taken earlier in Moscow. Most republican ministers depended more on the corresponding central body than on the republican Council of Ministers.[4] The activity of the republican governing elite was limited essentially to the execution of decisions made by the centre.

Therefore the republican ruling elite was not a political elite *stricto sensu* from either a structural or a functional point of view. The positions occupied by republican authorities were located at the middle level of the Soviet political system and their competencies were reduced to the management of public policies defined by the Union centre. At the same time the Belarusian ruling elite was extremely well integrated into the Soviet *nomenklatura* structure and devoid of specific national characteristics.[5]

It is not surprising that Gorbachev's liberalisation in the mid-1980s did not cause many splits within the monolithic ruling elite in Belarus. The conservative character of the Belarusian ruling elite in the Soviet era exerted a profound influence on the further development of the national political elite and facilitated the reconstruction of an authoritarian model of power in the late 1990s.

Elite and institutional changes during the transition period

A national political elite in Belarus formally appeared with the acquisition of independence. On the one hand, the former republican elite was automatically granted the formal status of a national political elite because of the institutional changes due to independence. On the other hand, the creation of a new national state implied the necessity of elaborating and implementing some national public policies. It was therefore necessary to involve the former republican ruling elite in the decision-making process in order to determine the country's development priorities. Nevertheless, the formal change of status did not imply an immediate change in the competencies and responsibilities of members of the ruling elite. The situation in Belarus was further complicated by the fact that, despite the changes in the institutional structure, no important changes took place either in the top-level positions or within the ruling elite during the first years of independence.

The Council of Ministers and the twelfth Supreme Soviet

Even though the Supreme Soviet formally became the supreme political institution after the disappearance of the Communist Party,[6] its new relations with the Council of Ministers were not clearly defined. The Belarusian Council of Ministers benefited from many powers liberated from the control of the CPB Central Committee as well as from the supervision of Moscow. At the same time, the composition of the government, whose top level was staffed mainly by Central Committee members, remained unchanged until 1994. This explains why during the first three years of Belarusian independence all government actions were naturally directed towards the reinforcement of government autonomy and the enlargement of the competencies of the executive body in relation to the legislature. In this period Prime Minister Viacheslau Kebich became the most influential political actor in Belarus. He also enjoyed the support of the largest parliamentary fraction, 'Belarus', composed of 119 conservative MPs who hoped that the Prime Minister would be able to protect their interests.

In fact, Kebich was a perfect example of a successful Soviet manager from the former ruling elite who had easily adapted to the new conditions, illustrating the conversion of former *nomenklatura* members into a new political elite. In August 1991, he was one of the first members of the establishment to reject Communist Party membership, as it was no longer useful for professional and social advancement. This pragmatism was followed by a large number of members of the Belarusian ruling elite.

The function of legislative bodies at different levels[7] had been quite symbolic in the Soviet political system. Their top positions of Chairman and Deputy Chairman had often been taken by party or state officials, as was also the case with the twelfth Supreme Soviet, when at the beginning of its activity the First Secretary of the CPB, Nikalai Dementei, was designated as Chairman of the Belarusian Supreme Soviet.

The twelfth Supreme Soviet was formed after the first multi-party elections to the republican Supreme Soviets, on 4 March 1990. Despite the domination of the 84 per cent of Communist Party members, there were 25 MPs from the opposition Belarusian Popular Front (BNF). More than 90 per cent of MPs were elected to the Supreme Soviet for the first time. Nevertheless, one-third of them were composed of members of the Communist Party apparatus and the Soviet executive body, and almost one-third of industrial and agricultural managers.[8]

This composition reflected the conservative nature of the Belarusian Supreme Soviet, which did not initiate any important political or economic reforms during its five-year mandate. The fact that the conservative majority lost its ideological cohesion with the disappearance of the dominant role of the Communist Party did not mean that it was ready to adopt new ideas or to share its power with the opposition. Therefore, the

Belarusian Supreme Soviet was a rare example among the republican Supreme Soviets inherited from the Soviet Union, which managed to stay in place until the legal end of its activities in 1995.[9]

Most of the conservative MPs and members of the government were perfectly adapted to the centralised model of power that relied on chains of personal dependence between leaders and their subordinates. On the one hand, the lack of personal initiative and freedom in this model was compensated by reduced competencies and responsibilities. On the other hand, this system of 'patrimonial communism'[10] favoured the practices of patronage and clientelistic networks. It explains why the members of the former elite chose an institutional design that could favour recognition of the local and national leaders of clientelistic networks.

Despite the general conservative character of the parliamentary majority, the Supreme Soviet became a public political scene where new personalities could appear. The best example was Stanislau Shushkevich, elected to the presidency of the Supreme Soviet in August 1991 after the departure of Dementei. Unlike the majority in parliament, he did not make his career in the party apparatus or in executive bodies. He was a researcher in nuclear physics, and later became Head of the Nuclear Physics Department in the Belarusian State University. Before he was elected to the Supreme Soviet, he was a Deputy Director of Education, in charge of scientific researchers in the State University. His political engagement started at the end of the 1980s when he criticised government policies for the management of the consequences of the Chernobyl nuclear catastrophe.

These minor changes in the Supreme Soviet and the neutralisation of the most conservative part of the Belarusian ruling elite from the CPB apparatus were not sufficient to introduce radical changes in the political elite in Belarus between 1991 and 1994. The members of the former ruling elite managed to keep their positions in the government and in the parliament. The absence of legislative elections in this period prevented the renewal of the Belarusian political elite and reduced the possibilities for the opposition to influence Belarusian politics.

Creation of the presidential institution and the first Belarusian President

The presidential institution appeared in Belarus later than in Russia or Ukraine, despite the fact that the same model was desired in all three cases: a famous Soviet administrative manager, who had been in charge of some high offices in the Communist Party apparatus and in central executive bodies, organises the transfer of his position of power in the new presidential institution.[11] Its new legitimacy, due to elections based on universal suffrage, empowered him to go ahead with his own policies, independently of the legislative will represented by the Supreme Soviet, which had been elected while the Soviet Union still existed. In Belarus, this office was created for the Prime Minister Kebich, who urged the Supreme Soviet to adopt a new constitution on 15 March 1994. This constitution was based substantially on the old Soviet-era one, with one major difference: the introduction of the presidential office.

However, this model of power transfer did not work in Belarus. First, the time factor was very important for a successful realisation of this model. The sooner elections were held, the stronger the probability of the absence of any real competition from other candidates. The shorter the period of governance of the main candidate, the better his chances were of being elected on promises of economic and social miracles. Early elections also ensured greater influence on the electorate, because of the control of the mass media.

In the case of the Belarusian Prime Minister, it was rather difficult to build a presidential campaign on promises of positive changes in the economic and social situation after four years of deepening crises under his government. Moreover, media pressure in favour of the Prime Minister had the opposite effect, provoking irritation among the population. In addition, these years also witnessed the arrival of new political actors.

Kebich's main rival during the electoral campaign became Aliaksandr Lukashenka. A graduate of the history faculty of the Mahileu Teachers' Training Institute in 1975 and of the Belarusian Agricultural Academy in 1985, he served in the military service in 1975–7, and subsequently in 1980–2 in the frontier troops of the Soviet army, and in 1977–8 worked in Komsomol and administrative bodies in the city of Mahileu. From 1982 he worked as deputy head of a collective farm, deputy manager of a building materials factory, then head of the state farm 'Gorodets' in the Shklov district.

It was the mandate as an MP of the twelfth Supreme Soviet, which he gained in 1990 that enabled this unknown state farm director to enter into national politics. The new political situation and the increasing importance of the Supreme Soviet allowed Lukashenka to gain some popularity as the head of the anti-corruption commission (April 1993 to July 1994). At the end of 1993 he sued the two chief government officials, who were at that time Kebich and Shushkevich, charging them with abusing their office and using state services for their personal benefit. These actions gave Lukashenka the aura of a politician fighting for justice. In March 1994 he announced his entry into the electoral competition for the presidential office during a speech on television denouncing the corruption of some other high officials. Even though his electoral programme was rather similar to that of Kebich, based on economic conservatism and the restoration of close ties with Russia, his fiery campaign rhetoric was sufficient to bring him 85 per cent of the votes in the second round of elections on 10 July 1994.

Mechanisms of elite recruitment under Lukashenka's presidency

Lukashenka's accession to the presidency was marked by a significant turnover in the Belarusian political elite. The specificity of the Belarusian case consists of the fact that once in the presidential office, Lukashenka received an important power of appointment to the newly created Presidential Administration and the government. At the same time he did not represent any political force and did not have many human resources to fill the positions in these political institutions. This is why he naturally based his recruitment mostly on his connections to the Mahileu *oblast* where he had previously been a state farm director, and on his contacts with other MPs in the twelfth Supreme Soviet. Moreover, his wish to reinforce his personal power obliged him to select his new collaborators according to the criterion of personal loyalty rather than on the basis of other credentials like competence and experience.

His recruitment policy was not completely new: it reproduced some characteristics of the Soviet model of elite recruitment. Nevertheless, there were some significant differences. Under Soviet-type systems the appointments were hierarchical ones made by superiors sitting in judgement on their administrative inferiors. Even if this judgement was sometimes based on performance as assessed by superiors rather than by abstract rules, few people were chosen solely on the basis of personal knowledge or personal bonds. Advancement to the top of the Soviet political system was more a result of the collective sponsorship of the whole Communist Party oligarchy, taking into account objective criteria based on candidates' independent political resources or appropriate professional qualifications.[12]

An analysis of the appointments made after the election of Lukashenka shows the insignificance of objective criteria in the majority of nominations of high officials to the main political institutions of the country. All the mechanisms of recruitment that he introduced reveal different forms of patronage whereby personal considerations are decisive in the appointment. We should note that patronage is defined in this case as the creation of patron–client bonds through personnel policy or by drawing on pre-existing bonds. We can distinguish pure patronage by the unexpectedness of the appointments when people are recruited to important staff positions without any qualifications and, in the majority of cases, from among old associates ('favouritism towards old associates'). Another form of patronage is characterised by an extremely fast promotion of persons with some educational credentials but without any appropriate professional experience ('sponsorship of outsiders'). There is also a patronage of former members of the elite who have been confirmed in positions equivalent to the ones they held in the past because of their demonstration of personal allegiance to the new President ('adaptation by loyalty').

Patronage networks in the Presidential Administration and the government

The main recruitment strategy used by Lukashenka to create the staff of the Presidential Administration was recruitment from old associates, mainly from his supporters during the electoral campaign. This is why Leanid Sinitsyn, who was a manager of the electoral team, became the chief of the Presidential Administration. Ivan Titenkou, in charge of financial support for the electoral team, obtained the post of Presidential Manager ('upravliaiushii delami presidenta'). Viktar Sheiman, formerly responsible for Lukashenka's security, was appointed as Secretary of the National Security Council. Uladzimir Kanapleu, an MP and Lukashenka's assistant who had been responsible for collecting votes in Mahileu *oblast* during the electoral campaign, became First Adviser to the President. In the same manner most of the electoral campaign team members were rewarded for their support by new appointments.[13]

In fact, the bonds existing between some of Lukashenka's supporters dated back quite a long way. For instance, despite their membership in the twelfth Supreme Soviet, Lukashenka had got to know Titenkou and Sinitsyn from their work in the Committee of the CPB in Mahileu *oblast* (*obkom*) in the 1980s, under the direction of the First Secretary Vasil Leonau, who became Minister of Agriculture in 1995. A significant number of appointees with experience of work in Mahileu *oblast* led some analysts to conclude that 'the Mahileu clan' had risen to power.

Nevertheless, the cadre resources of Mahileu *oblast* were not inexhaustible, and the twelfth Supreme Soviet became another important source of recruitment for new appointees whose professional profiles were rather close to those of their Mahileu collegues. MPs with experience of work in party and Soviet executive organs at the regional level were appointed to the government, for example Uladzimir Garkun, First Secretary of Dzerzhinsk gorkom, who became Deputy Prime Minister; Vladimir Rusakevich, former Deputy Chairman of the Brest *oblispolkom*; Ivan Kenik, Chairman of the *ispolkom* in Mozyr *gorsovet*; and others.

Previous experience of work in party and Soviet executives was not the sole criterion for recruitment. Many MPs coming directly from management positions in enterprises or organisations were appointed to the government. For example, MP Vasil Dalgaleu, Deputy Manager of the factory 'Diaproektor' in Rogacheu, who became Deputy Prime Minister in 1995; or Inessa Drabysheuskaia, head of the Oncology Centre in Homel, who became Minister of Health.

In most of the aforementioned cases, the people appointed to the highest positions in the government and the Presidential Administration had neither particular qualifications nor experience of working in government. Experience as a plant manager or district party committee member was sufficient in the eyes of Lukashenka and his close collaborators.

Personal loyalty to the President and readiness to implement his policies were also reinforced by the fact that almost none of the candidates had any objective reasons for occupying the positions to which they had been appointed. If, in a general way, the absence of appropriate qualifications or experience and the presence of personal obligations do not necessarily entail incompetence, some appointments were more than surprising and introduced some doubts about the capacities of appointees to perform their professional obligations. For example, Piotr Prakapovich, who became Deputy Prime Minister in 1995, was at the summit of his career the head of the state agricultural building firm (obselstroi) in Brest *oblast*. More surprisingly, he was appointed in 1998 as head of the National Bank without any, even rudimentary, knowledge of economy and finance. The professional experience of Aliaksandr Sasnouski, who had previously been head of a technical secondary school, and Deputy Chairman of Minsk *gorispolkom*, was also unprepared for the responsibilities conferred on him as Minister of Culture.

Nevertheless, the personal networks of Lukashenka and his closest entourage were not sufficient to fill all the main offices of the Belarusian state. Thus, Lukashenka was led to search for candidates in the former ruling elite, and even in the enemy camp at the previous elections. This adaptation of former elite members, who were used to administrative discipline, helped him to gain the loyalty of broader layers of the government bureaucracy. Therefore, some of the main governmental positions under Lukashenka's presidency are occupied by former members of V. Kebich's team,[14] such as the head of the Presidential Administration since 1995, Mikhail Miasnikovich (formerly Kebich's First Deputy Prime Minister), or Sergei Ling, Prime Minister from 1997 to 2000 (Kebich's former Deputy Prime Minister) and Uladzimir Zamiatalin, First Deputy Chief of the Presidential Administration (1994–7) and Deputy Prime Minister since 1997 (Kebich's former press secretary).

Cases of outsider sponsorship to top political positions are rare in the recruitment mechanisms used by Lukashenka. One can mention Ural Latypau, who entered the Presidential Administration in December 1994, after some years spent at the National Institute of Security in Minsk. Nevertheless, one cannot ignore the fact that he had previously made a brilliant career in the Soviet KGB. The economist Piotr Kapitula, a BNF sympathiser at the beginning of 1990s, who joined the electoral team of Lukashenka before becoming presidential adviser on economic issues in 1994, is another exception to general trends of recruitment.

Extension of the patronage network to the parliament

The recruitment strategy described above allowed Lukashenka to create the basis of his power support inside the Presidential Administration and extend his control over the central government. Reinforcement of presidential power was followed by the construction of the 'presidential vertical': the chain of administrative dependence through the regional and district level that gave Lukashenka, among other things, control over the appointment of regional and even district heads of executive bodies.

This same ambition to build a hierarchical state power structure without any counterbalance led Lukashenka to realise the necessity of reducing the importance of the parliament. Besides its constitutional right to influence Belarusian politics, the Supreme Soviet could easily provide opportunities for the appearance of new popular political actors. As Lukashenka could not personally designate and support every candidate for MP during the 1995 parliamentary election, he tried to discredit the electoral process.[15] This explains why he preferred to favour low-level voter mobilisation, extending the elections for a long period and thus delegitimising the parliamentary system.[16] Finally elected by the end of 1996, parliament was dominated by communists and agrarians. Nevertheless, even this conservative parliament was considered by Lukashenka as an obstacle.

In order to eradicate any possibility of legal opposition to his policies Lukashenka proposed a new draft constitution, which was approved by a popular referendum on 24 November 1996. A new National Assembly, composed of two Chambers, the Council of the Republic and the Chamber of Representatives, was created. Only 110 MPs from the former Supreme Soviet manifested their loyalty to the President and managed to keep their mandates. Thus, MPs who previously represented the political opposition were out of the new parliament.

It is therefore not surprising to find in the top positions of the National Assembly former Lukashenka associates such as Uladzimir Kanapleu, Viktar Kuchynski and Iuryi Malumau (members of the Council of the Chamber of Representatives), as well as reconverted members of the former Soviet *nomenklatura*, like, for example, Anatol Malafeeu, the former Secretary of the CPB Central Committee who became the Council Chairman.

An important trend in elite recruitment and mobility, which became more marked after 1997, is the simultaneous or sequential overlap of high officials. One can mention the example of Uladzimir Zamiatalin, Deputy Head of the Presidential Administration, who after being appointed in January 1997 as the Chairman of the State Committee for Printing, became five months later Deputy Prime Minister in July 1997, and also of Uladzimir Rusakevich who quit his position as Deputy Prime Minister in July 1997 for the position of Deputy Head of the Presidential Administration. A classic example is also Ural Latypau who after four years as a presidential adviser became Minister of Foreign Affairs and Deputy Prime Minister in December 1998. These cases testify that there is a great difficulty in recruiting new members for elite positions. This difficulty is often resolved by the transfer of existing members from one position to another in order to avoid new recruitment.

The bases of Lukashenka's power were consolidated at the beginning of 1997 through formal control over the main political institutions of the country granted by the new constitution, as well as by informal control through the creation of a patronage system of elite recruitment.

Main career patterns of Belarusian officials

In order to provide a more general understanding of the elite mobility process in Belarus by the end of the 1990s, it is necessary to analyse the biographies of the main political officials. We include in this analysis the President, the Chief of the Presidential Administration, his deputies, and the President's advisers; the Prime Minister, his deputies, and the ministers; the members of the Presidium of the Council of the Republic and members of the Council of the Chamber of Representatives.[17]

Despite the dominance of personal criteria in recruitment to the top positions within the political elite, the choice of candidates is generally limited by the social structure. An analysis of career types reveals some general trends in the elite circulation process. It indicates the rise of the representatives of certain particular social and institutional groups to elite positions.

Four main career types that led to the current Belarusian political elite can be distinguished: industrial managers, agricultural managers, members of the armed forces and security services, and the intelligentsia. The assignment of individuals to a particular career type is based on the following criteria: type of education, type of occupation the individual pursued prior to recruitment to the political elite, and type of task orientation that can be ascribed to most of the posts the individual held. Each case has been judged individually.

The first career trajectory of 'industrial manager' starts with an educational background in engineering and some professional experience inside an industrial company, where the individual climbs different levels of the administrative hierarchy from specialised positions at a medium level to management positions at the top level. Then the person acquires in most of the cases some experience in the district or regional executive bodies or, sometimes, can directly integrate into the central executive or legislative institutions.

A typical representative of this career type is the President of the Council of the Republic, Pavel Shypuk. A chemical engineer who graduated from the Belarusian Polytechnical Institute, he made his professional career in different posts in the Homel glass plant before becoming its general manager. Then he worked as Chairman of Homel *oblispolkom* before entering the Council of the Republic in 1997.

The career of 'agricultural manager' in many cases includes the following stages: graduation from the Belarusian Institute of Agricultural Mechanisation or the Belarusian Agricultural Academy with some professional experience at the head of a collective farm (*kolkhoz* or *sovkhoz*), completed by management experience in the district and then regional executive or legislative bodies before joining the central executive or legislature.

An example is Iurii Moroz, who graduated from the Belarusian Institute of Agricultural Mechanisation, worked as a mechanical engineer in the Borysau complex of pork production, then from 1975 to 1980 as chief engineer in Borysau *sovkhoz-kombinat*, and later in the Orsha livestock complex. He became a head of the *sovkhoz* 'Belovezhskii' in Kamenets district in 1982. In 1996 he was head of the agricultural and product department in Brest *oblispolkom*. In November 1997 he was appointed Deputy Minister and a month later, Minister of Agriculture.

The police, KGB and armed forces were also used to form today's Belarusian political elite, especially those who are responsible for the strategic tasks of state building, national security and foreign relations. This career type, which one can label as 'state coercive', begins with graduation from the Law Faculty of the Belarusian State University or from a military-political school; then the future members of elite acquire their professional experience in the different levels of the Committee of State Security (KGB) or Ministry of Internal Affairs (MVD) and its subsidiaries, or in the Soviet/Belarusian army. They enter the political elite through election as an MP or by climbing to the top positions in one of the coercive ministries.

For example, Uladzimir Zamiatalin graduated in 1973 from Donetsk (Russia) High Military-Political School and from the Military-Political Academy in 1983. He made his military career on different levels of the military hierarchy, becoming by the end of the 1980s deputy head of the political department of the tank division, supervisor in the political department, head of the military-political department of the okrug and deputy head of the information department in the Ministry of Defence. In 1994 he was appointed press secretary to the Prime Minister. In 1995 he became a head of the information department in the Presidential Administration and in 1996 First Deputy Head of the Presidential Administration. In January 1997 he was appointed Chairman of the State Committee for Printing and in July 1997 Deputy Prime Minister.

There are some other career trajectories that can be classified as 'intelligentsia'. This type concerns people with experience in a 'liberal profession': economists, doctors, teachers, lawyers who made professional careers corresponding to their educational background. One of the rare women in the Belarusian political elite, Inessa Drabysheuskaia, graduated from Vitebsk Medical Institute and then worked as a doctor in one of the medical centres of Homel. In the late 1980s she became deputy head, then head of the oncology centre for Homel *oblast* before her election to the twelfth Supreme Soviet in 1990. In 1994 she was appointed Minister of Health and since 1997 she has been Head of the Social Policy Commission in the Council of the Republic.

We should also note that there are a significant number of cases which are difficult to classify, when initial education does not correspond to professional occupation or to any particular career type. The importance of such cases confirms the fact that their entry into the Belarusian political elite is still not generally institutionalised and its members are recruited in a rather arbitrary way.

Conclusion

There was neither a significant democratic opposition, nor a split inside the ruling communist elite in Belarus at the end of the 1980s, as was the case in other European republics of the USSR. Nevertheless, political democratisation created conditions for the diversification of the political elite in the mid-1990s through free elections. In practice, it favoured the rise of some members of the regional elite to the national level and led to the reconstruction of a hierarchical system of power as the basis of the personal authority of the President, Aliaksandr Lukashenka, elected in 1995. The main mechanisms he used for recruitment to the Belarusian political elite included the selection of political staff from among past associates, the personal patronage of outsiders and the co-option of some members of the former communist elite. The main credential for recruitment has been personal loyalty to the President.

Since 1997 Lukashenka has exercised total control over the Belarusian political elite and no one could be nominated to any important office without his approval. The reconstruction of the hierarchical political system dominated by the executive has been facilitated by the weakness of the political opposition and the articulation of interests within the new Belarusian elite. In the absence of economic reforms and state decentralisation there has been no opportunity for the emergence of powerful groups with particular economic interests or regional groups battling for more autonomy. This also helps to explain the extreme conformism of the current political elite, because there are not many opportunities for promotion outside the political and administrative institutions controlled by the President and his entourage.

The apparent cohesion of the official Belarusian political elite is closely related to the personality of Lukashenka. The functioning of the political institutions designed during Lukashenka's presidency excludes any prospect of a change of power. In these conditions, unless the task of elaborating less arbitrary mechanisms of recruitment to the political elite remains unfulfilled, the future of the current high officials is unpredictable. New elections for the office of president, who is normally elected every five years, will provoke considerable instability inside the political elite whose members occupy their positions not by virtue of their professional competencies but thanks to their personal dependence on Lukashenka. This eventual turnover within the political elite will inevitably bring about a revision of the political agenda showing the necessity of change both in political institutions and procedures and in the mechanisms of recruitment and functioning of the national political elite.

The Belarusian case shows that even though the appearance of new national political institutions and free elections may give an opportunity for circulation within the governing elite, it does not necessarily provide the conditions for the emergence of fundamentally new political actors ready to implement a new type of politics. Democratic institutions cannot function if there are no political actors able to use them efficiently. Existing political actors tend to modify normal functions of these institutions for their own purposes, thus creating hybrid regimes with a minimum of democratic institutions and procedures and practices of power verging on authoritarianism.

Notes

1 A. Przeworski, *Democracy and the Market: Political and Economic Reforms in Eastern Europe and Latin America* (Cambridge: Cambridge University Press, 1991), pp. 37–40.
2 Concerning the state of elite research in Eastern Europe, see H. Best and U. Becker (eds), *Elites in Transition: elite research in Central and Eastern Europe* (Opladen: Leske und Buldrich, 1997).
3 The principal political institutions in Belarus are the Administration of the President, the Council of Ministers and the National Assembly (parliament) composed of the House of Representatives and the Council of the Republic. The presidency was established as the result of the adoption of the new constitution on 28 March 1994. The National Assembly replaced the previous parliament, the Supreme Soviet, after the referendum on the constitution held on 24 November 1996.
4 For instance, in 1977, 21 out of 28 Belorussian ministries were subject to the dual federal-republican authority and only seven were exclusively republican.
5 As Rainer Lindner notes, for a long historical period Belarusians were governed by other ethnic groups (Russians, Poles) or by assimilated Belarusians. See R. Lindner, 'Gruppy liderstva v Belarusi: proshloe i nastoiaschee', *Vektor* (Minsk: IIPS), No. 2 (1997): 11–16. The experience of national elite formation at the beginning of the twentieth century was interrupted by Stalin's purges, reducing the status of the Belarusian elite to tabula rasa. This facilitated the alliance of the national elite with the Soviet one. The loyalty of the Belarusian establishment to Soviet power and the absence of political ambitions and nationalist tendencies were well analysed by G. Drakokhrust, E. Drakokhrust and D. Furman, 'Transformatsiia Beloruskoi partiinoi sistemy', in D. Furman (ed.), *Belarus i Rossiia: obshchestva i gosudarstva* (Moscow: Prava cheloveka, 1998), pp. 106–52.
6 Following their support for the self-proclaimed State Committee for the State of Emergency organised by conservative leaders of the CPSU on 18–21 August 1991 in Moscow, the leaders of the Belarusian Communist Party were forced to resign, and the CPB and CPSU activities in Belarus were suspended, as was the case in Russia and Ukraine.
7 On the central level it was the Supreme Soviet, on the city level the *gorsovet*, on the regional one the *oblsovet* and for the district, the *raisovet*.
8 *Sovetskaia Belorussiia*, 18 May 1990, p. 1.

9 For instance, the Russian Supreme Soviet ceased its activity in October 1993 after a violent conflict with the President, Boris Yeltsin. Ukrainian MPs voted for the early dissolution of their Supreme Soviet in February 1994 as a result of the country's deep economic and political crisis.

10 This notion of 'patrimonial communism' is elaborated by H. Kitschelt, 'Formation of Party Cleavages in Post-Communist Democracies', *Party Politics*, Vol. 1, No. 4 (1995): 447–72.

11 This model was introduced by Mikhail Gorbachev, who after being General Secretary of the CPSU (1985–91) was elected first President of the USSR by the Congress of People's Deputies on 15 March 1990. A former member of the CPSU Politburo, elected Chairman of the Supreme Soviet of the RSFSR on 29 May 1990, Boris Yeltsin was voted into office as the first President of the Russian Federation on 12 June 1991. In Ukraine, Leonid Kravchuk, former Second Secretary of the Communist Party of Ukraine (PCU), was also elected Chairman of the Ukrainian Supreme Soviet on 23 July 1990 before winning the first presidential elections on 1 December 1991.

12 J.H. Miller, 'Putting Clients in Place: the Role of Patronage in Cooption into the Soviet Leadership', in A. Brown (ed.), *Political Leadership in the Soviet Union* (London: Macmillan, 1989), pp. 64, 83–4.

13 Lukashenka preferred to abandon some of his best team members who had supported him during the presidential campaign, such as Viktar Hanchar, Anatol Liabedzka, and Dzmitry Bulakhau, who manifested too much political ambition. This will be the case every time someone displays his political personality and expresses disagreement with presidential policies, and this is why Lukashenka's high officials continue joining the ranks of the Belarusian opposition. The most famous examples are ex-Prime Minister Mikhail Chyhir, who after his dismissal became the candidate in the unofficial presidential elections organised by the opposition in May 1999, or Stanislau Bahdankevich, former head of the National Bank, who has become head of the opposition United Civic Party.

14 Even the former Prime Minister Kebich was not totally excluded from the political scene and found a seat as MP in the House of Representatives.

15 This strategy was easy to implement because the new parliamentary elections were held according to the majoritarian second ballot principle retained from the former Supreme Soviet. It means that in any given geographic constituency the candidate is elected if he gets more than 50 per cent of the votes, with the condition that more than 50 per cent of the electorate has participated in the elections.

16 This strategy succeeded because after two rounds of voting, on 14 and 28 May 1995, only 119 MPs out of 260 had been elected. Therefore, the parliament could not start its activities: a quorum required the presence of 174 deputies. It was only seven months later, after two supplementary rounds of voting fixed on 29 November and 10 December 1995, that the parliament started to work with 198 deputies. Nevertheless, the organisation of the parliament's work was complicated by the difficulties in creating an effective majority due to the low number of MPs with party affiliations and the huge number of independent MPs (95 MPs).

17 Here we consider the 1998 composition of the political elite. The main sources for these data are *Parliament: National Assembly of the Belarus Republic* (1997), the daily papers *Narodnaia gazeta*, *Sovetskaia Belorussiia*, *Belorusskaia delovaia gazeta* and its web directory (http://www.bdg.minsk.by/whoiswho, retrieved December 2000), as well as the website of the government (http://www.president.gov.by, retrieved December 2000).

5 Party system development in post-communist Belarus

Elena A. Korosteleva

Introduction

This chapter outlines the problematic development of the political party system in Belarus. After a decade of transition the country remains effectively in a pre-*perestroika* era with limited economic or political restructuring. This is manifested in a centrally controlled state economy; state-owned media; power lying in the hands of a *nomenklatura* that closely resembles the pre-*perestroika* ruling elite; low-level public contestation; and even lower inclusiveness in the decision-making process.

Concurrently, Belarus has not genuinely enjoyed the practice of free and fair elections and the growth of a non-governmental sector. This is due in part to its ineffective legal framework and hollow system of representation inherited from the previous regime,[1] and to the weakness of political players. Political parties, a cornerstone of most democratic regimes, are becoming increasingly less influential, suffering partisan decline and lacking power.

The principal purpose of this chapter will therefore be to develop an understanding of the protracted party system development in Belarus, which is characteristic of many new transitions, but especially of the Commonwealth of Independent States (CIS). This chapter aims to demonstrate that the failure of the political party system to consolidate in Belarus cannot be explained purely in terms of the failure of parties to grow into a coherent system that would offer a forum for public contestation and inclusiveness.[2] It will be argued that inherited structures – especially a weak state, the *nomenklatura*'s control over the decision-making process, and lack of reforms – and their subsequent *institutional reinforcement* have also affected successful democratisation and party system institutionalisation in the republic.

The chapter will include three sections. In section one, party system development will be viewed from a three-dimensional perspective, which includes analysis of (i) parties in public office; (ii) parties as organisations; and finally (iii) parties *vis-à-vis* their voters. Section two will briefly refer to structural and institutional arrangements that continue to impede parties' consolidation in Belarus. A concluding section will offer further discussion of the prospects for party system institutionalisation in Belarus.

The party system in Belarus: a three-dimensional enquiry

Political parties are a necessary component of a democratic polity, and their emergence is fundamental to achieving political stability in the newly emerged democracies. Yet there is much evidence to suggest that political parties are having trouble establishing themselves as credible institutions in the post-communist regions. Belarus, Russia, Ukraine and other post-Soviet republics are good examples of such behaviour. These democracies seem to be characterised by relatively stabilised parties with recognisable names and limited but loyal partisan support. The paradox, however, is that these legitimate parties do not necessarily develop into a stable party system in order adequately to underpin public interests with power institutions. As the experience of many former Soviet states reveals, the anticipated consolidation, or even a tendency towards it, has never taken place.

The political situation in Belarus is such that the party system remains incipient, and legitimate national parties are powerless. This is primarily determined by parties' incapacity to organise and unite into a coherent system of interest representation, and to engage in coalitions and negotiations in support of their political strategies. Additionally, there are also structural and institutional arrangements that negatively affect party system development in Belarus. They will be discussed in section two of this chapter.

Two distinct periods of party development can be observed in Belarus. The first is associated with a slow but steady move towards consolidation between 1990 and 1996, when the leading parties enjoyed growing public support as well as the benefits of public office. The second period is characterised by the retreat of anti-system parties into a 'parallel society' and their self-defeating strategies after the dismissal of the publicly elected parliament by the President in 1996, whereas those parties that remained loyal to Lukashenka and re-entered the new parliament, continue receiving benefits negotiated with the President.[3]

Parties in public office

The first parliament was elected in Belarus in 1990, and in the best Soviet traditions was dominated by a majority of communist *nomenklatura*. According to law, 50 places out of 360, elected on a plurality basis, were allocated to a conservative group of veterans, and the remainder was shared between nominees of work organisations and candidates from single member constituencies. In these circumstances, the Belarusian Popular

Front (BNF), a nationalist party, appealed for the organisation of a broad coalition of pro-democratic forces in parliament. The Democratic Club of 100 deputies was established soon after. It consisted of 25 members of the BNF and democratically minded MPs, including Aliaksandr Lukashenka. Given their public support, the party *nomenklatura* had to make concessions to the democratic bloc. On a consensual basis Stanislau Shushkevich, a popular moderate MP from Minsk, was elected as First Deputy Chairman of the Supreme Soviet.

Muddling through the overcrowded issue arena, the domination of the conservative wing, and the indecisiveness of the three successive spokesmen (Nikalai Dementei, Stanislau Shushkevich and Miacheslau Hryb), the parliament, nevertheless, took some decisive steps towards further democratisation. The 'Party of Power' composed of the government and its allies in parliament (with Kebich as head) soon emerged, although its political position at first was undefined. The toleration of freedom of speech and political expression by the authorities was considerable; and moderate economic liberalisation took place. From 1993, however, the Belarusian political arena became characterised by a rather antagonistic, although non-violent, confrontation between the Party of Power and the BNF-led opposition. This configuration of political forces was similar to that in Ukraine, where the party *nomenklatura* also maintained a strong power position, led by President Kravchuk, and was opposed by a moderate democratic and nationalist opposition. The Belarusian Party of Power was, nevertheless, remarkably more conservative, even reactionary, than that in Ukraine or Russia at the outset of reforms, and this conservatism, supported at grassroots level, over time helped to install the individual authority of Aliaksandr Lukashenka.

New and much freer parliamentary elections took place in 1995. Nevertheless, the thirteenth Supreme Soviet appeared to be even more controversial than its predecessor. The newly elected communist and agrarian MPs declared their allegiance to Lukashenka. Yet, it was not clear whether the parliament would have the chance to convene at all, as only 119 out of 260 deputies were elected. Lukashenka publicly declared that he would introduce presidential rule if the second round of elections did not succeed. This was stimulating enough to have 196 MPs elected to the short-lived thirteenth Supreme Soviet by December 1995. The new parliament was dominated by the Left – pro-government deputies, communists and agrarians – who held almost half of the seats, and together they could vote for or promote almost any decision. The Speaker of the new parliament, Siamion Sharetski, was the head of a collective farm representing the Agrarian Party. The left-wing factions, nevertheless, soon found themselves in disagreement with Lukashenka over his attempts to concentrate power in his hands at the expense of parliament. As a consequence, political parties and parliamentary factions, except for 60 members of the pro-Lukashenka faction 'Zgoda' and a few others, moved closer to each other.

In 1996 the newly elected parliament was 'dissolved' by the President on the basis – in Lukashenka's words – of its inefficiency and inability to make adequate decisions. The new parliament was enacted in January 1997, and was composed of 110 MPs from the previous Supreme Soviet of the thirteenth convocation, which had convened on Lukashenka's conditions. The new legislature became bicameral, non-partisan, and unanimous in the best Soviet traditions.

Continuing decline of membership/voters and party influence on national decision-making might lead one to the conclusion that undeveloped parties have already failed in Belarus. In accord, Rose and Mackie[4] note that if a party does not partake in more than two elections in a new democracy, it can be regarded as an ephemeral party. This, however, may not necessarily be the case. What, for example, can be said if parties refused to partake in elections as a motion of protest against the regime and the President's violations of the rule of law? Or in effect, how 'free' might the expression of the electoral will be to judge party performance, if public opinion was carefully manipulated and 'streamlined' with the opinion of government officials? In other words, the party–voter relationship in the newly emerged democracies seems to be much more complex than that on the surface, and needs to be analysed using a multi-dimensional approach. Even though there have only been two official parliamentary elections in Belarus – in 1995 and 2000 – one presidential election in 1994 and one anti-presidential election campaign in 1999, it would still be misleading to deliver judgement regarding parties' survivability – and this is the peculiarity of Belarus as a new democracy! Parties were available for election, and were identified and supported by voters. However, there were also a number of predicaments, both institutional and human, which parties failed to overcome, in addition to their organisational failure. In the 1995 parliamentary elections, for example, (i) voter turnout was extremely low (just above 50 per cent), and those who turned up demonstrated, in the majority, their traditional loyalty to the communists; (ii) parties' canvassing strategies were overambitious and incongruent with their images; (iii) both institutional contexts (the electoral code, the constitution, the presidency) and structural contexts (the government structure, the economic crisis, the state-owned media, the scope for election fraud) were not in favour of the nationalist-minded BNF or the still indecisive liberals and democrats; and finally (iv) culturally the population in Belarus was not ready for a radical move to the wholesale restructuring of their society. In 2000 the oppositional parties simply boycotted the elections to protest against the gross violations of law by the President and his administration. This, however, was one of the limited opportunities for the opposition to enter into dialogue with the authorities, and to reinforce their mandate in voters' opinions.

Our analysis demonstrates the ambiguity and difficulty of structural and human circumstances for parties to consolidate. For example, the pre-1997

Belarusian parliament had the potential to remain in power, and to develop into a large democratic body that could have promoted the further democratisation of society.[5] However, political actors do not solely define the rules of the game, confronted by unaltered structures of regional power, the continuing authority of the *nomenklatura*, and their own limited skills and financial/human resources. The emerging democrats in Belarus were defeated by structural legacies of the past, and their sequential reinforcement by institutions. Hence, one continues witnessing intensive vote switching; legitimate, but voiceless parties; the tendency for the presidency to strengthen, and impending economic stagnation.

The 1990–6 Belarusian parliaments accumulated the 'cream' of political society in the sense that the majority of the party leadership was elected into public office. This allowed some parties like the Party of Communists of Belarus (PCB), Belarusian Popular Front (BNF), Agrarian Party (AP), and United Democratic Party (ODP)[6] to settle down further, and others – such as the Party of Civic Action (GD), Party of Popular Consent (PNS), and Belarusian Social Democratic Hramada (BSDG) – to be centrally launched. Largely oriented towards public office, parties were organised from the top down and had very weak links with their grassroots. They were and remained largely urban-based, having limited influence on voters in regions, who nevertheless, constitute 64 per cent of the entire population![7]

While in public office, parties were financially supported by the state. All party representatives had their own office, staff, technical, financial and media resources. These moves towards accommodation strengthened a tendency for the domination of parliamentary party over extra-parliamentary organisations. In 1996 there was an attempt to create a joint party–parliamentary office structure: the ODP and GD merged into the faction 'Civic Action' (GD) and set up the United Civic Party, largely based in parliament. The PNS in alliance with the BSDG NG found themselves in a similar situation: they formed a social-democratic faction, 'Labour Union', with the majority of their leadership in parliament. These tendencies have been concomitant with a reduction in numbers of party central office staff, and relocation of staff for public office by the majority of parties. By 1996 all parliamentary parties were using state resources to subsidise their own staff, including regional organisations: from technical equipment to free usage of communication sources and the state-owned mass media. The PCB and BNF were the only exceptions to a general tendency for co-operation with the state. They based their principal 'party machinery' outside of parliament, and had a comparatively large proportion of staff attached to the central office (about 10–15 paid staff). They represented a distinctive mass type of party with an extensive regional network and a relatively large membership of 16,000 for the PCB and 7,000 for the BNF[8] in 1996. The situation with the BNF in parliament was less favourable than that of any other party. It managed to promote 44 candidates during the parliamentary elections in 1995,[9] but failed to have a single candidate elected to parliament during the second election run in November–December. This allegedly occurred because of the party's radical and militant style of politics, especially during the election campaign, and reported fraud by the authorities, involving the addition of non-existent names (of people who had emigrated or deceased) to electoral lists in voting constituencies, and manipulating their vote to their own advantage.

Party competition in 1990–6 was organised along two principal conflict lines, 'conservative-reformist'[10] and 'power allocation'. The first divide highlights economic populism, authority, state social protection, reunion with Russia versus sovereignty, economic liberalism and support for orientation towards Europe. The second divide reflects the conflict over power distribution in the new democracy: this revolved around power arrangements between the legislature and the executive in the first instance, and with the introduction of the presidency, developed into a 'democracy–dictatorship' dilemma. The years 1990 and 1991 were characterised by a growing polarisation between existing political forces. The period between 1992 and 1995 displayed the opposite. The communist majority unequivocally dominated the reformist bloc of deputies, a process, that reached its culmination in the 1993 parliament. Stalemate was inevitable, and both blocs appealed for a presidential election in 1994. That year parliament proved to be an exception to the rule, with democratic forces breaking through and regaining the initiative. This was determined by the events of the political year: the unexpected victory for non-partisan candidate Aliaksandr Lukashenka during the presidential election, and the scandalous defeat of the old-style conservative forces that supported Kebich in his 'back-to-the-USSR' campaign for the presidency. The 1996 parliament was a watershed in conflict development between the legislature and the President, after which parliament was dissolved and reformed in favour of a more compliant one.[11]

During the period 1990–6 the communist bloc demonstrated unique organisational and ideological endurance. Historical legacies and institutional frameworks indeed had an effect on the discipline and structure of successor parties. Simultaneously, faction developments in the 1996 parliament revealed that, even though reformist parties were under pressure from the pro/anti-presidential divide, they had also become relatively unified. Three distinct faction blocs could be observed in the 1996 legislature. The largest two blocs, pro-presidential 'Zgoda' and non-partisan deputies,[12] were followed by the communists (PCB) and the Agrarian Party (AP). Civic Action (GD) and Social Democrats (CDC) formed the opposite pole of the spectrum. The principal issues that polarised the parliament were 'to interpret whether the dissolution of the USSR was legitimate', to discuss further actions towards reunion with Russia, the election/dismissal of Shushkevich as parliamentary Speaker, the dismissal of the Cabinet of Ministers, the change of the state coat of arms, the public right of ownership, new additions to the law on parliamentary elections, and so on. There was a distinct 'Left–Right' division, with 'Zgoda', non-partisan deputies, the PCB and AP on the left and the democratic bloc on the right. Interestingly, 'Zgoda' was the only faction that voted positively on the issues related to empowering presidential authority, being opposed by the rest of the parliament.[13]

The major concern of MPs was to maintain separation of powers between the legislature and the executive. For the first time, the most irreconcilable political opponents began working together (for example, the communists joined the reformist bloc). In addition, with Civic Action's insistence, many liberal economic laws were adopted. A broad political coalition of oppositional forces resisted Lukashenka's desire to establish one-man rule for at least a year.

Shortly after the dissolution of the Supreme Soviet of the thirteenth convocation in 1996, a new bicameral legislature was formed in Belarus. In January 1997, 110 deputies entered the House of Representatives of the National Assembly of Belarus. The upper house – the Council of the Republic – had 64 members; eight of whom were appointed by the President, and the rest were elected from the six regions of the republic and Minsk.[14] The aim of the new legislature was to work 'effectively', without any 'ideological' complications. This led to unified non-partisan voting, which 'undoubtedly' increased the efficacy of the new legislature. If the 1996 parliament (9 January–11 July) had considered only 59 bills, 399 decrees, and the quantity of rejected proposals was about 600, the new parliament produced 261 bills and 836 decrees for the two-year period (20 December 1997–10 February 1999).[15] According to the new regulations the President forms the parliamentary agenda and makes procedural suggestions. The new parliament became non-partisan and compliant, which was peacefully negotiated between the President and the new Members of Parliament. The former obtained a trouble-free existence from parliament, and the new MPs attained power and access to state resources, including relatively high salaries, and free accommodation in the capital of Belarus, Minsk.

The parliamentary arena is highly desirable for parties in the new democracies. It brings power, security and benefits by providing parties with a relatively independent existence from the electorate, especially in developing regimes. The Belarusian parties' conduct in public office, however, has been ambivalent. Parties indeed had an opportunity for institutionalisation and successful survival. Belarus's two pre-1997 parliaments had developed into a structured body with well-defined cleavages and organised competitive forces.[16] There was a certain degree of polarisation of interests, which under a moderate number of parties, with relative proportionality of forces, might have had the potential to result in a stable system.

Nevertheless, parties failed to remain in office and 'surrendered' their decision-making 'portfolio' in favour of an individual governance of the President, which now occurs in peaceful co-operation with the newly 'adapted' House of Representatives, the loyal Presidential Administration, the state-owned media, and the newly appointed Constitutional Court. Two equally important corollaries can be drawn from this discussion. The first and most obvious is that parties cannot fully sustain themselves in such an environment, where institutional and structural conditions *a priori* disregard opposition. Mainly urban-based, anti-system parties cannot bring together 'fringe' interests of civil society whilst struggling with the state and having limited financial resources.[17] In turn, governmental parties lack motivation in maintaining public support, having access to the state resources. This leaves disillusioned voters with an alternative: rationally to switch their votes away from the parties which have increasingly become their 'second choice', and to 'delegate' the President maximal authority to lead the country out of crisis. The issue of whether democracy can be possible at all, and without parties in Belarus, is presently at stake and at the centre of political discussion.

On the other hand, parties are still surviving and acquiring new features. The 'presidential divide' has turned out to be both damaging and stimulating for party political development. Government parties, by allying with the state, have negotiated their revenues for the 2000 parliamentary elections, and thereby secured their prospects for survival. Their 'well-being' has chances to improve again after the 2001 presidential election.

The situation of electoral and financial decline also stimulated oppositional parties to seek new organisational, ideological and economic opportunities for survival. Successfully or not, parties are developing a new image within civil society and the international community. They by and large have moved away from mass-type organisations, or remain such only formally. They utilise 'catch-all' strategies for their political campaigning, and have a relatively stable core clientele of voters. Politics as such has become more issue-based. Knowing their poor grassroots potential, parties have become more flexible in their membership: the best example is the Belarusian Popular Front. They are also more centralised and leadership-dominated.

In the light of the above discussion the logical question to ask would be whether or not parties are failing in Belarus. The analysis suggests that parties are actually adapting, but remain dormant in a situation of seeming stability, both political and economic. Public support lies with the President as a guarantor of stability. It looks as if parties are more likely to be a by-product of democratisation, rather than its initiator, especially when economic crisis is unleashed, or Russia considers an alternative leader for the Belarus–Russia Union.

Parties in central office and at the grassroots

Party 'central' organisation is known as a key independent element in explaining party 'effectiveness'. This implies that the way parties are organised and function can determine their prospects for adaptation and survival, especially in the changing environment of the new democracies of Eastern Europe.

On the extra-parliamentary level, two types of party organisation have developed in Belarus. The first group can be considered as a modified mass party organisation, having a relatively active regional network based on cells, clubs, and caucuses; flexible membership, associated not with fees, but commitment to promote the party's name and ideology; and intensive 'street canvassing'. The best examples of such developments are the nationalist BNF and neo-communist PCB. The aftermath of the 1996 crisis demonstrated the 'survivability' of mass-type organisations. Relatively successful examples were the BNF, PCB, CPB, neo-AP and LDPB. In addition, the BNF found ample support from the West. The PCB and LDPB largely remain afloat thanks to fraternal well-wishers in Russia. The CPB and neo-AP entirely depend on the state as their primary material source of existence.

The majority of reformist parties enjoy a 'new' type of organisation. As a rule, they are organised from the top down, having weak linkages to society, and a low membership base. They are generally located in urban areas and assign low priority to building up local structures. The OGP, BSDP NG and PNS are examples of modern types of party organisation. It appears that many new parties have become successful in establishing strong links with their western *familles spirituelles*. This co-operation is mainly available to them through a system of grants, bursaries, technical and educational assistance, as well as direct involvement in international projects.[18] New type pro-presidential parties (the PNS, for example) are more dependent on state resources than those of mass-type organisations, and are increasingly becoming serviceable parts of the state machinery. The management of new parties has undergone both 'generational' and methodological shifts. Contemporary parties rely more on opinion polls and market research, as well as Internet resources and public relations (seminars, conferences, publishing, and staff exchange for education purposes).

Pro-presidential parties[19] have their representatives in public office, although the latter remain non-partisan in parliament. They seem ultimately to rely on state resources, as their parties' leaders share key positions in government, or enjoy considerable benefit from their associates in parliament. They have no distinct ideological profiles or economic programmes, and definitively lack voters' support.

It has been interesting to establish a discrepancy between party rhetoric and action in relation to coalition potential.[20] In interviews, party leaders keep naming each other as political partners, which may not be effectively true in practice. For example, the OGP referred to the Belarusian Social Democratic Party 'People's Assembly' (BSDP NG) as their primary associate, and as their secondary associates, to the BNF, trade unions, Labour party (PT) and PCB. However, the BSDP NG, which found itself closer to the BNF and PT, did not enthusiastically confirm this linkage.

The BNF in turn affirms that as long as parties continue pursuing their personal ambitions, it will not form an alliance with any of them. The Labour party (PT) remains independent and hopes to collaborate with the communists if they 'tone down' their orthodoxy. The communists in turn assume that they already have a partner, namely trade unions, and are unwilling to support the liberals and democrats. Parties have recently tried to overcome their ideological differences in order to resist the move towards dictatorship altogether. In 1999 they attempted to organise a united movement with a single coordinating body to initiate an alternative presidential election, and spectacularly failed at the finale, due to ever-present disagreements. Two years later, on the eve of the presidential election, parties failed to demonstrate any unity or consensus over a single candidate for the presidential election campaign.[21]

Overall analysis suggests that parties in Belarus are highly fragmented, and have limited influence on voters in the regions. Oppositional party leaders are unable to overcome personal feuds and cannot attempt to campaign uniformly against the President. They are also limited by formal and informal institutional settings and legal rules. All parties lack clear ideological doctrine and policy manifestos, especially in terms of economic reforms, and have limited linkages with their voters. With weak party organisation, there is a greater scope for personalities, and a greater likelihood that individuals will be important contenders in the power game.

Parties and their voters

At present political balance in the country is weighed towards the President, which has enabled voters rationally to switch their choice away from parties which have become 'second-order preferences', and to 'delegate' maximal authority to the President to lead the country out of crisis. Lukashenka's public score has not much changed over the last three years and has remained consistently around 41–5 per cent on average, whereas the score of other political actors has significantly declined.[22] Simultaneously, voters continue to view parties as indispensable pillars of building democracy, despite the fact that their perceptions of parties as incapable of winning power make them seek immediate benefits and a sense of security from more powerful players in the country. Electors show positive and stable attitudes to further democratisation, resistance to the idea of dictatorial governance and no desire to retreat back to the USSR, which suggests that there is an apparent conflict between representation and leadership in Belarus. People conscientiously believe that, as representative institutions, parties are necessary. But as long as they are ineffective, 76 per cent of the population agree that, 'a strong leader can do more for the country than all the discussions in parliament'.[23]

Public opinion is presently very divided. Three distinct groups can be observed in the population: these are pro-governmental, oppositional and undecided voters. The latter group, which forms one-third of the voting electorate, has allowed considerable leeway for the President to manoeuvre in an attempt to recruit additional voters for the presidential election in 2001.[24] As research indicates, the pro-presidential part of the Belarusian electorate seems to be more consolidated in its opinion; whereas the 'protest electorate' is more critical, but less unified.[25]

Since 1997, on average 18–20 per cent of the population have supported political parties in Belarus, and less than 1 per cent of the population have been directly involved as party members. About 25 per cent of the population have an explicit awareness of the existence of political parties and their 'opposition' to the President.[26] Public trust of parties, nevertheless, has gradually declined. This may have the following explanation. In their earnest desire for social change, people are torn between parties, which ought to provide them with some representation and access to power for the citizenry to rule the country, and the President, who seems to them more capable of coping with public needs. Therefore, they often exchange their party loyalty for an opportunity to acquire immediate revenues pledged by the government. It is interesting to note that the electorates of the presidential and anti-system parties considerably overlap, and this forms an environment for vote switching along the 'president–anti-president' divide. In other words, contemporary voters demonstrate rational 'flexibility' in their voting behaviour, which allows them to pursue their own short-term policies despite their ideological motivations and personal beliefs.

Another explanation of the 'swing-or-not-to-swing' voting behaviour is undoubtedly parties' organisational insufficiency and their continuing inability to resist increasing power of the President. Parties act in accordance with their rationale and in pursuit of more accommodating strategies in order to survive voters' indifference and institutional predicaments. Nevertheless, their actions seem to be in continuing discrepancy with voters' rational choice. This is when the opportunities for populist leaders and perhaps other agencies for interest representation emerge. The latter (NGOs, new trade unions, and other interest organisations), though, express fringe interests and hence enjoy only limited support from the population. All these enhance the rudimentary image of parties within society, which if no consensus is achieved and no legal attempts by them are made to win public office, will bring parties to their political demise.

Structural and institutional arrangements

Our analysis of Belarus's political system suggests that there is a definite impact of structures and institutions on the process of building a stable party system, and democracy. In Belarus, limited economic reforms (including limited liberalisation and privatisation), a nominal rather than the essential rule of law, the *nomenklatura*'s control over state resources (including the mass media), and a pervasive system of patronage[27] have considerably inhibited the ways by which individual citizens can participate in decision-making through political parties and interest organisations.

According to UN estimates, the Republic of Belarus is presently characterised by regular paid but low wage and pensions, low-level unemployment, a relatively low external debt, apparently high growth rates, and the highest standard of living in the CIS since 1996. Nevertheless, there are grounds to question the sustainability of Belarus's progressive development in the future. Belarus's cumulative level of direct foreign investment *per capita* was the lowest in the CIS, its private sector contribution to GDP was also minimal and on average 45 per cent less than that in other newly independent states (NIS).[28] Belarus has not advanced in any of the principal reform directions, including (a) macroeconomic stabilisation; (b) private sector development; (c) liberalisation of prices and trade; (d) enterprise reform; and finally (e) development of financial institutions. In other words, the relatively progressive economic façade disguises a situation of impending economic crisis and the inevitable worsening of living conditions. Future economic uncertainty stemming from limited diplomatic relations with the West, and Belarus's obvious dependence on elite decision-making in Russia, further isolate it from the global economic community and make it an 'outsider', unlikely to engage in further democratisation.

Additionally, as a weak state, Belarus has not been legally or logistically prepared to embark on the course of democratic reforms, and subsequently has been manipulated by the former communist *nomenklatura* to their own advantage. Targeted privatisation and favourable conditions for certain business players widely promoted state monopolisation of the economy and limited the advancement of independent interests. The effective absence of reform at regional levels of power and direct presidential control over the decision-making process at all levels currently provide Lukashenka with the stable conservative support of around 40 per cent of the population. In addition, elite strategic considerations and public 'traditionalist' adherence to a strong leadership have institutionally reinforced the uneven power balance in society, which lies in the hands of the vested interests and away from the weak democratic forces. For example, the leftover socialist 'properties' allowed the communist majority to outplay the BNF's democratic initiative to get rid of a conservative parliament in 1992. A similar outcome took place during the 1995 election campaign, when the system simply did not allow the accession of nationalists to the new legislature. The 1996 crisis demonstrated the precedence of the decision-making of the President and the Moscow elites[29] over the national constitutional law, and the dissipated efforts of the opposition.

It is often suggested that the introduction of the presidency, as well as Lukashenka's outstanding ability to manoeuvre through the political landscape, were *the* crucial factors that brought the country to a political standstill. This certainly led parties to refocus their attention from pursuing their own mandates to embarking on a political battle with a much more powerful opponent – the President. In the short term Lukashenka has introduced his own system of personal rule, where governance by decree dominates the law; the separation of powers between legislature, the executive, and Constitutional Court is non-existent; and parties and other interest organisations are unrequited. In addition, the mass media have become 'nationalised' and the prospective union with Russia set in motion.[30] Naturally, the nation's cultural adherence to a strong leadership has ensured that a 'delegative' style of policy-making should remain dominant. This is to say that about 40 per cent of the electorate empowers the incumbent as seemingly more capable of initiating and pursuing change, rather than investing their 'political currency' in the pledges of parties. Another 40 per cent remain floating voters.[31]

Further discussion and conclusion

There is no 'recipe' for democracy. The efforts of parties alone cannot provide a suitable alternative to the current regime, especially when the electorate has its own rationale for supporting a strong president over parties. Cognitive frameworks and institutions cannot be altered on demand, and require careful revision. What is certain, though, is that in order to rebuild a ship at sea a floating dock is needed, and thus a joint approach to structure and agency would be advisable.

This chapter has demonstrated that parties' low ideological profile and their limited organisational and financial capacities explain why they remain legitimate but increasingly powerless players of the political game. This tendency has been reflected in parties' declining membership and partisan support, and their low impact on policy-making in the country. In addition, legacies and inherited structures, reinforced by institutional developments, have created an unfavourable environment for further party system consolidation in Belarus.

Popular interests are traditionally voiced through a panoply of mechanisms: unions, social movements, parties and other interest organisations. Voter–governor linkages may also be sought elsewhere. Nevertheless, parties continue to be seen as the most important mechanisms of interest mediation between society and state in contemporary Belarusian politics. When they are weakened organisationally, institutionally, or structurally, the power balance will be naturally transferred to the stronger 'player'. As Eijk and others have demonstrated in their research on the democratic deficit in the European Union,[32] party failure often does not lie with uncommitted voters or lack of media coverage; it is grounded within the weak powers of the legislature and the constitution. From the analysis of legislative–executive relations in Belarus it becomes clear that the parliament has no real power for decision-making and no incentive for partisan debates. In addition, power leverage on a regional level still remains in the hands of the Soviet-style *nomenklatura*. These all considerably undermine the influence of parties and other interest organisations in politics. The balance of power, hence, must be constitutionally reinforced, and players must be given equal chances to build their authority. Additionally, parties must offer clear and inclusive programmes of economic and political reform, and use them to manifest their readiness to play a fair and competitive political game.

Notes

1 There have been certain cosmetic alterations on the national power level (the introduction of the presidency, a bicameral parliament, the Presidential Administration, etc.). Simultaneously, there has been no change in the structure of regional legislative and executive powers. As a conservative stronghold, local 'soviets' were merely adapted to the needs of the 'new' system. In addition, from 1996 the heads of all-level regional executive committees were appointed by the president (Article 85). This phenomenon was subsequently named the 'presidential vertical'. Reformist political parties have limited influence in regions, which provides elected MPs in local councils with pro-communist, and often pro-Lukashenka majorities. In turn, local deputies appoint executive committees headed by Lukashenka's nominees. As a result, contemporary power distribution in regions exerts well-structured control over decision-making by the President and 'old-style' *nomenklatura*.

2 R. Dahl, *Polyarchy: Participation and Opposition* (New Haven and London: Yale University Press, 1971).

3 This in the first instance includes free accommodation and transport for MPs in Minsk, well-paid and secure positions in government on request, access to the mass media and other state resources, and full state protection, in many cases including MPs' re-election for a second term in public office.

4 R. Rose and T. Mackie, 'Do parties persist or fail? The big trade-off facing organisations', in K. Lawson and P. Merkl (eds), *When Parties Fail: Emerging Alternative Organizations* (Princeton, NJ: Princeton University Press, 1988), pp. 533–58.

5 Parliament had a swiftly developing faction structure, conflict polarisation, and high-level activity by MPs. For more details see E. Korosteleva, 'Explaining Party System Development in Post-Communist Belarus', unpublished PhD thesis (University of Bath, UK, 2001).

6 See the table of acronyms with a full description of the parties at the end of the chapter.

7 According to the 1999 census, 31.5 per cent live in villages, 16.44 per cent live in towns with less than 50,000 inhabitants, 6.03 per cent live in towns with 50,000–100,000 inhabitants, and 9.7 per cent live in towns with 100–200,000 inhabitants. This amounts to 63.7 per cent of the population living in regions (other than the capital and *oblast* centres).

8 The PCB had a compulsory membership fee – 1 per cent of monthly wages. With the 1996 financial failure, it changed its policy towards a more flexible and affordable form of co-operation with its members, on the basis of free donations and voluntary contributions. On the other hand, the BNF initially had a non-compulsory membership fee largely based on donations. One of the modern features of the BNF organisation is membership flexibility: there is no clear-cut distinction between members and non-members as long as the latter can contribute to the party's legitimising myth. For parties' membership refer to the Bulletin of the Ministry of Justice, 1999, pp. 43–44.

9 From interviews with party leaders (V. Viachorka, and a former member of Soim (Council), V. Tregubovich), 1999; and election archives (Election Committee, 1995).

10 Scholars avoid referring to a 'Left–Right' divide here due to the general confusion and the absence of any clear interpretation of the issue. It nevertheless has a particular meaning in relation to the post-Soviet states, with communist successor, agrarian, and labour parties on the left, and in opposition to them, social democratic, liberal, and nationalist parties.

11 See the graphic analysis in Korosteleva, 'Explaining Party System Development', Chapter 4.1.

12 It was not a bloc in strict terms; however, the conduct of non-partisan MPs was remarkably coordinated.

13 For detailed analysis, see Korosteleva, 'Explaining Party System Development'.

14 Despite the fact that Lukashenka appoints only eight members to the Upper House of parliament, he exerts full control over the nominees from the regions through his effective 'presidential vertical'.

15 *Parliamentary bulletins. Summary 1997–1999* (Presidential Library, Minsk).

16 See Korosteleva, 'Explaining Party System Development', Chapter 4.

17 The recently adopted Presidential Decree No. 8, 'On some measures concerning the rules of receipt and utilisation of foreign gratuitous aid', 12 March 2001, is now in force, and parties will find it more difficult to organise co-operation with the West by way of sponsorship and grants.

18 It is not yet known how the opposition parties will survive under the President's decree demanding full registration of foreign aid (No. 8, 12 March 2001). The West has already begun a boycott campaign against Lukashenka's decision (see EBRD's resolution, IMF conclusion, and the OSCE AMG in *Radio Free Europe/Radio Liberty Newsline*, Vol. 5, No. 70–4, Part 2, April 2001, http://www.rferl.org/newsline).

19 They can be found amongst both types of party organisations. Examples are the CPB as a mass type of organisation, and the PNS SD as a modern type of organisation.

20 See the analysis of interviews with the party leadership in Korosteleva, 'Explaining Party System Development', Chapter 4.2.

21 In 1999 the BNF literally withdrew its candidate and refused to participate in the election race at the very last minute, as it found that the OGP was dishonestly trying to promote its own candidate on others' behalf. In 2001, two weeks into the election campaign, the CCDF (Coordinating Council of Democratic Forces) was still uncertain about their decision over a joint candidate from the opposition.

22 For more details, see David Rotman and Aliaksandr Danilov, Chapter 7 below.

23 M. Wyman, 'Developments in Russian voting behaviour 1993 and 1995 compared', *Communist Studies and Transition Politics*, 12 (1996): 277–301.

24 See Chapters 6 and 7 in this book for further details.

25 O. Manaev, 'Belorusskii elektorat: za i protiv prezidenta', *NISAPI News*, Vol. 1 (1998): 22–8.

26 D. Furman (ed.), *Belorussiia i Rossiia: obshchestva i gosudarstva* (Moscow: Prava cheloveka, 1998).

27 ISA European Institute, Sussex University, 'Evaluation of the PHARE and TACIS Programme, 1992–1997': http://europa.eu.int/comm/europeaid/evaluation/reports/tacis/951432.pdf, retrieved March 2001. See also Olga Belova, Chapter 4 above for more details.

28 EBRD, *Transition Report 1999: Ten Years of Transition* (London: EBRD, 1999).

29 The same can be said about the practice of the 2000 parliamentary elections, when international observers claimed gross violations of the democratic laws,

and Russia was the only state to stand up clearly in support of the 'democratic' procedures in Belarus.

30 Full analysis of institutional and structural impediments is given in Korosteleva, 'Explaining Party System Development'.

31 R. Dobson, 'Belarusians want more freedom. But haven't given up on Lukashenka', Office of Research, 13 September 2000 (Washington DC: Department of State 20520).

32 C. van der Eijk *et al.*, *Choosing Europe?: The European Electorate and National Politics in the Face of Union* (Michigan: University of Michigan Press, 1996).

Table 5.1 Appendix: political parties in Belarus, January 2000

Party acronym or name	*Full English name of party*	*Date of foundation; membership; leader*	*Structure*	*Ideology*
AP	Agrarian Party	1992; 12,000 (in 1997); Mikhail Shymanski	Local branches in villages, *kolkhox*	Agrarian, Socialist
BNF	Belarusian Popular Front	1993, re-established in 2000; 2,500; Vintsuk Viachorka	Branches in all regions, especially western part of Belarus	Liberal nationalist, democratic
BPP	Belarusian Peasant Party	1991; +1,000; Iaugen Lugin	Local organisations in most regions	Nationalist, Liberal
BPP	Belarusian Patriotic Party	1994; +1,000; Anatol Barankevich	Not known	Communist; pro-Lukashenka
BPT	Belarusian Party of Labour	1993; +1,000; Aliaksandr Bukchvostau	Party clubs	Socialist
BSDG NG	Belarusian Social Democratic Party 'Narodnaia Hramada'	1991; 2,000; Nikalai Statkevich	112 regional organisations	Social-Democratic
BSDP	Belarusian Social Democratic Party	1998; +1,000; Stanislau Shushkevich	City and regional branches	Centre right
CCP	Christian Conservative Party	2000; +1,000; Zianon Pazniak	Branches in Minsk, and some regions of Belarus	Radical nationalist, democratic
CPB	Communist Party of Belarus	1996; 7,000; Viktar Chykin	90 District, regional and city branches	Communist
Green	Belarusian Green Party	1992; 1,000; Nikalai Kartash	Mainly in Homel, and Minsk	Ecological

Table 5.1 continued

Party acronym or name	*Full English name of party*	*Date of foundation; membership; leader*	*Structure*	*Ideology*
LDPB	Liberal-Democratic Party of Belarus	1994; 18,000 (in 1997); Siarhei Haidukevich	District and regional organisations, especially in eastern part of Belarus	Russian chauvinist
Nadezhda	Belarusian Women's Party	1994; 5,000 (in 1999); Valiantsina Paleviakova	Regional and city organisations in Minsk and Mohileu	Social-Democratic
OGP	United Civic Party	1995; 3,500; Anatol Liabedzka	Minsk, 6 regional; 28 city and 66 district branches	Liberal, conservative
PCB	Party of Communist Belarusian	1991; 15,000; Siarhei Kaliakin	143 local, 6 regional and Minsk branches	Communist
SD PNS	Social Democratic Party of People's Accord	1991, re-registered in 1997; 2,050; Leanid Sechka	50 regional and 135 primary units, mainly in Homel, Mohileu and Hrodno	Pro-presidential
RPTS	Republican Party of Labour and Justice	1993; 1,000 (in 1995); Anatol Niatylkin	Not known	Socialist
SSBR	Slavic Union 'White Russia'	1992; 1,500 (in 1997); Nikalai Siargeeu	Regional organisations in Homel and Vitebsk; local branches in eastern part of Belarus	Russian chauvinist
SSP	Belarusian Social Sports Party	1994; 7,000 (in 1995); Aliaksandr Aleksandrovich	Not known	Pro-presidential

Source: Ministry of Justice, 1999.

6 Electoral politics of Belarus compared

Christian W. Haerpfer

Introduction

This chapter analyses the political behaviour and attitudes of the electorate in Belarus during the period 1992 to 2000. The support for democracy on the one hand and the support for non-democratic alternatives, on the other, within the Belarusian population is compared with the democratic and non-democratic political behaviour in six other post-Soviet countries: the Russian Federation, Ukraine, Moldova, Estonia, Latvia and Lithuania.

The process of democratisation, which took place after 1989 in post-communist Europe, is part of 'third wave democratisation', in the terminology of Samuel Huntington.[1] This third wave democratisation started in 1974 and took place in Portugal, Spain, Latin America, and somewhat later in Central Europe and the former Soviet Union, after the *annus mirabilis* of autumn 1989.[2] The conceptual basis of this chapter is the 'transformation approach', developed by the author. This approach includes three central procedural stages:

- Process 1: democratisation towards democracy
- Process 2: marketisation towards a market economy
- Process 3: the creation of a civil society

A central conceptual assumption of my 'transformation approach' is that we should not speak of 'transition', but of 'transformation'. The term 'transition' implies that there is a passage from a stage A to a certain stage B, that is, from a communist political system towards liberal democracy, from a centrally planned economy to a market economy. The concept of transition suggests a clear end-point of political development, for example a pluralist and liberal democracy; the process of change, for theoreticians of transition, is a clear track from point A to point B; and transition theory involves defining the goal of change and deciding when this goal has been reached and transition completed. At the level of the political system, we see state A, a communist party system, a transition period away from state A and the arrival at state B, a liberal democracy. The pitfalls of this *static* approach are overcome by the transformation approach, which regards the variety of political changes after 1989 as dynamic and open. This approach does not aim at analysing the final destination of change as a system of democratic stability. This concept is valid only for those European countries, which extricated themselves from communism in the late 1980s and are in the process of seeking stability.[3] These countries are labelled as 'post-communist countries', and include the following:

1 Central Europe: the Czech Republic (1), Hungary (2), Poland (3), Slovakia (4), Slovenia (5)
2 The Balkans: Bulgaria (6), Croatia (7), the Federal Republic of Yugoslavia (8), Romania (9)
3 The Former Soviet Union: Estonia (10), Latvia (11), Lithuania (12), Belarus (13), the Russian Federation (14), Ukraine (15), Moldova (16)

The database source for this chapter is the New Democracies Barometer, an international survey project implemented between 1991 and 1998 under the author's guidance.[4]

Support for the new political regime in post-Soviet Belarus

When support is measured for the new political regime in Belarus, it should reflect a degree of satisfaction with the current political system. One should analyse the reaction of post-Soviet citizens to the form and structure of a democratising system. For this analysis, only those respondents were selected who gave the current government in Belarus an evaluation in the range between +10 and +100 on the democracy-scale (see Table 6.1). Within the range of all seven post-Soviet countries, the Belarusian electorate shows the third highest level of support for the current government.

At the beginning of political transformation in 1992, only 35 per cent of the Belarusian electorate had a positive assessment of the national government of Belarus. This rating improved up to 1998, when 48 per cent of the citizens of Belarus thought in a positive way about their incumbent government. Since 1998, almost half the population of Belarus have supported the current government. In 2000, 47 per cent of the post-Soviet citizens in Belarus displayed a positive opinion about the national government of their country. Regarding support for the incumbent government, the electorate of Belarus shows attitudinal patterns, which are very similar to the behaviour of the electorate in the Baltic States, especially citizens of Latvia and Lithuania. The behavioural patterns concerning regime support are quite different in Belarus, as compared to Russia, Ukraine and Moldova. As in Belarus, about half of the electorate in Lithuania (45 per

Table 6.1 Support for the current government

Q. Here is a scale for ranking how the government works. The top, +100, is the best; at the bottom, –100, is the worst. Where on this scale would you put the CURRENT regime in your country?

	(Respondents with positive attitudes: +10 to +100)						
	1991	*1992*	*1994*	*1996*	*1998*	*2000*	*Change*
Central Europe	56	59	61	66	55	*	–1
Balkans	67	56	57	57	46	*	–21
Post-Soviet Union	*	41	43	40	*	47	+6
1 Estonia	*	58	75	69	*	70	+12
2 Latvia	*	43	45	37	*	49	+6
3 Belarus	*	**35**	**29**	**35**	**48**	**47**	**+12**
4 Lithuania	*	46	34	37	*	45	–1
5 Russia	14	36	48	26	36	37	+23
6 Ukraine	*	25	24	33	22	31	+6
7 Moldova	*	*	*	*	*	23	*

Source: New Democracies Barometer, 1991–2000. See note 4 for details.

cent in 2000) and Latvia (49 per cent in 2000) show their positive assessment of the current regime. The same pattern of electoral support for the regime is to be found in Belarus, Estonia and Latvia, but also in the Balkans, with an average of 46 per cent in 1998. The regime support in Estonia is very high, with 70 per cent of the Estonian electorate having a positive assessment of their current government. The behavioural pattern in Estonia is similar to the electorates in Central Europe. The post-communist states, which have applied for accession to the European Union, supported their own governments within a range of between 55 and 70 per cent throughout the 1990s (Table 6.1).

The pattern in Russia, Ukraine and Moldova is different from that observed in Belarus. In the Russian Federation, more than one-third of Russian citizens supported the current regime throughout the period between 1991 and 1998, which is less than in Belarus and more than in Ukraine. In 1998, 36 per cent of the Russian electorate gave the current regime a positive evaluation, which means, on the other hand, that more than 60 per cent of the Russian electorate were dissatisfied with the way democracy worked in 1998. The level of regime support in Russia remained the same between 1998 and 2000. Currently, 37 per cent of post-Soviet citizens within the Russian Federation give the incumbent Russian government a positive rating, which is much lower than in Belarus. Nevertheless, it has to be said that support for the political regime in Russia increased from as low a point as 14 per cent in 1991 to 37 per cent in 2000. In Ukraine the level of regime support went up from 25 per cent in 1992 to 31 per cent in 2000, which is a sign of the absence of political transformation at the level of the national government. Almost 70 per cent of the

Ukrainian electorate was against the current government of Ukraine in the year 2000. The situation of the national government before the general elections in 2001 in Moldova was even worse than in Ukraine. In 2000, only 23 per cent of Moldovan citizens showed a positive evaluation of their government. Analysis of public support for the government had in Belarus displayed similar patterns of political behaviour to those of the citizens of the three Baltic States, which were different from the patterns occurring in the Russian Federation, Ukraine or Moldova.

Popular support for democratic national parliaments

Another indicator of democratic behaviour in Belarus is the support of parts of the electorate for the national parliament in Minsk. This support has been measured by the disapproval of a potential suspension and dissolution of the national parliament as a non-democratic action (see Table 6.2). An analysis of how deeply embedded Belarus's national parliament is in the system of political values of the electorate will be given below.

Since 1992, an absolute majority of the Belarusian electorate has been against the destruction of the national parliament in Minsk. In 1992, an absolute majority of the Belarusian population was against a non-democratic suspension of the national parliament. This figure went down to 57 per cent in 1994. Since 1994, however, support for the Belarusian parliament against suspension grew to 60 per cent in 1996 and to 72 per cent in 1998, which was a level similar to that in Romania in the late 1990s. In 2000, popular support for the national parliament in Minsk went down to 56 per cent. Again the attitudinal political pattern in Belarus with regard to the defence of the national parliament is very similar to the political behaviour of the Lithuanian and Latvian electorates. A majority of 65 per cent of Lithuanian citizens and of 51 per cent of Latvian citizens are openly against the suspension of their national parliaments. In those two Baltic countries, as in Belarus, the level of democratic legitimacy decreased to some extent between 1996 and 2000 from majorities above 60 per cent to majorities above 50 per cent.

Support for the Russian Duma (parliament) against non-democratic attacks was very low in 1994, when only 40 per cent of Russians disapproved of a potential coup against the 'White House' in Moscow. The legitimacy of the Russian Duma has improved since 1994: in 1996, 61 per cent of the Russian electorate supported the Duma as a political institution of the new Russia and 62 per cent of the Russian mass public gave the Russian parliament a general legitimacy in 1998, despite the general political crisis. The level of popular support for the Duma remained the same until 2000, when 61 per cent of the Russian electorate was prepared to support the national Russian parliament. Contrary to the attitudinal pattern in Belarus, Lithuania, Latvia and post-Soviet Russia showed very low support for their parliament at the beginning of political transformations and gradually increased it over time between 1996 and 2000.

The behavioural pattern in Belarus concerning popular support for the national government is quite different from that in Ukraine and Moldova. The lowest extent of popular support for the national parliament in comparison with other post-Soviet countries and Belarus in particular can be found in Ukraine and Moldova. Support for the Ukrainian national parliament had a downward tendency between 1992 and 1996: in 1992, an absolute majority of 58 per cent of all Ukrainians was prepared to defend the national parliament against non-democratic coups. This figure decreased from 56 per cent in 1994 to 39 per cent in 1996 – the lowest support for a national parliament throughout post-communist Europe. This dangerously low extent of popular support for the Ukrainian parliament recovered slightly to 55 per cent in 1998. In 2000, however, only 43 per cent of the Ukrainian electorate were prepared to endorse a vote of confidence in their parliament.

Support for the national parliament is even lower in Moldova: only 41 per cent of Moldovan citizens are against the suspension of their national parliament in Chisinau, which is the lowest level of parliamentary legitimacy in all post-Soviet and post-communist countries. The fact that only a minority of the electorate in Ukraine and Moldova is prepared to defend their democratic parliaments in the case of a non-democratic coup demonstrates that democracy has not yet been established in public perception in these two post-Soviet countries, and that non-democratic alternatives have a certain chance of success, due to the lack of popular support for democracy within the electorate at large (Table 6.2).

Table 6.2 Extent of support for the national parliament

Q. If parliament were suspended and parties abolished, would you approve or disapprove?

	(Percentage respondents disapproved)						
	1991	*1992*	*1994*	*1996*	*1998*	*2000*	*Change*
Central Europe	80	76	75	77	78	*	–2
Balkans	85	82	77	83	76	*	–9
Post-Soviet Union	*	60	57	63	63	55	–5
1 Estonia	*	61	84	82	*	*	8
2 Lithuania	*	60	54	77	*	65	22
3 Russia	*	*	40	61	62	61	22
4 Belarus	*	**68**	**57**	**60**	**72**	**56**	**4**
5 Latvia	*	54	51	61	*	51	10
6 Ukraine	*	58	56	39	55	43	–3
7 Moldova	*	*	*	*	*	41	*

Source: New Democracies Barometer, 1991–2000. See note 4 for details.

In Central Europe a constant level of support for the newly created national parliaments can be found in that region, ranging between 75 and 80 per cent of public support in Central and Eastern European countries (CEECs). They are also notable for having the most advanced political and economic life. In the Balkans, support for parliaments decreased from a record level of 85 per cent in 1991 to 82 per cent in 1992 and 77 per cent in 1994. The legitimacy of parliaments recovered to 83 per cent in 1996, but fell again in 1998 because of the low level of parliamentary legitimacy in the Federal Republic of Yugoslavia in the era of former President Miloševich.

Alternatives to democracy: support for an authoritarian leader in Belarus

In this section the extent and structure of popular support for a 'strong and authoritarian leader' in Belarus and other countries of the former Soviet Union will be analysed. The overall result of this research confirms that support for a strong leader, as the opposition to a pluralist democracy, is melting away during the course of transition from communist rule to pluralist democracy.

The main outcome of this analysis is that the Belarusian electorate is the most democratic public in comparison with seven other post-Soviet states (see Table 6.3). In 2000, only 23 per cent of Belarusian citizens favoured the idea of strong leadership over the power of parliament, parties and a pluralist society. This represents a dramatic decline in support for a non-democratic leader in Belarus, since it decreased by 53 percentage points between 1992 and 2000. At the start of political transformation in 1992, a record level of 76 per cent of the electorate of Belarus was in favour of a strong, non-democratic leader without democratic institutions. This amazing majority shrank to 57 per cent in 1994, decreased further to 37 per cent of the Belarusian electorate in 1998 and finally, in 2000, reached a low level of 25 per cent of those who are in support of the idea of authoritarian leadership without democratic institutions.

The non-democratic adherence to a strong leadership is one of the few elements that make public behaviour in Belarus similar to that in the Russian Federation. The public wish for a 'strong man' in Russia was 33 per cent lower than that in Belarus in 1994, but reached 47 per cent by 1996. Since 1996, however, the desire of Russian citizens and voters to have a strong leader instead of a pluralist democratic system decreased to 36 per cent in 1998 and finally to 29 per cent in 2000. Similar patterns of behaviour can be found in Belarus, Russia and Latvia. At the beginning of the political transformation in 1992 in Latvia, a clear electoral majority – 62 per cent – liked the idea of having a strong leader instead of a pluralist democracy. The group of supporters of individual rule in Latvia melted down to 45 per cent in 1996 and finally to 33 per cent in 2000.

Table 6.3 Alternatives to democracy: support for an authoritarian leader

Q: Do you agree or disagree with the view that it is best to get rid of parliament and elections and have a strong leader who can decide things quickly?

	(Percentage persons agreed)					
	1992	*1994*	*1996*	*1998*	*2000*	*Change*
Central Europe	27	27	23	19	*	–8
Balkans	47	28	19	20	*	–27
Post-Soviet Union	63	46	55	43	38	–25
1 Belarus	**76**	**57**	**56**	**37**	**23**	**–53**
2 Russia	*	33	47	36	29	–4
3 Latvia	62	34	45	*	33	–29
4 Ukraine	53	56	67	55	45	–8
5 Estonia	61	34	51	*	*	–10
6 Lithuania	64	62	62	*	58	–6
7 Moldova	*	*	*	*	59	*

Source: New Democracies Barometer, 1991–2000. See note 4 for details.

In Ukraine and Estonia the desire to have an authoritarian leader is still very much alive. In both countries, around 50 per cent of the electorates supported an authoritarian leader as an alternative to democracy, in Estonia at least until 1996. Nevertheless, the majority within the Ukrainian population in favour of a strong man has decreased steadily from a peak of 67 per cent in 1996 to 55 per cent in 1998 and 45 per cent in 2000. There is still an absolute majority for a strong leader to be found in Lithuania (58 per cent in favour) and in Moldova (59 per cent in favour) (Table 6.3).

Support for an authoritarian leader as a non-democratic option is lowest in the CEECs. In the accession countries the public share in favour of a strong man decreased – on average – from 27 per cent in 1992 to 19 per cent in 1998. This shrinking interest in having one-man-rule instead of a fully fledged democratic system is even more striking in the Balkans. A clear majority of 47 per cent of citizens of, for example, Bulgaria and Romania, had the desire for a strong man at the beginning of their political transformations, in 1992. That non-democratic group of post-communist citizens in Southern Europe shrank to 28 per cent in 1994 and finally to 20 per cent in 1998, which is well below the mean values for the post-Soviet region of 63 per cent in 1992 and 38 per cent in 2000.

Alternatives to democracy: support for a military regime in Belarus

Another alternative to democracy, which is less popular than a strong authoritarian leader within post-communist Europe, is the wish for the replacement of democracy by a military regime. That wish was measured by asking the question of whether the national army should govern the country (see Table 6.4).

Support for a military regime in Belarus as an alternative to democracy is getting smaller during the course of the political transformations. In 1994, 15 per cent of the Belarusian public thought that military rule was a viable alternative to democracy. This share of Belarusians in favour of military rule decreased to 13 per cent in 1996 and 10 per cent in 1998. In 2000, finally, only 9 per cent of the electorate in Belarus considered a military regime as something desirable. The level of support for military rule in Belarus is situated somewhere between the Baltic States on the one hand and the other NIS (newly independent states) on the other. In the Baltics, a military coup is basically out of the question: only 4 per cent of the Latvian or the Lithuanian electorates are thinking about that alternative to democracy. A military coup is a realistic option only for one-tenth of the post-Soviet citizens in the Russian Federation and in Moldova. The desire for a military regime amongst the Russian electorate decreased from 15 per cent in 1998 to 11 per cent in 2000; popular support for a military takeover in the Russian Federation is dwindling. The only post-Soviet country where a military regime could receive a significant and sufficient level of public legitimacy is Ukraine. At the beginning of political transformations in Ukraine in 1994, only 10 per cent of the electorate were in favour of a military coup. Contrary to Belarus, the public support for a military regime increased in Ukraine to 15 per cent in 1996 and finally – quite dramatically – to 32 per cent in 2000. This change of public mood in Ukraine seems to indicate that a military regime could – eventually – gain significant support and some political legitimacy in this post-Soviet country.

Table 6.4 Alternatives to democracy: support for a military regime

Q. Do you agree or disagree with the view that it is best that the army should govern the country?

	(Percentage persons agreed)				
	1994	*1996*	*1998*	*2000*	*Change*
Central Europe	5	3	3	*	–2
Balkans	12	9	12	*	0
Post-Soviet Union	16	8	13	12	–4
1 Estonia	1	2	*	*	+1
2 Latvia	3	3	*	4	+1
3 Lithuania	7	6	*	4	–3
4 Belarus	**15**	**13**	**10**	**9**	**–6**
5 Russia	10	11	15	11	+1
6 Moldova	*	*	*	11	*
7 Ukraine	10	15	14	32	+22

Source: New Democracies Barometer, 1991–2000. See note 4 for details.

Very few people in Central Europe (3 per cent) believe that the army should govern the country. In the Balkans a similar level of support for a military regime can be found as that in the former Soviet Union. In both regions 12 per cent of the electorate are – on average – in favour of military dictatorship. Hence, it appears to be justified to talk about a convergence between the post-Soviet countries on the one hand and the Balkan region on the other with regard to support for a military regime as an alternative to democracy (Table 6.4).

Alternatives to democracy: support for a monarchy in Belarus

In a variety of post-communist as well as post-Soviet countries we find the historical experience of a king or a tsar as a widespread form of political regime in the past. The issue is whether nostalgia for monarchy and a wish for the establishment or renaissance of a king or a tsar figurehead exist amongst the electorate of the newly emerged states (see Table 6.5). It turned out that in Belarus, about one-tenth of the population support a return to a monarchy as an alternative to a democratic political system. In 1994, 8 per cent of the Belarusian electorate were in favour of a new tsar; this share increased to 10 per cent in 1998 and remained at this level of 10 per cent in 2000. The pattern regarding a revival of a tsarist regime in Belarus is very similar to the attitudes towards a monarchy in Russia (10 per cent in 2000), Ukraine (10 per cent in 2000) and Moldova (12 per cent in 2000). The wish for a return to monarchy is quite high in Ukraine and increased from 7 per cent in 1994 to 12 per cent in 1998, indicating again the deep dissatisfaction of the Ukrainian mass public with the current democratic regime in Ukraine. The desire for a return of the Romanovs in Russia grew from 9 per cent in 1994 to 11 per cent in 1998.

Table 6.5 Alternatives to democracy: support for a monarchy

Q. Do you agree or disagree with the view that a return to a monarchy would be better?

	(Percentage respondents agreed)			
	1994	*1998*	*2000*	*Change*
Central Europe	4	4	*	0
Balkans	14	14	*	0
Post-Soviet Union	8	10	10	+2
1 Ukraine	7	12	8	+1
2 Russia	9	11	10	+1
3 Belarus	**8**	**8**	**11**	**+3**
4 Moldova	*	*	12	*

Source: New Democracies Barometer, 1991–2000. See note 4 for details.

More than one-tenth of Russian citizens preferred a tsarist regime to the current Russian democracy.

The highest level of support for the revival of a monarchy was found in the Balkans. A constant share of 14 per cent of all southern Europeans, especially in Serbia, Bulgaria and Romania, favours a return to monarchy.[5]

Creation of a new Index of Democracy in Belarus and other post-Soviet countries

On the basis of an analysis of findings of the New Democracies Barometer, an 'Index of Democracy' has been developed.[6] It reflects public perception of regime change (see Table 6.6). The aim of this index is to measure the extent of democratisation at the level of the individual of societies in transformation from non-democratic to democratic regimes. The Index of Democracy is designed to identify those segments of post-Soviet societies which one can label as 'democrats' or 'democratic citizens', people who identify themselves with the concept of pluralistic democracy without necessarily supporting the existing political regime, who could be democratic to a greater or lesser extent or non-democratic to the same degree. This index does not measure the rating of the performance of the current government at a given point in time; it is supposed to measure the support for democracy as a principle and a form of regime, as opposed to other, non-democratic forms of political regime.

This Index of Democracy consists of nine different characteristics:

1 Negative rating of communist political regime in the past
2 Positive rating of New Democracy or current political regime
3 Optimism about the future of democratic parliaments
4 Support for democratic national parliament
5 Rejection of an authoritarian leader as an alternative to democracy
6 Rejection of a military regime as an alternative to democracy
7 Rejection of a monarchy as an alternative to democracy
8 Rejection of a return to a communist political regime as an alternative to democracy
9 Optimism about the future of democracy

The Index of Democracy consists of ten values. Value 10 means, for example, that a person is 'democratic' on all nine items, value 9 means that a respondent is democratic on eight out of nine items, value 1 means that a person is 'non-democratic' on all nine items.

The resulting groups are defined as follows:

A	Democrats:	values 9–10
B	Weak democrats:	value 8
C	Weak non-democrats:	value 7
D	Non-democrats:	values 1–6

Table 6.6 Index of Democracy in Belarus and other post-Soviet societies (= Index of Democracy, values 8–10)

Country	*1994*	*1996*	*1998*	*Change*
Central Europe-Mean	57	52	61	4
Balkans-Mean	56	52	55	–1
Post-Soviet Union-Mean				
1 Estonia	43	46	*	3
2 Belarus	**23**	**15**	**41**	**18**
3 Lithuania	18	27	*	9
4 Latvia	22	18	*	–4
5 Ukraine	25	12	19	–6
6 Russia	15	*	*	*

Source: NDB 3 (1994), NDB 4 (1996), NDB 5 (1998), Russian Federation Survey 1994, New Baltics Barometer 1994, New Baltics Barometer 1996.

Only those people have been included in the calculation of the Index of Democracy who are democratic on either seven out of nine items, eight out of nine items or on all nine items, which ensures a very strict definition of 'democrats'. The Index of Democracy encompasses the category of 'democrats' (=values 9–10) as well as the group of 'weak democrats' (=value 8) (Table 6.6).

If in a given society more than 60 per cent of the population can be labelled as 'democrats', then I am talking about a 'consolidated democracy'.[7] This notion of consolidated democracy refers to the individual level of the post-communist citizen. The process of consolidation of democracy at the medium level and at the macro-level has to be measured with other methods. The extent of democratisation at the level of elites and of institutions should be analysed with other political science research methods. I am focusing here on the extent of democracy at the micro-level of transforming societies. If in a given society more than 40 per cent of the electorate are identified as 'democrats', then one can discuss the case of an emerging democracy. All societies with a share of less than 40 per cent democrats are transforming societies, where democracy is one path of political development amongst a variety of regime forms; the outcome of transformation in those societies is uncertain and does not lead inevitably towards democracy.

In the region of the former Soviet Union, no consolidated democracy can presently be found. Only Estonia can be qualified as an 'emerging democracy' with a share of democratic Estonians of 46 per cent in 1996. Behind Estonia, we find Belarus as a political system with the second highest share of 'democrats' within the national electorate amongst all post-Soviet countries. In 1998, it was found that 41 per cent of the Belarusian population are 'democrats' in terms of their political attitudes and their political behaviour. The level of democratisation of the Belarusian public is quite astonishing. In 1994, only 23 per cent of the post-Soviet citizens in Belarus could be characterised as pluralistic democrats. In the four years between 1994 and 1998, the number of Belarusian 'democrats' almost doubled, reaching a level of 41 per cent, which is much higher than the spread of democratic attitudes in Lithuania or Latvia, not to mention Ukraine or Russia. A similar level of democratisation of the electorate was found in Lithuania, where 27 per cent of the citizens can be labelled as democrats.

The number of democrats is extremely low in Latvia (18 per cent in 1996), Ukraine (19 per cent in 1998) and in the Russian Federation (15 per cent in 1994). These three post-Soviet countries are at the very bottom of the list of post-communist countries on the basis of the size of the share of democrats within the respective electorates. Russia, Ukraine and Latvia form one cluster with an extremely low level of democratisation of the mass public, whereas Belarus forms together with Estonia and Lithuania another cluster of post-Soviet political systems with a rather high level of democratisation of the electorate. The empirical evidence justifies the characterisation of Belarus and Estonia as 'emerging democracies', at the level of mass politics, of course.

Conclusions

This analysis demonstrates in a very clear way the varied extent of democratisation in post-communist Europe. In Central Europe an average of 61 per cent of the mass public can be described as 'democrats'. One can therefore confirm the hypothesis that the countries of the Central European region are more consolidated democracies in relation to the state of the public mind. In the Balkans, one will find that the majority favours democracy. The average share of 'democratic citizens' in the Balkans is 55 per cent. However, there are no consolidated democracies yet to be found in Southern Europe.

The main aim of this chapter was to analyse political attitudes and the political behaviour of the mass public in Belarus in a two-dimensional comparative perspective. The first dimension was formed by a comparison of the Belarusian electorate over time, between 1992 and 2000, thus covering nine years of political transformation. The second dimension consisted in a comparison between the Belarusian mass public on the one hand with the electorates of six other post-Soviet countries – Estonia, Latvia, Lithuania, Moldova, the Russian Federation and Ukraine – on the other.

One major outcome of this empirical comparative study was that the Belarusian electorate does not fulfil the popular expectations nourished by international publications and media, which suggest that Belarus and, by implication, its population, are non-democratic and somehow politically backward. In an empirical ranking of the six post-Soviet countries analysed, the population of Belarus came second behind Estonia with regard to support for pluralistic democracy. Only Estonia and Belarus fulfil the criterion of an 'emerging democracy' with a share of more than 40 per cent of the electorate being 'democrats' in a very strict definition. An absolute majority of the Belarusian electorate is prepared to defend the national parliament in Minsk if it were threatened with suspension, together with the dissolution of other democratic institutions like parties or general elections. The desire for a strong leader instead of a pluralist democracy is lowest within the Belarusian population in comparison with the six other post-Soviet populations.

With regard to a variety of indicators of democratisation, the electorate of Belarus shows political attitudes and values, which are very similar to those in Lithuania, Latvia and Estonia. Belarus appears to be forming a North–South cluster together with these three Baltic States, whereas the Russian population seems to constitute a different and much bigger political compound together with Ukraine and Moldova. The electorates of Ukraine and Moldova show an extremely similar pattern of political attitudes and behaviour, unfortunately at the bottom of the scale of democracy, which was developed in this chapter.

In this analysis such a phenomenon as the 'Belarusian paradox' has been revealed implying the contrast between a partially democratic mass public and an authoritarian political system. This, however, turned out to be a puzzle only at first glance. First of all, 59 per cent of the Belarusian electorate are not 'democrats', they are either neutral or non-democrats. This implies that there is still an absolute majority of the adult population in Belarus, which is not democratic and could be mobilised for alternatives to democracy. This Belarusian paradox shows a pattern which is very similar to the political situation in the Federal Republic of Yugoslavia in 1998 under the regime of Slobodan Miloševich. In Yugoslavia as well as in Belarus, we find a split electorate with about 40 per cent 'democrats' and about 40 per cent supporting the incumbent authoritarian political regime and approximately 20 per cent of the mass public, who are located between these two broad political camps. In 1998, 92 per cent of the democrats in the Federal Republic of Yugoslavia were against a strong authoritarian leader instead of elections; the Pearson-correlation[8] between being democratic and being against an authoritarian regime of one strong leader was 0.60. A very similar picture was visible in 1998 in Belarus: 82 per cent of all democrats in Belarus were against a strong authoritarian political leader; the Pearson-correlation between Belarusian democrats and citizens against a dictatorship in Belarus was 0.48. Nowadays, nobody is surprised that there is a considerable group of democratic post-communist citizens in Serbia and Montenegro, so why should it be otherwise in Belarus? The crucial question is not the supposed paradox of political behaviour in Belarus, but how the political elite, the political actors and institutions in Belarus are resolving the current political situation and – of course – in which direction, towards democracy or towards an authoritarian dictatorship. Belarus is literally at the crossroads of political transformation.

Notes

1 S.P. Huntington, *The Third Wave: Democratization in the Late Twentieth Century* (Norman: University of Oklahoma Press, 1991).
2 See J.J. Linz and A. Stepan, *Problems of Democratic Transition and Consolidation: Southern Europe, South America, and Post-Communist Europe* (Baltimore: Johns Hopkins University Press, 1996).
3 See the excellent overview in K. Henderson and N. Robinson, *Post-Communist Politics: An Introduction* (Hemel Hempstead: Prentice-Hall Europe, 1997).
4 The data in Table 6.1 to Table 6.6 are taken from sources given below: Christian Haerpfer is the director and principal investigator of the New Democracies Barometer. He conducted the following academic surveys:

1 Belarus 1992/1994/1996/1998 = New Democracies Barometer
2 Ukraine 1992/1994/1996/1998 = New Democracies Barometer
3 Russia 1994 = New Democracies Barometer
4 Central Europe 1991/1992/1994/1996/1998 = New Democracies Barometer
5 Balkans 1991/1992/1994/1996/1998 = New Democracies Barometer

The data for surveys 1 to 5 come directly from the machine-readable multinational database of Christian Haerpfer. All calculations are made by the author. Richard Rose, University of Strathclyde, is the director and principal investigator of the New Baltics Barometer and the New Russia Barometer:

1 Russia 1991/1992/1996/1998/2000 = New Russia Barometer

The Russian data are cited from the following sources: R. Rose, *New Russia Barometer V: Between Two Elections* (Glasgow: Centre for the Study of Public Policy, 1996); R. Rose, *Russia between Elections: New Russia Barometer VIII* (Glasgow: Centre for the Study of Public Policy, 2000); R. Rose, I. Boeva and V. Shyronin, *How Russians are coping with Transition: New Russia Barometer II* (Glasgow: Centre for the Study of Public Policy, 1993); I. Boeva and V. Shyronin, *Russians between State and Market: The Generations Compared* (Glasgow: Centre for the Study of Public Policy, University of Strathclyde, 1992).

2 Estonia 1992/1994/1996/2000 = New Baltics Barometer
3 Latvia 1992/1994/1996/2000 = New Baltics Barometer
4 Lithuania 1992/1994/1996/2000 = New Baltics Barometer

The Baltic data for 1994 and 1996 have been made available to the author within the framework of the ESF-Network 'Citizens in Transition', which is co-ordinated by the author together with Richard Rose. The Baltic data for 1994 and 1996 come directly from the machine-readable multinational database of Christian Haerpfer. All calculations are by the author.

The Baltic data for 1992 and 2000 are cited from the following sources: R. Rose, *New Baltics Barometer IV: A Survey Study* (Glasgow: Centre for the Study of Public Policy, 2000); R. Rose, *New Baltics Barometer III: A Survey Study* (Glasgow: Centre for the Study of Public Policy, 1997); R. Rose, *New Baltics Barometer II: A Survey Study* (Glasgow: Centre for the Study of Public

Policy, 1995); R. Rose and W. Malei, *Nationalities in the Baltic States: A Survey Study* (Glasgow: Centre for the Study of Public Policy, 1994).

The data for Ukraine and Belarus for 2000 are cited from the following source: S. White and R. Rose, *Nationality and Public Opinion in Belarus and Ukraine* (Glasgow: Centre for the Study of Public Policy, 2001).

The data for Moldova in 2000 are cited from the following source: S. White, *Public Opinion in Moldova* (Glasgow: Centre for the Study of Public Policy, 2000).

5 The return of King Simeon as Prime Minister of Bulgaria in recent elections is one of the examples of such a tendency.

6 See R. Rose, W.T. Mishler and C.W. Haerpfer, *Democracy and its Alternatives. Understanding Post-Communist Societies* (Oxford: Polity Press and Baltimore: Johns Hopkins University Press, 1998); R. Rose and C.W. Haerpfer, *New Democracies Barometer II: Adapting to Transformation in Eastern Europe* (Glasgow: Centre for the Study of Public Policy, 1993); R. Rose and C.W. Haerpfer, *New Democracies Barometer III: Learning from What is Happening* (Glasgow: Centre for the Study of Public Policy, 1994); R. Rose and C.W. Haerpfer, *New Democracies Barometer IV: A 10-Nation Survey* (Glasgow: Centre for the Study of Public Policy, 1996); R. Rose and C.W. Haerpfer, *New Democracies Barometer V: A 12-Nation Survey* (Glasgow: Centre for the Study of Public Policy, 1998); R. Rose and C.W. Haerpfer, *New Democracies between State and Market: A Baseline Report of Public Opinion* (Glasgow: Centre for the Study of Public Policy, 1992); R. Rose and C.W. Haerpfer, *New Russia Barometer III: The Results* (Glasgow: Centre for the Study of Public Policy, 1994); R. Rose and C.W. Haerpfer, *Trends in Democracies and Markets: New Democracies Barometer 1991–98* (Glasgow: Centre for the Study of Public Policy, 1998).

7 See the overview of the concept of 'consolidation of democracy' in L. Diamond, *Developing Democracy toward Consolidation* (Baltimore: Johns Hopkins University Press, 1999).

8 Pearson's correlation coefficient (r) demonstrates a degree of linear relationship between two variables that have been measured on interval or ratio scales (e.g. height in inches and weight in pounds). It is calculated by multiplying the z-scores of two variables by one another and then calculating the average of their 'relationship'. For more details see W.P. Vogt, *Dictionary of Statistics and Methodology* (Sage Publications, 1993).

7 President and opposition

Specific features of the Belarusian political scene

David G. Rotman and Aliaksandr N. Danilov

Introduction

The aim of this chapter is to outline general features of the electorate of the contemporary government and opposition in Belarus, to analyse the distribution of political forces and to study the motives for their behaviour.

The past 10 to 15 years in the life of a relatively small country like Belarus, years coinciding with the change of millennium, were transitional. And as time goes by, both professional commentators and the general public are becoming less and less certain about their opinions on these dramatic events. What was 'the station' where 'the train to the bright future' left from, and what is the definition of 'the station' and the direction the train is going in? In our view, in the case of system transformations in the post-Soviet states, debate continues about the fundamental processes, which caused such a major geopolitical upheaval. And it will be a long time until the world gains its lost balance back again.

Today the world is looking for a new paradigm of global development, applying old models and appealing to historical experience, but old formulae do not work, and the situation makes everybody change – both in the East and the West. The principles of a new morality are being established: what was acceptable in the past is not possible today. The process of transformation, which started according to a single pattern, is taking a different form in every newly emerged post-Soviet state. A specific variant of market economy and political regime is taking shape in every country.

The complexity of this process lies in the fact that there is no single mechanism of transformational changes, and every country has to work out its own politics of transformation, mostly by the method of trial and error. That is why it is not so easy to assess the changes taking place on post-Soviet territory, to evaluate them in historical perspective. In addition, a contemporary researcher cannot fail to be concerned about the price of every 'achievement', about social and moral payment for it in the present and the future.

Choosing the path

In such conditions, the role and responsibility of the authorities and the opposition, the new political elites that are being formed in the post-Soviet states, are radically increasing. Many of the institutions of civil society have proved to be only partly formed and thus unable to carry out democratic functions in full. We have in mind political parties, the mass media and representative institutions. The reasons for such a situation should be sought not only in the present, but also in the past of Belarus. Most probably, a traditional Belarusian caution, a lack of undue haste in making decisions, has saved the country, more than once, from devastation. The citizens of Belarus have traditionally respected power and relied on its help in hard times. That is why new market relations and individualism have not been so easily established in the country.

After the collapse of the USSR, the authorities had at their disposal two possible courses of action for escaping from crisis: swift and decisive changes in the economy ('shock therapy') or the gradual reform of economic relations. The first variant could have led to a steep increase in unemployment and to mass popular discontent due to deterioration in the standard of living. The second variant might lead to the same result but at a slower speed, and in the meantime would allow the population to adjust to the changing situation. The second variant afforded fewer problems for the authorities, so a socially oriented model of the economy became dominant. More and more often Belarus approached its eastern neighbour Russia in search of markets for manufactured goods and to buy cheap raw materials. This helps to explain the Belarusian government's efforts to create a close union between the two countries. It should also be emphasised that the second variant was chosen by the government of the country after the collapse of the USSR, that is, before the election of the first president.

As a result, Belarus adopted the second path as its strategic model – a socially oriented market economy, which, on the one hand, permits the preservation of the people's social achievements, and, on the other hand, involves the use of various mechanisms to increase the effectiveness of the economic system and to promote the introduction of new innovative technologies. This policy is successful to some degree, as it keeps the country out of chaos. In spite of economic hardships, the majority of the population is not inclined to blame the authorities and the President for inaction and the lack of ability and skill to correct this state of affairs. This demonstrates the authorities' shrewdness in taking the opinion of the electorate into account and correcting their policies in good time.

Power and society

In the Belarusian political arena power functions as a complex, multilevel, but quite monolithic and co-ordinated mechanism. The measures to strengthen his authority which President Aliaksandr Lukashenka took in 1994–5 made it possible to solve many problems of governing the country in the period of transition, and were similar to those taken by President Vladimir Putin when he came to power.

The contemporary authorities in Belarus enjoy serious social support among different layers of society, and the head of state constantly emphasises in his statements that his politics is of 'the people', without referring to any definite social group or political force whose interests he represents. Taking into account our long Soviet past and the high level of nostalgia among the population, the political authorities regard such a position as a logical one, ensuring the stability of power.

It can be stated quite firmly that a social explosion is unlikely at present. There are factors blocking such a possibility. Among them are:

1 The stable authority of the President of the country
2 The absence of any real influence on the 'protest' electorate by the political opposition
3 The economic position of the Belarusian population which is to some extent better than that of the citizens of other CIS countries

The high, stable rating of the President of Belarus Lukashenka can be regarded as some kind of achievement for the post-Soviet countries. Let us now study the recent ratings of Belarusian political actors (Table 7.1).

This table contains the names of famous Belarusian politicians who influence (to different degrees) the situation in the country. The absolute leader of the political field is A.G. Lukashenka. From the beginning of the presidential election campaign in 1994 his rating indices have been distributed in the interval from 42.0 to 54.2 per cent. The leaders who

Table 7.1 Ratings of political leaders,[1] 1993–2000

	1993	*1994*	*1995*	*1996*	*1997*	*1998*	*1999*	*2000*
Bahdankevich		2.0	1.1	3.1	1.5	1.5	0.9	1.7
Haidukevich	–	0.2	0.1	–	0.1	0.3	0.1	0.4
Hryb	–	0.7	0.1	0.9	0.8	0.5	–	–
Iarmoshin	–	–	–	–	0.2	0.6	0.2	6.6
Kaliakin	–	–	–	0.5	0.2	0.2	0.2	0.2
Liabedzka	–	–	–	–	0.3	0.4	0.1	2.1
Lukashenka	0.3	54.4	49.0	43.6	46.0	50.7	54.2	42.0
Miasnikovich	–	0.3	0.2	0.8	0.3	0.9	0.5	0.7
Pazniak	3.3	7.9	8.6	4.4	0.4	0.2	2.8	3.4
Chyhir	–	1.0	0.9	2.4	2.2	0.9	3.8	6.3
Sharetski	–	–	0.2	2.3	0.8	0.7	0.3	0.7
Shushkevich	4.1	7.4	6.4	5.9	5.1	4.2	4.3	6.1

Source: For this and following tables, see the Archive of the Centre for Social and Political Research, Belarusian State University.

initiated the national democratic movement – S. Shushkevich and Z. Pazniak – have stable ratings, but of a different, obviously lower order. Other politicians included in the table lag behind considerably in political weight and the stability of their positions. All this shows an imbalance in the Belarusian political field, which may have determined the formation of authoritarian tendencies in the style of the leading political actor – some would say, against his will. The topicality of this argument is supported by sociological data.

One can conditionally divide the politicians included in the rating table into four groups:

1 President A.G. Lukashenka
2 The President's closest companions-in-arms (Ermoshin, Miasnikovich)
3 The opposition to the authorities consisting of politicians who had previously supported the President, but left his team for various reasons (Chyhir, Bahdankevich, Liabedzka)
4 Representatives of democratic movements formed before Lukashenka came to power (Pazniak, Shushkevich, and others)

Reality shows that the first two groups are quite monolithic (outwardly, at any rate), but the last two, representing the opposition, are disunited. The group, which has left power, is trying to move away from the group of representatives of national democratic movements. This testifies to the stability of the government, and the disunity and weakness of the opposition.

We will now look at the data characterising the levels of trust, which different social groups have in the authorities (Table 7.2).

One can see from the table a definite tendency towards a decline of trust in the various branches of power, but, at the same time, stable support for the authorities. We note that this level of trust is largely determined by attitudes towards the head of state. As a result, we will study in detail the electorate's views on the President.

The President

Using methods developed by the Centre for Social and Political Research, Belarusian State University, we will now attempt to define the attitudes of the population to the President of Belarus Aliaksandr Lukashenka.[3] At the first stage of the analysis a so-called rating '*Sito*' ('Sieve') has been calculated. To interpret it according to the range of questions about the President's activity, a complicated sorting of data has been conducted. Such a sorting allows one to select three main categories: 'total supporters' (people who always have a positive attitude to the President's activity), 'total opponents' (people who always have a negative attitude to the President's activity), and 'those who hesitate'. Calculation of the rating 'Sieve' gave the results shown in Table 7.3.

Table 7.2 Degree of trust in various political institutions of the country, 1997–2000

Q. What is the degree of your trust in . . . ?[2]

	1997	*1998*	*1999*	*2000*
President of Belarus A.G. Lukashenka				
Trust completely	30.0	26.7	28.2	17.5
Quite trust	29.7	30.3	33.0	31.7
Don't quite trust	15.0	14.2	13.7	21.9
Do not trust at all	13.7	12.6	13.2	16.1
Don't know	11.6	16.3	11.8	12.8
Parliament of Belarus				
Trust completely	11.3	10.2	10.4	6.6
Quite trust	25.5	25.1	30.3	22.8
Don't quite trust	24.5	21.0	22.9	31.8
Do not trust at all	16.8	15.7	15.0	16.9
Don't know	21.9	28.0	21.3	21.9
Belarusian government				
Trust completely	13.6	13.3	12.0	8.8
Quite trust	28.3	27.4	31.8	24.9
Don't quite trust	21.2	19.8	21.9	29.8
Do not trust at all	15.3	13.7	15.5	17.5
Don't know	21.6	25.8	18.9	19.5
Constitutional Court				
Trust completely	12.1	11.9	11.2	7.9
Quite trust	26.0	26.0	30.7	23.9
Don't quite trust	15.9	12.9	17.9	21.5
Do not trust at all	16.8	13.1	13.3	14.9
Don't know	29.2	36.2	26.8	31.8

Table 7.3 Correlation of the number of total supporters and total opponents of President Lukashenka, 1997–2000

Groups	*1997*	*1998*	*1999*	*2000*
Total supporters	15.6	16.0	17.9	16.5
Total opponents	29.4	27.2	28.4	29.6
Those who hesitate	54.9	56.8	53.7	53.9

From the table it can be seen that the basis of the President's support represented by his total supporters is constantly about 16 per cent. Moreover, the group of those who hesitate amounts to more than 50 per cent of the total number of electors. It should be noted that the number of total opponents is always larger than the number of total supporters. The main question is: what is the relationship between the President and the electorate? A response to this question will be given after examining the rating 'from the past to the future'. Measurement of this kind of rating is calculated on the basis of answers to sociological questionnaires: 'For whom did you vote at the last elections?'; 'For whom would you vote if the presidential elections were held on Sunday?'

Using the grouping (sorting) method, the following categories were selected: 'firmly pros' (those who voted for Lukashenka last time and are going to vote for him next time as well), 'firmly cons' (those who have never voted for Lukashenka), 'loss' (those who were for the President in the past, but are now against him), and 'gain' (those who were against the President, but are now for him).

Table 7.4 shows the distribution of the electorate in groups that was obtained.

From the table it can be seen that the President's gain from the electorate is higher than his loss. For further analysis, a calculation was made of the correlation between the data obtained from the two ratings (the 'Sieve', and 'from the past to the future'). We used here the results of the measurements calculated from the representative sample in 1999. The sample included 2,001 respondents (Table 7.5).

In this table the data concerning the hesitating group are the most interesting. In total, there turned out to be 1,074 people (in the rating 'Sieve') out of 2,001 respondents (the number questioned in this research), which constitute 53.7 per cent. Those who were 'totally for' the President amounted to 466 people, or 23.3 per cent of the total number of respondents in this study. Those who were 'totally against' numbered 226 people,

Table 7.4 Distribution of the electorate in groups within the framework of the rating 'from the past to the future', 1998–2000

Groups	*1998*	*1999*	*2000*
Firmly pro	37.2	38.2	38.2
Firmly contra	38.1	34.0	34.0
Loss	13.8	13.3	13.3
Gain	11.0	14.5	14.5

Table 7.5 Correlation of the results of the complex rating measurements

Groups	*Hesitating*	*Total supporters*	*Total opponents*	*In total (in row)*
Firmly contra	226	–	445	681
Loss	152	–	114	266
Gain	230	60	–	290
Firmly pro	466	298	–	764
In total	1,074	358	569	2,001

Note: Calculation is made in absolute numbers, based on a representative nationwide sample.
Source: Centre for Social and Political Research, BSU.

or 11.3 per cent. The loss of President Lukashenka's electorate was 152 people, or 7.6 per cent. The gain was 230 people, or 11.5 per cent.

Using these data it is possible to calculate the totality of the electorate that would have been most likely to vote for the President if the elections had been held at the moment of the rating measurement. For these calculations we will take: 'total supporters' – 17.9 per cent (Table 7.3); 'firmly pro' – 23.3 per cent (in the number of the 'hesitating', Table 7.5). Thus, the total percentage of electors who are ready to vote for Lukashenka is 41.2 per cent today. The number who constituted the 'gain' (from the number of the 'hesitating') is most likely to be added to these groups – another 11.5 per cent. Thus the total expression of the number of the supporters of the head of state could constitute 52.7 per cent. That would mean victory for Lukashenka in the first round of the elections.

The number of those who are likely to vote against the President can be calculated in the same way. Among those, first, there will be 'total opponents' and 'firmly contra'. Some of the 'loss' group may be included as well. In the struggle for votes between the President and the opposition, the position of that part of the Belarusian electorate whose ideological and social choice has not yet formed might play a decisive role. This group is hesitating, and according to different estimates, could constitute up to 50 per cent, and furthermore, could change its configuration depending on the situation.

The characteristics of the situation in the country are highlighted in the index of political stability. This represents a correlation of estimates of trust in the presidential power and in the opposition. The measurement on the basis of which the summary index of 'trust in the authorities' was calculated was obtained according to the following parameters: trust in (i) the President; (ii) the government; (iii) the local authorities; (iv) the heads of the regional administrations. The summary index constituted 0.50. This number, which is situated right in the middle of the level scale (the interval of the index calculation is from 0 to 1), means that trust in all the authorities is expressed by half of the electorate. However, the index of trust in the President individually constituted 0.62, while the government received an estimation of 0.49; the local authorities – 0.42; the heads of the regional administrations – 0.45. From these data it can be concluded that the fixed degree of trust is situated right in the middle of the scale simply because of the fairly high index of President Lukashenka.

In the context of this measurement the summary index of 'trust in the opposition' was also calculated. It constituted 0.15. The index of the population's satisfaction with their standard of living was calculated as well. It constituted 0.22. From the data presented above it can be concluded that just half of the population trusts the authorities. This can be explained by the low index of the population's satisfaction with their standard of living. Because 80 per cent of the population is dissatisfied (according to the index – 0.22), trust in the authorities is likely to decline in future.

The opposition

The logic of political life and common sense would lead us to assume that a decline of trust in the authorities should necessarily result in an increase in the population's trust in the opposition. However, this has not taken place. The level of trust in the opposition is low – 0.15. This means that the opposition does not enjoy any popularity at all. The authorities' loss of influence and power is not benefiting the opposition, but is situated on some hypothetical point of the political field where the potential basis for the emergence of a new, alternative political power is being created. The inability of the political opposition in Belarus to win trust demands particular analysis.

We have already mentioned that the opposition is disunited, which means that the opposition's problems lie in the opposition itself. This involves its inability to co-operate with the electorate on a broad scale, an absence of will to co-ordinate the efforts of various opposition trends, a lack of professionalism to create its own popular mass media (not today, but in 1992–4), and many other factors.

Today it would be more correct to speak not about the destruction, but the self-destruction of the opposition. Here are the landmarks in this process:

1. August–September, 1991 – lack of political will to force the deputies of the Supreme Soviet (to be more exact, the communist majority frightened by the failure of their wager on the coup in Moscow) to make a decision about the abolition of parliament and the conduct of pre-term elections.
2. Autumn 1992 – obstruction of the Belarusian Popular Front's intention to hold a referendum on the abolition of parliament and the conduct of pre-term elections; this blocking was carried out on behalf of the Supreme Soviet (and included the democratic deputies headed by Shushkevich).
3. The first half of 1994 – absence of any desire on the part of the democratic leaders to negotiate about a single candidate to stand for the presidency of the country.
4. September–December 1996 – compromise tactics of the democratic Members of Parliament about the referendum on amendments to the constitution.
5. April–May 1999 – failure (or complete absence) of any attempt to hold unofficial presidential elections.
6. October 2000 – refusal to participate in the parliamentary elections.

In the course of preparing for these events, serious strategic and tactical mistakes were made by the leaders of the opposition. This list of events could be easily continued. But this is not the point. The important thing is the situation these mistakes have led to. Today there is no active, effective and influential opposition in the country.

The absence of any well-developed structure of political parties and trends is very characteristic of Belarusian politics. Naturally, political parties do exist in Belarus. Today there are 17 of them, which is enough for a small country. However, support for these parties among the population is very low. The conscious population's support for political parties from survey to survey has remained constant at a level of 20 per cent.

About 20 per cent of the population of the country are aware of the existence of certain parties. It might be assumed that the authorities have prevented the development of the party structure. But the same situation could be seen during the questioning of the population in 1991, and in 1992 and 1993 as well. How can one explain such a state of affairs? It is probably because political parties appeared in Belarus not as a natural expression of the positions, wishes and preferences of certain social groups, but as an elementary mirror reflection of those that appeared and functioned in Russia, Ukraine and Lithuania, or in Germany and Poland.

It should be noted that this reason for the unpopularity and weak activity of the parties fits in very well with the picture of the contemporary opposition. Close analysis suggests that the opposition exists only for its own sake.

The electorate of the presidential power and the opposition

We will now attempt to analyse the electorate of the presidential power and the opposition. The political arena in Belarus used to be quite homogeneous, but has changed significantly in the past ten years. The transformation of society, the absence of definite moral values, the vague prospects for the future and the growing material divisions in society find their expression in electoral preferences. Today, like ten years ago, among the problems causing the citizens anxiety are price rises, inflation, crime, and the social protection of the population.

Every political force in the country offers its own solution to the country's problems, defining Belarus's path of development. The current government, proceeding from contemporary circumstances, is implementing social and political reforms, applying to the full the experience of the past as building material for the future. Citizens with conservative views predominate among the President's electorate. Belarus has rejected 'shock therapy', preferring quiet, evolutionary reforms. As a matter of fact, the speed of reform is still a highly topical issue.

The opposition's electorate adheres to the view that market transformations are impossible without mass privatisation, the creation of a strong private sector of the economy, and the initiative and activity of the country's citizens. However, the idealised image of the market economy and its corresponding political policy is in conflict with the social reality of the post-Soviet countries, and is consequently beginning to be eroded.

It is no surprise that the majority of Belarusian citizens have adopted the position of observer in the social experiment developing on a large scale.

Let us look at the sociological research data obtained from a national sample in 1994 and 2000 by the Centre of Sociological and Political Research of the Belarusian State University (Table 7.6).

The presidential electorate did not change significantly, except in age, during the period from 1994 to 2000. During these six years the number of people of pensionable age supporting the current authorities increased and their educational level decreased slightly.

From the point of view of the President's supporters, during the last seven years the authorities have managed to preserve relative stability in the country, and, at all events, the 'appearance' of social justice. On account of its Soviet mentality and the negative experience of economic and political reform in the newly independent states after the collapse of the USSR, the presidential electorate gives a positive assessment of the gradual character and social orientation of Lukashenka's unhurried reforms. In the voters' view, order has been preserved in the country, national, religious and other conflicts have been avoided, salaries have been paid regularly and on time, a high level of education, science and medical services has been maintained, the pension system has been adapted to the

Table 7.6 Characteristics of the electorate of the President and the opposition[4]

	Authority		*Opposition*	
	1994	*2000*	*1994*	*2000*
Sex				
Male	33.3	35.6	43	50.4
Female	66.7	64.4	57	49.6
Age				
18–29	11.46	8.0	25.0	35.7
30–44	30.6	6.9	40.0	33.4
45–59	23.0	23.0	28.0	21.3
60 and older	34.8	62.1	5.0	9.5
Place of residence				
Capital	17.9	19.5	23.0	17.3
Regional centre	17.0	9.2	14.0	27.7
Other towns	23.7	26.4	37.0	32.3
Countryside	37.9	44.8	25.0	22.8
Education				
Primary	25.5	23.0	5.0	1.7
Incomplete secondary	10.9	20.7	10.5	7.2
General secondary	32.2	21.8	28.5	21.9
Professional	17.3	6.9		11.2
Technical		17.2	31.0	25.9
Incomplete higher	1.8	2.3	7.5	7.8
Higher	11.8	8.0	16.5	24.2

changing circumstances, and social security has been retained for groups in need.

A peculiarity of the presidential election of 2001 is that the authorities managed to forestall a massive growth of the protest vote without making their socio-economic or political mistakes visible to all levels of Belarusian society. The administrative resources of the current regime are still strong enough to pose other questions about the need for a radical change in the state's domestic and foreign policy and the necessity for a complete reshuffle of government personnel.

Among the small opposition electorate there have not been any significant changes either. There is a preponderance of young people between the ages of 18 and 29 (35.7 per cent) and between 30 and 44 (33.4 per cent), with a technical education (25.9 per cent) or a higher education (24.9 per cent), who live in the regional centres (27.7 per cent) and towns (32.3 per cent). These people believe that the radical market reforms proposed by the opposition could significantly improve living conditions and bring the country closer to European standards.

The absence of real political dialogue between the authorities and the opposition, the lack of an exchange of ideas and the absence of public expertise in the conduct of policy definitely lower the level of political analysis, and to some degree exhaust the content of the politics conducted in the country, where emphasis is more frequently laid on administrative resources. Experience shows that without a strong opposition and the developed institutions of civil society the strengthening of personal power is inevitable – and this is hardly possible for a long period in a modern European state.

Conclusions

In the eyes of Belarusian voters, proposals for a mutually profitable economic and political co-operation between Belarus and Russia and other countries of the CIS act as a kind of drug making them believe that a socially oriented state policy will be successfully implemented. At the same time, the geopolitical position of Belarus, the historical experience of the Belarusian people, the weakness of the political opposition and the lessons of Yugoslavia make a policy conducted from a position of force completely unacceptable and ineffective.

One cannot but notice that the changes taking place in the newly independent states, and general global tendencies such as participation in world policy and the work of international organisations, albeit considerably restricted, exert a positive influence on the internal and external policy of Belarus. Independent observers notice some movement towards market reforms, an increase in the number of supporters of change, some democratisation of the system of government, a diminution in the excessive power of the President and the expansion of international contacts.

The economic behaviour of different groups of the population is changing, along with their values and political preferences. Open confrontation between political and economic conservatism and liberal market tendencies is a thing of the past and has become transformed into practical competition in real life. In these conditions the authorities balance skilfully, holding the initiative in their hands – and hence, retained the controlling interest in the presidential election campaign of 2001.

Notes

1 The table of Belarusian politicians has been compiled from the database collected as a result of measurements conducted by the Belarusian sociological service 'Public opinion' and by the Centre for Sociological and Political Research, Belarusian State University.

2 Data of the Centre for Sociological and Political Research, Belarusian State University.

3 A detailed description of these methods is presented in the article by David G. Rotman, 'Sotsial'naia i politicheskaia situatsiia v strane: metodicheskie podkhody k analizu resul'tatov issledovanii', *Sotsiologiia*, No. 2 (1999): 54–64.

4 Data of the Centre for Sociological and Political Research, Belarusian State University.

8 Belarus

In search of national identity between 1986 and 2000

Jan Zaprudnik

In my view, the problem of saving the [Belarusian] nation is directly related to the degree of national self-awareness. (Vasil Bykau, *Belaruskaia dumka*, 7 (1992), p. 43)

Geopolitical background

The geographical location of Belarus severely affects its geopolitics. In the pre-1991 period, the occasionally used nickname of the Belarusian SSR as 'the Western Gate of the Soviet Union' aptly reflects the country's geostrategic significance. One fateful aftermath of this was the physical destruction of Belarus in World War II, including a heavy demographic loss, known as 'every fourth one', when 25 per cent of the nation were wiped out. As a consequence, the number of Russians in the republic rose by about one million between 1945 and 1985. This increase was even more significant among the intelligentsia as a result of the disproportionately high destruction of native cadres in the Stalinist purges.

Another feature of Belarusian society as it emerged from the Soviet era was its deep-rooted provincialism and difficulty in thinking of itself as an entity apart from Russia. A telling incident illustrating this occurred in 1992 during a visit of Polish journalists to Minsk. 'The guests from Warsaw', reported a newspaper, 'were quite surprised to learn from Mr Butevich [Belarusian Minister of Information] that the Polish ethnic minority is the largest in Belarus. When the Minister was reminded that there are Russians, too [by far the largest minority], he said: "Russians are not a minority!" At which the Poles were sincerely astonished.'[1]

Many Belarusians still cannot think of themselves as a self-sustained nation, especially in terms of economic relations, which enhances linguistic and cultural attachment to their eastern neighbour. A group of international analysts agrees that 'Belarus is, in a geopolitical sense, a crossroads state' and that Russia remains 'the single most important external factor in Belarus's evolution'.[2]

Russia's intentions towards Belarus can be seen through the recently adopted 'Theses of the Council on Foreign and Defence Policy', where

Belarus's national agenda is also mentioned. The 'Theses' include the merger of the two countries' armies 'into a single system with a single command and control structure' and make the following projection: 'Since the processes of restoring national self-consciousness are being accelerated in Belarus, time is working in favour of the opponents of "integration". So the unification process should be speeded up.'[3] As a result, during the last two years elite shifts in Minsk have led to a dramatic increase in ethnic Russians occupying top positions in the Belarusian government, with the national Prime Minister, his deputies and heads of the power ministries, as well as a number of deputy ministers and the Speaker of the lower chamber of parliament, all being Russian-born.

The beginning under Gorbachev

Mikhail Gorbachev's programme of restructuring, announced in 1985, facilitated a collective complaint by 28 intellectuals in hitherto-silent Minsk to the top Soviet leader. This move was rather unusual for Belarus, a country known for its subservient Communist Party leadership and silent intelligentsia. In their letter to Gorbachev, the 28 signatories entreated the recipient to help save the Belarusians from 'spiritual death'. The threat of demise was seen in the fact that the national language, which the petitioners saw as 'the soul of the nation', and 'one of the foundations upon which the statehood of the Belarusian people rests', had been 'squeezed out of almost all spheres of life'. The writers of the petition pointed out that discrimination against Belarusian culture had given rise to a 'noticeable growth of national awareness', which, in turn, 'is provoking a hostile reaction from the bureaucracy'. To prevent a rise in tension, the authors suggested that the Belarusian language 'must be protected by legislation'.[4] The national Supreme Soviet subsequently provided legal protection on the issue in 1990.

Political fallout of Kurapaty and Chernobyl

In the late 1980s, two major developments had a strong impact on Belarusians' sense of identity – the publication of an account of mass graves of victims of Stalinism in the Kurapaty forest near Minsk and revelations about radiation fallout from the Chernobyl nuclear disaster. Kurapaty immediately became a generic symbol of Stalinist repression of the nationally conscious Belarusian intelligentsia, which had taken place in the ideological and ethnic cleansing of the 1930s. The name 'Kurapaty' became a powerful catalyst for national awareness and a patriotic political movement. To accelerate investigation of the crime, a civic group called the 'Martyrology of Belarus' was founded in October 1988. Its spokesman, the most prominent Belarusian writer Vasil Bykau, said that the inquiry into 'our losses and our martyrs would be laid as a cornerstone in the foundation of our national consciousness'.[5]

In February 1989, a rally of 40,000 young people in Minsk displayed such slogans as 'sovereignty for Belarus' and 'Official Status for the Belarusian Language'. The Communist Party bosses admitted that the previous policy of suppression of national culture had led to 'an emotional "explosion" among the intelligentsia'. The 'Martyrology of Belarus' became a stimulus for the creation of the Belarusian Popular Front 'Renewal' (BNF) in June 1989. Chaired by Zianon Pazniak, the BNF played an exceptionally important role in securing for the Belarusian language the status of sole official language (although for a brief period from 1990 to 1995) and proclaiming Belarus's sovereignty (27 July 1990) and independence (25 August 1991).

Another important factor that influenced the rise of national self-awareness toward the end of 1989 was the revelation that over 70 per cent of the radiation of the 1986 Chernobyl disaster had landed on Belarusian territory. A public outcry and pressure for investigation of the Chernobyl cover-up had significant political and psychological repercussions. The leadership was accused of subservience to Moscow at the expense of national interests. 'The Chernobyl tragedy has demonstrated', wrote one critic, 'that the Belarusian people needs indispensably to raise its self-awareness. If our leadership had high national self-awareness, this would not have happened.'[6]

The national idea

With the advent of sovereignty and independence, much discussion has revolved around the closely interrelated concepts of the Belarusian 'national idea', 'national consciousness', and 'national identity'. In August 1992, an international conference was held on the subject of the formation and development of national consciousness among the Belarusians.[7] Soon afterwards the Academy of Sciences took upon itself the task of providing a 'scientifically grounded Belarusian national idea'. The daily *Zviazda* published a series of articles under the heading 'We need a vivifying idea that will save Belarus'.[8] The key element of this quest was to be sought in the spheres of culture and history. The multi-confessional and multi-ethnic make-up of Belarusian society, divided between East and West, became highlighted. It was found to possess a distinct type of mentality characterised by tolerance, humanistic values, the absence of extremist views, and having peaceful intentions toward its neighbours. It was claimed that Belarusian culture was a 'synthesis' of eastern and western types, without dogmatic collectivised Byzantism, on the one hand, or western individualism, on the other.[9] However, public awareness of these qualities was low. Researchers found that only 5 to 6 per cent of the population 'possesses the necessary knowledge of the history of [our] national culture'.[10]

There has been little change over the past years. A nationwide representative opinion poll conducted in March 2000 in Belarus, a country with 81 per cent of Belarusians, revealed an amazing lack of national self-awareness. Respondents were asked to give a cultural definition of Belarusians, saying whether they are 'a separate self-sustained (*samastoinaia*) Belarusian nation', or 'a branch of the triune Russian nation', or 'other'. Only 49.8 per cent said that Belarusians are a separate nation, while 42.6 per cent chose the second answer, with 2.1 per cent pointing at Russian roots; 5.5 per cent said they did not know how to answer. Interestingly enough, in response to the question of whose citizens they felt to be first, 75.9 per cent of respondents named the Republic of Belarus. Russia was named by only 2.2 per cent, and the USSR by 12.4 per cent.[11] This shows the importance of statehood in the formation of a sense of national identity.

It would be useful to find out the position of official ideologues towards the issue of a 'national idea', as many commentators claim that Lukashenka has destroyed the Belarusian character of the state and sold statehood to Russia. It must be noted that they do not shy away from discussing their version of Belarus's nationhood. For example, the editor of the newly launched presidential monthly *Belaruskaia dumka* (*Belarusian thought*), Uladzimir Vialichka, wrote in 1996: 'We need like fresh air a consolidating national idea. The formulation of the latter is an honorary common obligation of politicians and representatives of the social sciences.'[12] Two years later, the journal devoted an entire issue to the subject, announcing that: 'The intellectual elite is busy looking for a universal national idea', since 'attempts to organise one's life according to an alien pattern and image are not successful'.[13] There are definite differences between government, independent intellectuals and politicians in their understanding of the meaning and practical applications of the 'national idea'. While independent writers advocate full sovereignty and independence for Belarus, on the government side there is plenty of double-talk, inherited from the Soviet era, which allows officials to speak of Belarus's 'independence' under a union with Russia. Nevertheless, there is also a general consensus that the concept of a national idea should be developed, and some see it as being already in motion. Here is one explanation of this phenomenon and an optimistic projection: 'Having been born later than other national ideas', wrote one of them, 'and facing hardships in search of historical justification and acceptance for the future, "the Belarusian idea" nevertheless has been alive and gaining ground. And for the young people who are growing up in an independent state, the ideas of the Belarusian people and the Belarusian state will, obviously, become something so familiar and natural that they will never be lost.'[14]

Language, culture, religion

Traditionally, to be Belarusian meant to be a Belarusian speaker. In Belarus, as in Eastern Europe generally, the notion of nationality has been based on ethnicity. According to the outstanding Belarusologist, Academician

Iaukhim Karski (1861–1931), author of the monumental three-volume monograph, *Belorusy* (1903–22), the Belarusian language was 'an inseparable indicator of the Belarusian nationality during its centuries-old history'.[15] Conversely, the use of the Russian or the Polish language among Belarusians generally has been seen as an indicator of cultural and political allegiance to Russia or Poland. The conceptual fusion of language and nationality (citizenship), although challenged by some, is still brimming with political implications. 'If the entire official documentation in our country is conducted exclusively in the language of a neighbouring state, i.e., in Russian', says one critic of the present-day abandonment of Belarusian in official usage, 'then perhaps we, the Belarusians, are not any longer citizens of Belarus, but of boundless Russia?'[16]

During the 1990s, the status of the Belarusian language went through a series of reversals. In January 1990, the Supreme Soviet of Belarus, in the wake of prolonged and heated public debates, adopted the 'Law about languages in the Belarusian SSR'. Belarusian was proclaimed to be the sole official language of the country. Minority languages were to be protected, and a period of up to ten years was given to make a transition from Russian to Belarusian. The preamble to the law declared: 'Language is not only a means of communication, but also the soul of a nation, the foundation and the most important part of its culture.'[17] Implementation of the language law, however, was slow and difficult. First, there was stubborn resistance by the bureaucracy against the use of Belarusian, even by those who knew it. Second, the language itself, in the mind of the population, was stigmatised as 'peasant' by years of disuse by the higher power echelons. According to some polls, less than 25 per cent of Belarusians knew their native tongue sufficiently well and less than 50 per cent were willing to advance their knowledge.[18] Nevertheless, efforts under the Kebich government (1990–4), with the Speaker Stanislau Shushkevich using Belarusian in his parliamentary proceedings, led to some increase in the role of the national language in education and the media. It regained its position in the field of publishing, education and public usage, reminding one of its status during the 1920s. However, after Aliaksandr Lukashenka was elected President in the summer of 1994, a reversal took place, especially after the May 1995 referendum. One of the four questions asked was whether the voters would agree to give the Russian language 'official status equal to Belarusian'. In spite of ardent protests by some legislators and members of the intelligentsia, the answer was a firm 'Yes', explained by the following: (a) decades of Russian being used as the official language; (b) weak national self-awareness on the part of a majority of Belarusians; and (c) intensive government propaganda, including by the President himself, on behalf of the Russian language. Soon, further legal steps narrowed the use of Belarusian in public life. In 1998, the 'Law about languages' was amended in a peculiar way: the choice between Belarusian and Russian for official usage was left to individual bureaucrats, with freedom to choose either one. Even more: the updated law, in saying that 'In the Republic of Belarus the languages in the sphere of culture are Belarusian and (or) the Russian language', made possible further elimination of Belarusian from public life.[19]

Currently, the mass media, including the TV and radio which are totally owned and controlled by the state, use overwhelmingly Russian. In the capital of Minsk, there is not a single college or high school where classes are taught in the language of the titular nationality. Only in a few schools are there exclusively Belarusian-language classes. The number of books and periodicals in Belarusian has been diminishing from year to year. For example, in the three-year period 1995–7, Belarusian-language publications dropped from 12.5 per cent of the total to 5.5 per cent.[20] Thus, linguistically, in 2000 Belarus has been pushed back almost to the mid-1980s, when the 28 signatories entreated Gorbachev to save their nation from 'spiritual death'.

Opinions differ on whether the linguistic and cultural death of the nation will ensue. David Marples suggested in 1999: 'For Belarus, national development without the native language, especially under the shadow of a much larger Slavic neighbor with a lengthy historical tradition as an empire, was virtually impossible.'[21] The Belarusian language indeed has been losing ground in favour of Russian since 1995. According to the 1999 census, the Belarusian language is now spoken at home by 36.7 per cent of the population and Russian by 62.8 per cent. The question, however, should be asked as to whether Russian, spoken by Belarusians, is unavoidably a carrier of Russian cultural and political identity. Apparently not, if one analyses Belarus's urban centres where 69 per cent of the entire population live, and the rural areas. For example, the predominantly Russian-speaking capital of Minsk (population 1.7 million) has become a hotbed of political activism in defence of Belarus's sovereignty and independence. Meanwhile, the Belarusian-speaking villages have turned themselves into fortresses of conservatism and nostalgia for Soviet times and reintegration with Russia. There is a growing distinction between linguistic and political Russification. Russian in Belarus in many cases is as much a language of cultural renewal of the country and its independence as Belarusian. There may be, even if the comparison is distant, a similarity to English in Ireland or German in Austria. The Minsk researcher Oleg Manaev, in his analysis of the republic's electorate, provides a 'sociological photo' of a voter who is 'almost undoubtedly an opponent of Lukashenka': 'a young educated Minsker, actively engaged in entrepreneurship, who speaks Russian, supports Belarus's independence and is West-oriented'.[22] Other examples of Russian being used to raise national self-awareness are bilingual independent newspapers, such as *Narodnaia volia*, *Nasha svaboda*, *Rabochy* and others, where Russian-language commentaries expose the nature of the Lukashenka regime and advocate preservation of national independence.

It is true that defenders of Belarus nationhood insist that free development and wide public usage of the native language is a *sine qua non* for fully fledged national statehood. They are not only right in their insistence, but also stand on solid constitutional ground. The country's 1994 constitution, even as amended by Lukashenka in 1996, names two 'state languages' – Belarusian and Russian – and in that order. Recently only Belarusian has been used on national money and postage stamps. Names in foreign passports are also inscribed in the Belarusian version only. On the official level, the ideal of a Belarusian-speaking nation has not been abandoned. Aliaksandr Sasnouski, Minister of Culture until November 2000, explaining the policy of his ministry, said: 'The Belarusian people bind up their future with national culture, which serves as a guarantor both of their sovereign existence and integration into a kind of bicultural community and, eventually, into world culture.' According to Sasnouski, the desirable 'linguistic person' of tomorrow 'should speak', among other languages, 'his native, national language; a language of interethnic, international relations (Russian, English) and the languages of Belarus's neighbours'.[23]

Belarus currently contains many vestiges of the past Soviet era: the KGB; the statues of Lenin; the official holiday of the October Revolution; a disproportional number of Russian names of streets and collective farms; the (wordless) national anthem, and so on. On the other hand, however, there is a slow institutionalisation of nationhood. Thus, the former Supreme Soviet was renamed the National Assembly; the Academy of Sciences, the National Academy of Sciences; the Central Historical Archive; the National Historical Archive. Belarus today is a participant in the Olympic Games. The phrase 'our country' (*nasha kraina*, in Belarusian; *nasha strana*, in Russian), which used to mean 'the Soviet Union' before 1991, now means 'Belarus'. All this is accompanied by ongoing, albeit slow and unspectacular, cultural processes, with scores of small youth groups involved, that are contributing to the sense of national identity and patriotic impulses. The following is one of a number of new occurrences – an interesting relationship between musical creations by young people and national identity: 'The programme "I was born here", writes a musicologist, 'can do what parliamentary commissions and ideological organs were incapable of doing . . . The two dozen songs, many of which have been known for a long while, in their new reading and new context contain not simply a strong artistic potential, but also that idea which is able to become a unifying and directing power [a reference to the past leading role of the Communist Party].'[24]

Religious revival in Belarus has also affected the rise of national consciousness. A recent study by the Institute of Sociology of the National Academy of Sciences has shown that 47 per cent of the population are believers, while 20 per cent are non-believers and 33 per cent could not provide an answer as to their religious conviction. Among the believers,

78 per cent are Orthodox Christians, 9 per cent Catholics and the rest belong to other denominations.[25]

Orthodox Christian believers are organised in the Belarusian Orthodox Church (BOC), since 1989 an exarchate of the Russian Orthodox Church. The BOC is headed by an ethnic Russian, Metropolitan Filaret (Vakhrameeu), and has been a potent factor in the cultivation of the 'Russian spirit' among the population. During the 1989–94 period, in tune with the general Belarusianisation of cultural life, the Belarusian language and local traditions gained acceptance in some areas of religious activity of the BOC. The Feast of All-Belarusian Saints was established, translation of the Gospel into Belarusian began, publication of Belarusian-language calendars and a periodical was launched, and Belarusian was allowed in certain religious services. Nevertheless, the idea of the autocephaly of the BOC, recently aired by some clergy and laymen, has a long way to go. As one of its protagonists puts it, 'the path toward a Belarusian national [Orthodox Christian] church goes through an INDEPENDENT NATIONAL BELARUSIAN STATE! [emphasis in the original] . . . Only then could one speak also about autocephaly.'[26]

As for the Roman Catholic Church in Belarus, it is characterised, as a result of history, by a close pro-Polish orientation in its linguistic and cultural expression. The equation of Orthodoxy with Russianness and Catholicism with Polishness is still deeply ingrained in the popular mind. Nevertheless, in both of these confessions there are priests and lay people who appreciate the significance of the Belarusian language in religious life. Belarusian-language books and a periodical have also been published for Catholic believers. Fully devoted to the cause of religious and national rebirth is the small Belarusian Greek-Catholic (Uniat) Church, which uses Belarusian exclusively in its services and publications, but faces serious hurdles from both the leadership of the BOC and lay authorities, compliant to the official pro-Moscow policies.

Historical scholarship and education

The end of ideological control by the Communist Party and the 1990 declaration of sovereignty loosened constraints on historical scholarship, opened up new layers of the past and gave freedom for interpretation. The new coat of arms and the national flag, adopted in 1991, harked back to the history of the medieval Duchy of Polatsk and the Grand Duchy of Lithuania, where Belarusian culture flourished, as well as the 1918 Belarusian National (*Narodnaia*) Republic that preceded the establishment of the Belarusian Soviet Socialist Republic. The past, it seemed, would become a prologue for a new future.

At the end of 1992, Prime Minister Viacheslau Kebich laid out the views of his government on the role of national culture in the reconstruction of the nation's damaged spirit. In a speech that was advertised as a major address to the intelligentsia, Kebich said: 'If we are a nation, we should by all means have our own national holy places. It is not easy for us to shape our national self-awareness with the national heritage we have received, not easy to reconvince our contemporaries and successors that we have a history of our statehood, that we are not some rootless Ivans . . . That is why any efforts, state and public initiatives, to revive our national history are so necessary and valuable.'[27]

Vasil Kushner, editor-in-chief of the newly launched quarterly, *Belaruski histarychny chasopis* (*Belarusian historical journal*), spelled out the approach to be taken: 'We openly and sincerely state that our policy and the main goal of the journal will be to contribute to the process of national rebirth and deepening the national consciousness of the Belarusian people . . . This is the national policy, enshrined in a series of legislative acts of the Republic of Belarus.'[28]

In the article, 'On the national conception of historical education in the Republic of Belarus', a different ethnogenesis of the Belarusian people was observed. The Belarusians were viewed no longer as a branch of the nationality of 'ancient Rus', but as a Slavicised mixture of Slavic and Baltic tribes (a thesis forcefully advanced, among others, by the Russian Soviet historian Valentin Sedov). Teachers of history were advised to replace such appellations of pre-1917 Belarus as 'Western Rus', 'West-Russian lands', 'West-Russian population', 'West-Russian culture' by the terms 'Belarus', 'Belarusian people', and 'Belarusian culture'.[29] The 1994 constitution of the republic stated in its preamble that the Belarusian people have a 'centuries-old history of development of Belarusian statehood'. Emotional historiography along these new historic lines, expressed by such writers as Uladzimir Arlou, Kastus' Tarasau, Volha Ipatava, Leanid Daineka and others, gained a great deal of support from publishers. To substantiate a new view of the past and assist in educational efforts, the publication of major information sources was launched: a six-volume encyclopaedia of the history of Belarus, an 18-volume universal Belarusian encyclopaedia, single-volume encyclopaedias of the Belarusian language, Belarusian thinkers, an illustrated chronology of the history of Belarus, and several others.

All these trends have been slowed down as a result of the 1995 referendum. Conservative historians and government watchdogs raised their voices against an 'extreme nationalistic' interpretation of the past. Soon, an 'adjustment' followed with replacements in institutes, universities, and editorial boards, including the encyclopaedia of the history of Belarus and the universal Belarusian encyclopaedia. In February 1999, Radio Liberty reported that Deputy Prime Minister Uladzimir Zamiatalin had ordered the elimination of 'seditious material' from a textbook on Belarus's history, in which the past was depicted from the 'positions of the nationally radical Belarusian opposition'. In particular, Zamiatalin denounced the textbook for mentioning repression of Belarusian national culture by

Stalin's totalitarian regime in the 1930s. He labelled the book as a 'falsification', pointing to the 'lack of a single official view of the country's history in line with the demands of the President of the Republic of Belarus'.[30]

Not everyone fell in line with Zamiatalin's criticism. For example, we have quite a different view on Stalin's repression: the newly published textbook for college students of law and history, approved by the Ministry of Education, speaks, albeit briefly, of 'mass repression', 'Bolshevik terror' and the 'total Russification' of Belarus under Stalin.[31] It would appear that the confrontation between officialdom and nationally minded elements of Belarusian society is being played out not only in the streets of Minsk, but also in the ministries and other official places.[32]

Civil society and civil liberties

In Belarus, the Soviet regime left an atomised society, associated with low political culture and a low level of knowledge about national life. For example, when recently asked to pick the country's Prime Minister out of three names, 58 per cent of respondents around the country, and 81 per cent in the eastern region of Mahileu, said they did not know the name.[33] The past decade of independence has seen efforts to raise society's awareness of its power potential. Scores of non-governmental organisations (NGOs) are trying to increase citizens' civic assertiveness, political activism and national consciousness. There are good reasons for this. One is that, in innumerable cases, authorities at higher and lower levels are guided in their decisions by secret instructions and sublegal acts, often in contravention of constitutional principles. NGOs are counteracting such misuse of power, especially rampant in the field of culture and human and minorities' rights. The mobilisation of society is steadily growing.

In early December 2000, a congress of Belarus's democratic NGOs took place in Minsk. Two hundred and eighteen delegates decided to participate in its activities, which included social, cultural and political goals. The nationwide Assembly of NGOs, aiming at the creation of 'a strong and influential third sector', numbers 430 members.[34] Activation of NGOs is hampered by a lack of financial support from the private sector. On coming to power with the idea of 'market socialism', President Lukashenka reversed the process of privatisation and imposed stringent regulations on any economic activity. As a result, private capital was drastically reduced and placed under strict state control.

The participation of young people in the activities of civil society reflects general attitudes among the population. According to some estimates, only about 5 per cent of young people are engaged in public affairs. But most of those so engaged appreciate the values of democracy and national culture. And the capital of Minsk is not the only place where civil liberties are asserted. There are numerous regional clubs, bulletins, small circulation journals (many of them supported financially by the West) advancing the cause of national identity and the country's political independence. Street demonstrations and arrests that have taken place during the last two to three years show the increasing assertiveness of the young who have grown up under conditions of independence. The latest development in this area is the formation in the autumn of 2000 of a new coalition of youth groups under the name 'Changes!'. To counteract young people's grassroots civic initiatives, the government established a 'patriotic youth' union in 1997, pouring into it lavish state subsidies. This organisation, however, is heavily bureaucratised and politically inert.

Civic disobedience in defence of national culture has been stimulated by the voluntary exile from their native country of a number of prominent figures, who are now active abroad. They include writers Vasil Bykau, often characterised as 'the conscience of the nation', Uladzimir Niakliaeu, president of Belarus's Writers' Union, politicians Zianon Pazniak, Siamion Sharetski and Siarhei Navumchyk, civic leader Hanna Surmach and others. They all are active abroad, each in his/her own field.

Another significant influence on the activities of civil society in Belarus comes from western states. Sharp criticism of Lukashenka's domestic and foreign policies by western governments, as well as in the western press, has strong repercussions among the democratic opposition of Belarus.

Statehood as a source of national identity

Of all the elements that contribute to the formation of national identity, statehood is gaining predominant significance. 'Historical experience shows', wrote one scholar in the pre-Lukashenka period, 'that neither union with Poland, nor being a part of Russia and then of the USSR allowed the Belarusian people fully to realise their creative potential. It is obvious that only within the framework of its own statehood will such a possibility will become a reality.'[35] Lukashenka himself vows to preserve his republic's sovereignty in a union with Russia, doubtful as that seems. In these circumstances, for many the search for national identity has become a quest for ways and means to reduce the antinomy between formal national statehood and its heavily Russified content. At a recent Belarusian–Polish round table on the idea of Belarusianness and Polishness, Belarusian discussants defined the essence of their national idea as a 'conception of a distinct national state of the Belarusian people' and stressed that the 'main strategic goal of national identity is the survival of the nation'.[36]

There is a view that the government, which has vested interests in independence, has no choice but to resort to the national awareness of the population as a sort of barrier against absorption of national sovereignty by Russia, which would unavoidably reduce the status and role of Belarusian bureaucrats, including that of Lukashenka. 'Gradually', writes one analyst about recent trends, 'the government's rhetoric began to emphasise the need to maintain Belarusian statehood and sovereignty, no matter how advanced the integration process became.'[37] Some outside observers agree: 'Each day that passes strengthens the sense of national consciousness among Belarusians – most rapidly among the young, the intellectuals, and those who hold the reins of power and see the advantages that independence has brought.'[38]

Conclusion

If saving the Belarusian nation depends on national self-awareness, as Vasil Bykau has postulated, there are indications that these efforts may succeed. The main hope for these lies with the younger generation of Belarusians and the preservation of Belarusian political statehood. The maintenance of the latter is not only in the interest of the Belarusians themselves, but also of their immediate neighbours and the democratic West as a whole. The world needs to see democratic states along the western borders of Russia stabilised and strengthened. This would be the best way to reduce the threat of Russian imperialistic schemes, which, as history has proven, never vanish and have the ability to reincarnate. Contemporary Belarus is the best proof of this.

Since national identity has been gaining ground in Belarus, the only way for Russia to maintain its dominion over the 'western-gate' country is through suppression of its identity in the hands of an autocratic regime. Strongman Aliaksandr Lukashenka has been demonstrating this stratagem. Therefore, at this historical juncture, it appears that the cause of democracy in Belarus and international security in Europe most need continuous moral, political and financial support for the Belarusian democratic opposition and NGOs, which are the best hopes for a peaceful Eastern European future.

Notes

1 *Znamia iunosti*, 16 December 1992.
2 S. Garnett and R. Legvold (eds), *Belarus at the Crossroads* (Washington, DC: Carnegie Endowment for International Peace, 1999), pp. 6, 7.
3 S. Shushkevich, 'Belarus: Self-identification and Statehood', *Belarusian Review*, No. 2 (Summer 2000): 10.
4 *Letters to Gorbachev: New Documents from Soviet Belorussia*, 2nd ed. (London: The Association of Belorussians in Great Britain, 1987), pp. 20–1.
5 *Press-hrupa 'Navina pavedamliae'* (Minsk: Samizdat press release, n.d.), p. 2.
6 *Sovetskaia Belorussiia*, 20 January 1990.
7 See the result of the deliberations in the 400-page volume *Farmiravanne i razvitstsio natsyianal'nai samasviadomastsi belarusau* (Minsk, 1992).
8 *Zviazda*, 18 March 1993.
9 V. Konan, 'Arkhetypy belaruskaha mentalitetu: sproba rekanstruktsyi pavodle natsyianalnai mifalohii', in *Farmiravanne*, p. 21.
10 O. Gapanovich, 'Nam iavno ne khvataet svezhego vozdukha kul'tury', *Belaruskaia dumka*, No. 10 (1993), p. 13.

11 A. Vardamatski, 'Belarus i svet', *Belaruskaia perspektyva*, No. 9 (2000), p. 7.
12 *Belaruskaia dumka*, No. 1 (1996), p. 19.
13 *Belaruskaia dumka,* No. 10 (1998), p. 7.
14 V. Nosevich, 'Belorusy: stanovlenie etnosa i "natsionalnaia ideia"', in D. Furman *et al.* (eds), *Belorussiia i Rossiia: obshchestva i* gosudarstva (Moscow: 'Prava cheloveka', 1998), p. 28.
15. Y. Karski, *Etnograficheskaia karta belorusskogo plemeni* (Petrograd, 1917), p. 1.
16 A. Astapenka, 'Rolia i mestsa pravaslaunai tsarkvy u nezalezhnai Belarusi', in *Ad 'tuteishastsi' da natsyianalnai dziarzhaunastsi* (Warsaw, 1999), p. 67.
17 J. Zaprudnik, *Belarus: At a Crossroads in History* (Boulder, CO: Westview Press, 1993), pp. 137–41.
18 Gapanovich, 'Nam iavno ne khvataet', p. 14.
19 L. Lych, 'Belaruskaia mova iak ab'ekt dziarzhaunai dyskryminatsyi', in *Aniamenne* (Vilnius: 'Gaudas', 2000), p. 26.
20 V. Hrytskevich, V. (2000) 'Linhvatsyd, albo Znishchenne movy', in *Aniamenne*, p. 91.
21 D.R. Marples, *Belarus: a denationalized nation* (Canada: Harwood Academic Publishers, 1999), p. 52.
22 O. Manaev, 'Elektorat Aleksandra Lukashenko', in Furman *et al.*, *Belorussiia i Rossiia*, p. 289.
23 A. Sasnovski, 'Nivelirouka kultur? Ne – ikh samabytnasts', *Belaruskaia Dumka,* No. 2 (1997), pp. 9–10.
24 D. Podberezski, 'Eta pesnia khorosha – nachinai snachala', *Belorusskaia delovaia gazeta*, 7 December 2000.
25 *Belarustoday Online,* Internet Journal, 13 November 2000.
26 *Radio Free Europe/Radio Liberty (RFE/RL) Newsline*, Vol. 2, No. 186, Part 2, 25 September 1998.
27 *Zviazda*, 23 December 1993.
28 *Belaruski histarychny chasopis*, No. 1 (1993), p. 5.
29 M. Bich, 'Ab natsyianalnai kantseptsyi historyi i histarychnai adukatsyi u Respublitsy Belarus', *Belaruski histarychny chasopis*. No. 1 (1993), p. 19.
30 *RFE/RL Newsline,* Vol. 3, No. 39, Part 2, 25 February 1999.
31 V. Krutalevich and I. Yukho, *Historyia dziarzhavy i prava Belarusi (1917–1945)* (Minsk: 'Belaruskaia navuka', 2000), pp. 193, 228, 229.
32 R. Lindner, *Historiker und Herrschaft: Nationsbildung und Geschichtspolitik in Weissrussland in 19. und 20. Jahrhundert* (Munich: R. Oldenbourg, 1999).
33 Vardamatski, 'Belarus i svet', p. 7.
34 Belarusian Association of Resources Centers, BARC_List NEWS (barc@user.unibel.by), No. 121, 4 December 2000. According to *Belorusskaia delovaia gazeta* (No. 883, 7 December 2000) 'about 500' NGOs belong to the assembly.
35 V. Miskevich, 'Chas vybora', *Belaruskaia dumka*, No. 8 (1993), p. 12.
36 E. Dubianetski, 'Idei belaruskastsi i polskastsi', *Kantakty i dyialohi*, No. 10 (2000), p. 62.
37 A. Rozanov, 'Belarus: Foreign Policy Priorities', in Garnett and Legvold, *Belarus at the Crossroads*, p. 33.
38 Garnett and Legvold, *Belarus at the Crossroads*, pp. 177–8.

9 Path-dependence and the economy of Belarus

The consequences of late reforms

Colin W. Lawson

Introduction

There are some economies in former communist countries where the process of economic transition in the 1990s clearly failed: for example, the Russian and Ukrainian economies. We can learn something new about how any market system functions from an autopsy on such economies – most importantly about the roles of enterprise and system governance.

There are other economies in former communist countries where the process of economic transition has not really been tried, so it is wrong to speak of failure. The economies of Belarus and Turkmenistan clearly fall into this category. We can ask why the transformation was not seriously pursued, or why the process was reversed, though the answer usually lies more in politics than economics. We can also ask a much more difficult question, which is, 'What would happen if policy were reversed and a serious attempt made at economic transition?' This chapter tries to answer that question for the economy of Belarus.

The remainder of the chapter has three sections. First, we place economic transition in Belarus in perspective, in part to establish the location of the base from which further change might occur. Comparisons with other Commonwealth of Independent States' (CIS) economies are made, and the reasons for Belarus's move towards an administrative economy in recent years are discussed.

Second, we examine what might happen if a serious move were made towards a market system. To do this two types of evidence are used. Using data drawn from a wide range of transition economies, statistical associations between a range of transition dimensions and economic growth are established. The relations can be used to predict the output consequences of a policy. To this are added any special features that might influence Belarusian performance, specifically any advantages and disadvantages which might come from being a late reformer. It turns out that there are some strong reasons to expect that Belarus's economic course to date will exert a significant influence on future growth. Path dependence is significant, although we cannot quantify it precisely. A summary and discussion conclude the chapter.

The transition state of Belarus

Table 9.1 shows the transition position of CIS states during the mid- to late 1990s. The CIS states are sensible comparators for Belarus because of a shared length of time under planning and a similar degree of disruption caused by the disintegration of the Soviet Union.

The table shows that Belarus was a little below average as a reforming economy in the mid-1990s, and had become very obviously uninterested in reform by the end of the decade. Not only did the reform gap widen compared to other CIS states, but in fact between 1997 and 1999 Belarus marginally strengthened the administrative control and weakened market influences over the economy. The transition throughout the CIS obviously stalled towards the end of the decade, and after the 1998 crisis went into a marked retreat in Russia. But almost everywhere it stalled at a significantly higher level than in Belarus.

The transition scales used by the European Bank for Reconstruction and Development (EBRD) are subjective and not demonstrably of the 'equal interval' type needed to construct fully meaningful arithmetic averages. So any manipulation of the raw data needs careful and sceptical interpretation. In addition the base level is a score of 1, and a country gets that score merely by virtue of doing business with the EBRD and being assessed. So it would be reasonable to argue that the average CIS 1999 score was 1.3, on a scale of 0–3.3. So if the EBRD's transition indicators were fully equal interval then the transition would be 39 per cent complete for the CIS as a whole, but only 15 per cent complete for Belarus.

Table 9.2 shows the current position of Belarus in the transition process. The share of output generated in the private sector is the smallest of all the transition states. Its insignificant growth reflects the stalled privatisation

Table 9.1 Average core[1] transition indicators: CIS states

	1994	*1997*	*1999*
Armenia	1.8	2.5	2.7
Azerbaijan	1.4	2.0	2.2
Belarus	1.6	1.6	1.5
Georgia	1.3	2.7	2.7
Kazakhstan	1.6	2.7	2.7
Kyrgyzstan	2.8	2.8	2.8
Moldova	2.2	2.6	2.7
Russia	2.6	3.0	2.5
Tajikistan	1.6	1.6	2.0
Turkmenistan	1.2	1.5	1.4
Ukraine	1.3	2.5	2.5
Uzbekistan	1.9	2.2	2.1
Average	1.8	2.3	2.3

Source: European Bank for Reconstruction and Development (EBRD) Annual Reports: 1994, 1997 and 1999.

programme and the thicket of obstacles that face the creation of new firms. The situation in the enterprise sector is that there is little private ownership of large enterprises, though a substantial number of smaller enterprises have been privatised, especially former communal property. The pressure on firms to restructure has been minimal, as soft budget constraints have continued to be the norm in the state sector, and state orders have sustained otherwise bankrupt firms. As unsold stock was reported to stand at the equivalent of 40 per cent of GDP in the spring of 1999, one really has to doubt the meaning of the growth rates reported for 1996 (3 per cent), 1997 (11 per cent), 1998 (8 per cent), and the estimated 3 per cent for 1999. Improvements in corporate governance have been minimal. The process of re-registration of companies, to be completed in 2001, will have strong negative effects on the growth of the private sector.[2] There are two reasons for this. First, as owners and shareholders will be personally liable for company debts, the scale and risk reduction benefits of limited liability will be surrendered. Second, increasing capital requirements in line with the minimum wage will increase operating costs. Although both provisions of the September 1998 presidential decree on re-registration procedures are aimed at the problem of insolvent trading, an effective bankruptcy law would have the same effect at significantly lower cost.

The 'Markets and trade' average indicator in Table 9.2 reflects widespread price controls on basic foodstuffs and energy prices, significant restrictions on exchange convertibility and only very limited progress towards an effective competition policy. For financial institutions there has been little progress towards creating a fully functioning market system. Although a two-tier banking system is in place, state banks account for the majority of loans, and banking regulations are not rigorously enforced to limit the adverse effects of closures. Much of the commercial bank system, dominated by the state banks, is primarily engaged in delivering soft loans to enterprises, using earmarked state funds. There is limited trading of securities and government paper, but exposure to the Russian government's 1998 GKO (*gosudarstvennye kratkosrochnye kredity* – state short-term loans) scam drained reserves from the system, and the state-owned stock exchange is of little importance in raising new capital.

Table 9.2 Belarus: selected transition indicators[3]

	Private sector (% of output)	*Enterprises*	*Markets and trade*	*Financial institutions*	*Legal reform*[4]
1994	15	2.0	1.7	1.0	n.a.
1996	15	1.7	2.3	1.5	1.0
1997	20	1.3	2.0	1.5	2.0
1998	20	1.3	1.7	1.5	2.0
1999	20	1.3	1.6	1.5	2.0

Source: EBRD Annual Reports; various issues.

The fact that Belarus's transition performance is poor and (slightly) declining raises the question of whether this reflects a policy to return to a fully integrated planned or administrative economy. Certainly the scale of administrative intervention is very considerable and the government not only has a taste for intervention, but a clear preference for administration over market solutions. For example, at a cabinet meeting in December 1999 President Lukashenka instructed his government to 'raise wages in the budget sphere, eliminate unfounded differences in work remuneration between branches . . . and pay wage arrears . . .'.[5] The Index of Economic Freedom, produced by the Heritage Foundation and the *Wall Street Journal*, ranked the Belarus economy as 145th out of 161 – categorising it as 'repressed'.[6]

But a taste for economic or political repression and a lack of intention to pursue economic transition does not in itself constitute a carefully articulated plan to recreate a planned economy. A closer look at the reasons for the recent fall in the EBRD average ranking for Belarus demonstrates a more pragmatic approach by the government.

Table 9.2 shows a fall in the transition rating for the 'Enterprises' area of transition from 1994 to 1997, and in the 'Markets and trade' rating from 1996 to 1999. Tables 9.3 and 9.4 show the disaggregated assessments underlying these aggregate average rankings. From Table 9.3 it is clear that the fall in the average enterprises rating is due to a fall in the

Table 9.3 'Enterprises': subindices

	Large-scale privatisation	*Small-scale privatisation*	*Governance and enterprise restructuring*[7]	*Mean*
1994	2	2	2	2.0
1996	1	2	2	1.7
1997	1	2	1	1.3
1998	1	2	1	1.3
1999	1	2	1	1.3

Source: EBRD Transition Reports, various issues.

Table 9.4 'Markets and trade': subindices

	Price liberalisation	*Trade and foreign exchange system*	*Competition policy*	*Mean*
1994	2[8]	1	2	1.7
1996	3	2	2	2.3
1997	3	1	2	2.0
1998	2	1	2	1.7
1999	2–	1	2	1.6

Source: EBRD Transition Reports, various issues.

subrating for large-scale privatisation from 1994 to 1996, and in the governance and enterprises restructuring score between 1996 and 1997.

The fall in the large-scale privatisation score between 1994 and 1996 was due to the suspension of the 1993 privatisation programme in 1996, despite the fact that vouchers had been distributed as early as 1994. After 1996 little voucher privatisation occurred, and as late as 1999 only 40 per cent of the 1994 vouchers had been redeemed for shares. By then government plans to buy back the remaining 60 per cent of vouchers from the public and thus formally to end this approach to large-scale privatisation were only held in abeyance by a lack of finance.

The fall in the governance and enterprise restructuring rating from 2 in 1996 to 1 in 1997 looks like a downgrading of the earlier, perhaps optimistic, assessment. This emerges if we compare Belarusian reality with the EBRD criteria for a grade one score – 'soft budget constraints (lax credit and subsidy policies weakening financial discipline at the enterprise level); few other reforms to promote corporate governance'.[9] The consequences were that enterprise debts were 70 per cent of GDP at the end of 1998, unsold stocks were at 40 per cent of industrial output by March 1999, and 27 per cent of enterprises were loss making.[10] This may have improved slightly during 1999, for the economy minister reported 17.5 per cent of firms making losses in the January–September period, including 35.5 per cent of all agricultural enterprises and farms.[11]

However, a very limited amount of privatisation, mostly small scale, did continue after 1996, and although there was some nationalisation and re-nationalisation – for example, the stock exchange and a major department store – there was no further drastic change in policy. Even the re-registration order of 1998, referred to above, might, perhaps somewhat optimistically, be thought of as an ill-advised attempt to deal with tax evasion and insolvent trading.

Table 9.4 shows that the overall decline in the 'Markets and trade' aggregate index in Table 9.2 is due to declines in the underlying 'price liberalisation' index in 1998 and 1999, and to a decline in the 'trade and foreign exchange' subindex between 1996 and 1997. The latter decline was triggered by the reintroduction of convertibility of restrictions, whereby 40 per cent of foreign currency earnings were to be given up to the state at a disadvantageous exchange rate. The former decline in 1998 was due to the government's reintroduction of previously abandoned price controls, in response to a surge in inflation. In 1999 price liberalisation was further restricted by a presidential decree that extended strict price regulations to a wide range of products.

In fact both the external sector regulations and the extension of price have their origins in a rise in inflation caused by a failure to control monetary emissions and to put public finances on a sustainable basis. In 1997 the National Bank of Belarus increased domestic credit by 107 per cent. In part this seems to have been an attempt to direct subsidised credit to certain firms, and to replace the balances of loss makers, especially in agriculture. The credit injection produced a currency crisis and inflation, and the response to both has been piecemeal and interventionist.

The intervention has shown the limited effectiveness of administrative intrusion in a largely state-owned but market-determined system. For example, in 1998 both private and public enterprises were ordered to revert to pre-crisis level prices. Unsurprisingly this was not fully complied with, but shortages occurred and the government's response was to introduce rationing. Nevertheless the National Bank's inflation target of an upper limit of 2 per cent per month was consistently broken and there was demonetisation and currency substitution towards US dollars.

We can conclude that although there is a very strong bias towards intervention, and a desire to retain a dominant state sector, there is no evidence of any strong desire to return to full central planning. The slight fall in the admittedly already low EBRD transition scores in recent years is due to piecemeal interventions in situations created by policy failure. The fact that further interventions are then needed to deal with the (largely) predictable problems caused by earlier interventions suggests the strength of the almost reflex administrative response.

But the system is not inflexible. For example, currency restrictions led to a wide gap between administered and black market exchange rates, and this reduced the foreign exchange available to the state, and its ability to tax certain income sources. On 14 December 1999 the authorities admitted their failure to control this market by administrative means by authorising commercial banks to introduce freely determined exchange rates, and removing the requirement that they deliver 70–95 per cent of their foreign exchange holdings to the state.[12]

The transition outcomes for Belarus have so far been sufficiently disappointing to doubt the long-term viability of the present economic policies, or indeed in a democracy, of any government that pursued them. Real GDP *per capita*, measured against 1989 = 100, was estimated by the EBRD at 80 in 1999. That was up from a 1995 low of 62, but the validity of these figures from the viewpoint of economic welfare has already been questioned here, in view of large and growing stocks of unsold output.

The immediate scope for expansion looks limited, in view of the problems in other CIS economies. In the longer term growth will be limited by the recent low level of investment. The volume of investment stood at 57 in 1998, compared to a 1990 base of 100, and had been under 60 for five years.

The inflation performance is now much better than in the hyperinflationary period of 1992–5, but is still significantly worse than most other CIS states. For example, the 1999 estimate was 182 per cent, against a CIS median of 18 per cent.

Unemployment at the end of 1998 was a low 2.3 per cent, reflecting social, political and economic policies, but obviously hiding a vast amount of underemployment. The lack of output is much more accurately reflected in the 1993–5 poverty headcount of 22 per cent, up from 1 per cent in 1987–8, and based on a poverty line monthly income *per capita* of only US $19. Matching this impression was a fall in life expectancy from 72.3 years in 1985, to 68.5 years in 1997.

Given the generally discouraging attitude of the authorities towards private sector activities it is unsurprising that Belarus has attracted little foreign investment. During the period 1989–98 the CIS received $27.6 billion in foreign direct investment,[13] of which Belarus's share accounted for $444 million. In *per capita* terms Belarus's $44 compares to a CIS average of $69. Obviously in neither case would such investment make more than a trivial difference to living standards.

However, an authoritarian political culture may have had one slightly beneficial economic effect, in that corruption might be a little less widespread than in other CIS states. The 1999 corruption assessments of Transparency International cover 99 countries.[14] Denmark, the least corrupt of those assessed, scores 10.0 out of a maximum 10.8. Cameroon, the most corrupt, scores 1.5. Belarus ranks 58th on 3.4, but is comfortably ahead of its nearest CIS rivals, Moldova and Ukraine, joint 75th with a score of 2.6.

What emerges from this analysis of the Belarus transition experience is that the present policies hold out little prospect of sustained improvements in economic welfare. Lax subsidy policy, conducted from a shrunken tax base, invites continuing resort to the printing presses. A preference for administrative intervention including the perhaps unwitting creation of negative real interest rates, in the presence of substantial inflation, wrecks the efficiency characteristics of the price system and leads to irrational output mixes, input combinations and income distributions, and encourages demonetisation and currency substitution. Going back to a fully administrative economy should have few economic attractions, as there is no likelihood that Belarusian planners would perform much better than Soviet planners in creating a consistently dynamic and efficient system. Therefore at some stage it is likely that a serious move towards a market system will be made. The question is what would happen.

The consequences of a genuine transition

To predict the impact of a serious attempt at transition we can use evidence from the experience of all transition economies in the 1990s.[15] We used EBRD transition indicators for 1994–8 to test the impact of varying levels and rates of change of transition on rates of economic growth. The indicators were not constructed for periods before 1994, and given the current, very limited state of transition in Belarus it is evidence from the early years of other countries' transition that may help predict what will happen in Belarus.

The results of the impact of the levels and rates of change of transition on growth in 24 transition economies are shown in Table 9.5. This displays the ordinary least squares multiple regression results of nine different transition indicators on growth. The GDP growth rate for 1994–8 and for the shorter period 1995–6 are the dependent variables in separate equations to test for the stability of estimated relations. The relatively small changes in R^2 and coefficient values for the equations using different time periods give us some confidence that most of the relations are stable.[16]

With the EBRD indicators there seems to be a very powerful general result, namely that the greater the level of transition by 1994, the higher the rate of growth in 1994–6 and 1994–8.[17] This is true for six dimensions of transition: private sector share; large-scale privatisation; small-scale privatisation; enterprise restructuring; trade and foreign exchange liberalisation; and banking reform. It is also true for the composite indicator. In these dimensions the results are significant at better than the 5 per cent level. For price liberalisation the result is significant at the 10.3 per cent level (1994–6) and the 7.4 per cent level (1994–8). For security markets reform it is significant at the 6.5 per cent level (1994–6) and the 0.6 per cent level (1994–8). Taken together these results provide powerful evidence for the positive impact of transition on growth. The evidence on the effects of the speed of transition on growth is much weaker. It suggests only a weaker link between a faster rate of transition and a higher rate of growth.

A general explanatory framework for these results can be constructed.[18] This draws a distinction between the results, both in terms of level and rate of change, which can be attributed to the specific systems switch – from plan to market – and those which are due to change itself. For example, with the switch in economic systems the key change is to increase the ability of economic actors to make decisions in their own interests. In some cases this has led to increased internal and external competition in product markets, and in others to the open use of monopoly power, and to the seizure or consolidation of power by rent-seeking interest groups. These impacts are due to systemic change, indeed to the specific change being undertaken.

But change in any economic system may involve new products, processes, economic structure, governance or policy. In many cases the costs of such changes, that is the costs of transition, are positively and increasingly related to the degree and speed of change. Most change involves the reassignment of some resources. This takes time and so leads to output loss.

The possible system-switch specific aspects of the move from an administered to a market system are subtle and very difficult to capture in a formal model. It is not that the switched resources may be of above average productivity for their class of input. That is a common result in typical restructuring in a market system. Here the system change has much more significant impacts on the distribution of resources. For example, allowing

Table 9.5 The relationship between transition and growth

Explanatory variable		*Estimated coefficients and diagnostic statistics*	
		1994–6	*1994–8*
a. Private sector share (PSS)	Level of PSS	0.353 (4.446, 0.000)	0.197 (2.371, 0.027)
	Change rate of PSS	0.134 (1.531, 0.140)	0.038 (0.242, 0.811)
b. Large-scale privatisation (LSP)	Level of LSP	5.194 (2.885, 0.009)	3.829 (2.232, 0.036)
	Change rate of LSP	0.161 (2.555, 0.018)	0.182 (1.539, 0.138)
	R^2	0.303	0.187
c. Small-scale privatisation (SPP)	Level of SPP	5.104 (3.716, 0.001)	3.533 (2.892, 0.008)
	Change rate of SSP	0.027 (0.287, 0.777)	0.023 (0.180, 0.859)
	R^2	0.492	0.491
d. Enterprise restructuring (ER)	Level of ER	7.578 (3.549, 0.002)	5.691 (2.966, 0.007)
	Change rate of ER	0.124 (1.651, 0.113)	0.186 (1.468, 0.156)
	R^2	0.384	0.343
e. Price liberalisation (PL)	Level of PL	10.145 (1.701, 0.103)	6.303 (1.878, 0.074)
	Change rate of PL	0.122 (0.512, 0.614)	0.160 (0.555, 0.584)
	R^2	0.202	0.182
f. Trade and foreign exchange liberalisation (TF&EL)	Level of TF&EL	3.521 (2.692, 0.013)	2.469 (2.599, 0.016)
	Change rate of TF&EL	–0.028 (–0.477, 0.638)	0.010 (0.128, 0.899)
	R^2	0.554	0.401
g. Banking reform and interest rate liberalisation (BR&IRL)	Level of BR&IRL	7.620 (4.053, 0.001)	4.920 (3.648, 0.001)
	Change rate of BR&IRL	0.136 (1.856, 0.077)	0.176 (1.693, 0.105)
	R^2	0.458	0.402
h. Security markets and NBFIs (SM&NBFLs)	Level of SM&NBFLs	3.872 (1.944, 0.065)	4.337 (3.015, 0.006)
	Change rate of SM&NBFLs	0.197 (1.551, 0.135)	0.390 (3.044, 0.006)
	R^2	0.186	0.349
Composite indicators based on above (b) to (h) indicators (CI)	Level of CI	7.522 (3.617, 0.002)	4.865 (3.086, 0.005)
	Change rate of CI	0.122 (0.922, 0.367)	0.135 (0.769, 0.450)
	R^2	0.436	0.375

Note: Dependent variable is average annual growth rate of GDP in the period.
Level of variables is their value in the first year in the period.
The first and second values in brackets are t-values and significance levels respectively.
The GDP data comes from *World Development Indicators 2000 CD-Rom* (Washington, World Bank, 2000). The transition indicators come from the European Bank for Reconstruction and Development Transition Report, various issues (London, EBRD).

private business to exist will encourage, amongst other things the more entrepreneurial to leave other activities and to switch to the new private sector. The growth of this sector, which can offer higher wages, or the expectation of higher gains, will suck the more productive workers out of the rest of the system. In the longer run this may maximise output, but in the immediate aftermath of the system change a drop in output is possible as, initially, private output rises less than the fall in state output. The size of the effect increases with the speed and hence the size of the change towards a market system. In effect the change in system in this case is magnifying the effect of a given switch in resources.

Formal models of the transition process have, understandably, concentrated more on modelling change and resource redeployments, than on the characteristics of the specific system change.[19] The emphasis we have placed on change *per se* here, so far, is on its disruptive effects under any system. These negative effects on output are transitory, and disappear as new investments are brought up to rated capacity, as workers are retrained, or successfully learn by doing. But with some types of rapid systemic change, a too rapid speed of introduction may damage growth in the short and long run.

The results of Table 9.5 are clear. There is strong evidence that on a wide of indicators, the closer the approximation to an advanced market system the higher the rate of growth. It is important to note that Table 9.5 shows results from cross-sectional data. No country need conform to the aggregate average relations recorded there. But the fact that the coefficient estimates are reasonably stable across the two different sets of equations, for GDP changes in 1994–6, and in 1994–8, suggests that the findings are robust.

The implication for Belarus is that if it began to pursue a much more active transition policy, there would be significant early gains in output. The speed at which change occurs does not in itself generally seem to make much difference. This is signalled by the generally low significance coefficients picked up by the rate of change variables in the different transition dimensions. But note that this is not true of large-scale privatisation. There, the further and faster the change, the better: at least for the period 1994–6.

But the general result Table 9.5 indicates may be more or less pronounced for a late reformer, and while it is easy to argue for either case, it is difficult to anticipate which might turn out to be the case. The key factor may be the lateness of transition. Those interest groups which in all states opposed or came to oppose transition – from communists or ex-communists to trades unions, bureaucrats and many ex-state managers who are the new owners and rent seekers – have had much longer than similar groups in other countries to perfect blocking techniques. In addition in the foreign sector the long hiatus in Belarus's transition has created a credibility problem for reformers wishing to attract foreign investment.

Also, foreign markets that might have been exploited by a more market-oriented Belarus may have been occupied by others.

On a more positive note it may be possible for Belarus to use some of the expensively gained experience of other transition states to avoid the more obvious pitfalls of reform. It would be possible to design and implement a very effective transition, though hardly one without cost. Experience shows that its implementation would require sustained political will, and that that is very hard to exercise in a democratic system. There is a certain irony in this, for the political system that is the most likely to generate a genuine desire for change is in some ways one of the least likely to deliver it efficiently.

Conclusion

It has been shown that the transition in Belarus ceased to progress after about 1996, and in recent years has reversed to a slight extent. Most of the transition changes have been slight, and the major part of the process remains incomplete. This hiatus is clearly a political choice. In no sense could it be said that the transition process had failed. Indeed the existing market–administrative mix has been singly unsuccessful in delivering economic benefits to Belarus. Moreover it has been argued that because of internal contradictions in the present system of economic management it will be unable to deliver significant sustained growth.

The present system is characterised by soft budget constraints, non-market allocations of credit, administrative interventions and major obstacles to the growth of the private sector. However, a full-blown return of central planning is unlikely. It has been argued that although the government has a clear preference for the state sector over the private sector, and a taste for intervention, there is no clear move towards re-establishing the previous central co-ordination system. There is some pragmatism in economic policy, and it is possible to see the rise in administrative control since 1996 as in itself being little more than perhaps ultimately a mistaken response to perceived crises. This interpretation can be maintained for interventions as diverse as the reimposition of certain price controls, to limit inflation; or the reintroduction of obligatory work placements on students' graduation, to counteract a shortage of professionals in rural areas.[20]

Notes

1 For 1997 and 1999 the data sources give three indicators for enterprises, the degree of large-scale privatisation; small-scale privatisation; governance and enterprise restructuring. There are three indicators for markets and trade: price liberalisation; trade and foreign exchange system; and competition policy. There are two indicators for financial institutions; banking reform and interest rate liberalisation; and securities and non-bank financial institutions. The averages for those eight indicators are shown in Table 9.1. For 1994 the data source

gives three indicators for enterprises, but only the first two of the 1997 and 1999 indicators for markets and trade and only the first of those years' financial institutions indicators. To provide, admittedly imperfect, comparability it was assumed that the missing indicators had the same value or average value as the indicators provided for the core transition areas. For 1997 and 1999 where + or – has been attached to indicators they have been treated as +0.3 and –0.3 in calculating averages. The EBRD indicators range from 1 (no change or little change from an administrative economy) to 4+ (standard of a well-functioning advanced market system).

2 See EBRD, *Transition Report 1999: Ten Years of Transition* (London: EBRD, 1999). This source and other EBRD transition reports are used extensively in this section.

3 The indicators in columns 3–6 are averages of subgroup indicators. See note 1 to Table 9.1 for details.

4 Legal indicators were not constructed for 1994.

5 *Radio Free Europe/Radio Liberty (RFE/RL) Newsline*, Vol. 3, No. 248, Part 2, 23 December 1999.

6 Reported in *RFE/RL Newsline,* Vol. 3, No. 233, Part 2, 2 December 1999.

7 'Governance' was added to the category title in 1997, but noted in criteria for assessment before this date, so criteria are largely consistent across time for all categories and indices.

8 For 1994 price liberalisation and competition policy are included in the same category, and not separately assessed. Therefore they have been given the same value for 1994 in this table.

9 EBRD, *Transition Report 1998: Financial sector in Transition* (London: EBRD, 1998), p. 27.

10 EBRD, *Transition Report 1999*.

11 *RFE/RL Newsline*, Vol. 3, No. 232, Part 2, 1 December 1999.

12 Unless otherwise indicated, the data sources for the remainder of this section are EBRD, *Transition Report 1999* and EBRD, *Transition Report 2000: Employment, Skills and Transition* (London: EBRD, 2000).

13 Calculated from World Bank data cited in J. Coolidge, 'The art of attracting foreign direct investment in transition economies', *Transition*, Vol. 10, No. 5 (October 1999): 5–7.

14 See *Transition*, Vol. 10, No. 5 (October 1999): 1–3.

15 I am indebted to Anil Markandya for suggesting this type of empirical test, and to Haifeng Wang for research assistance. For an extended discussion of theoretical reasons for the results, see C. Lawson, 'Explaining the effects of the level and rate of transition on economic growth', mimeo (University of Bath, Department of Economics, 1999).

16 The diagnostics for the equations underlying Table 9.5 were all acceptable.

17 For similar results on the level of transition indicators and growth in 1994 see P. Brenton, D. Gros and G. Vandille, 'Output decline and recovery in the transition economies: causes and social consequences', *Economics of Transition*, Vol. 5, No. 1: 113–30 (1997). It is unclear whether some of their results are inconsistent with ours, because of differing methodologies.

18 See Lawson, 'Explaining the effects . . .' for others.

19 P. Aghion and O. Blanchard, 'On the speed of transition in central Europe', in National Bureau of Economic Research, *Macroeconomics Annual* (1994), pp. 283–320.

20 *The Times Higher Education Supplement*, 7 January 2000, p. 11.

10 Economic policy in Belarus from official and oppositional perspectives

Nadezhda Lisovskaia and Julia Korosteleva

Introduction

Taking the period from 1991 until 2000, the purpose of this chapter is to contrast official and oppositional approaches to economic policy in the Republic of Belarus. The types of policy we will be dealing with include fiscal, credit-monetary, investment and structural policy. The official position is represented by the policy of the Belarusian government. The alternative position is represented by five parties in opposition: the Party of Communists of Belarus, the Belarusian Social-Democratic Party 'Hramada', the Belarusian Popular Front, the United Civic Party and the Belarusian Republican Party.

The chapter is divided into four sections, corresponding to four types of economic policies, which will be analysed from official and oppositional perspectives. The conclusion will contain the main findings and observations revealed in the analysis.

Fiscal policy

Development of the official policy

The possibility of the conduct of fiscal policy is principally secured by the reform of ownership rights and method of resource allocation in the economy, which constitute formal conditions for fiscal policy, as well as by the state of public finances, which provides the actual possibility of the conduct of the fiscal policy, especially an expansionist one. Ownership rights, which have been hardly reformed during transition, will be discussed below. As far as the state of the public finances is concerned, most of the post-socialist countries had deficit budgets by the beginning of transition. The main budgetary pressures of transformation origin include increased difficulties in tax collection, the profound crisis of the remaining state enterprises, the spread of barter operations and servicing the foreign debt. Regardless of these factors, Belarus generally had one of the smallest deficits amongst transition states.[1] However, this cheerful observation points to the hypothesis that, starting from 1995, the mechanism of fiscal regulation has been similar to the one used under central planning.

To trace this, let us look at the revenue and expenditure sides of the budget. Here two peculiarities attract our attention. First, taking the low *per capita* income of Belarus, which was only US $1,396 in 1998, it is curious that it was possible to reach a relatively high level of revenue: 36.6 per cent of GDP in 1999. This phenomenon can be attributed to the strengthening of the mechanism of tax collection, the decreasing role of income and profit taxes and the influence of inflation. The second peculiarity is the budget's chronological unevenness. The years 1993–4 stand out with high levels of both expenditures and revenues, as compared with the years before and after. This correlates with the phase of relatively active economic reforms that took place in those years, when Stanislau Shushkevich was in power and when many state enterprises were privatised and massive price liberalisation took place. These two years, in our view, were the most trustworthy over the years of transformation in terms of the accuracy of the official fiscal statistics. The point is that in 1991–2 Belarus had still not got rid of the mechanism of fiscal regulation practised under central planning; since 1994, with the change of government, Belarus has been reintroducing this mechanism. In both cases many fiscal elements could not be traced in the official budget statistics: these elements referred to implicit taxes and subsidies.

The development of fiscal policy over the years of Belarusian transformation has been characterised by, first, changeability, second, exorbitant taxation (almost looting), and third – paradoxically enough – the seemingly liberal character of fiscal policy. The first observation can be easily explained by taking into account the necessity for the transitional economic system to find its new equilibrium. Constant changes in economic legislation are common in transitional countries, and Belarus is no exception.

The second feature can be attributed to the fact that the abolition of the plan has, on the one hand, created a monetary vacuum, and, on the other hand, suddenly required the budget to perform a more significant role, similar to that in market-type economies. In order to fill the vacuum, or at least to secure budgetary allocations for social and other important items of expenditure, governments of post-central planning countries have been faced with the necessity to tax heavily. This situation is vividly illustrated in Belarus, where there are presently about 30 taxes, with the main ones being profit, payroll, VAT, excise tax and customs duties. Their totality, significantly stifling commercial activity in Belarus, cannot therefore be interpreted as an illustration of state protection of domestic industry.

The last feature of central planning – the seemingly liberal character of the fiscal system – can be explained if we recall the specificity of the transitional structures – the co-existence of central planning and market elements. In such a situation, given an adequate political commitment, the central planning method of resource allocation takes over market institutions. The latter are alien to a central planning system and therefore still undeveloped. It is the persistent macroeconomic crisis which spurs the Belarusian government into implementing command-administrative measures at the expense of market ones. The market instruments, which include protectionist policy (because protectionism is an element of the market, not of a central planning system) therefore remain underdeveloped and manifest themselves as liberal ones. These liberal fiscal institutions can be seen in the low level of tariffs, the loosely differentiated types of tax and non-tariff protection, and the only limited preferences given to domestic producers.[2] The persisting command-administrative instruments, on the other hand, can be traced in fiscal policy itself and, especially, pricing policy, to be discussed later. As for the former, implicit forms of taxation and subsidisation[3] have been observed in Belarus.

Thus, we see that the change of political power has caused an inconsistent development of fiscal policy in Belarus in 1991–2000. In the early 1990s, when the administrative leverages were weakened, the fiscal problems in the Belarusian economy became acute. Starting from 1994, with the advent of Lukashenka into power, one could get an impression of the imminent stabilisation of Belarus's public finances. Closer investigation reveals that this is no more than window-dressing, since administrative-command methods of expropriation and allocation of resources have been lagging behind. However, the specificity of fiscal policy cannot be attributed only to the change of political regime. As we have seen, governments of all colours and political convictions had to face some unprecedented and objective dilemmas caused by the transition from central planning.

An alternative approach

Since the programmes of the Party of Communists of Belarus and the Belarusian Communist Party[4] are, in substance, a call to bring back central planning, the place of fiscal policy in the view of communists has an interesting implication for our discussion. The notion of fiscal policy did not exist in the vocabulary of central planners, nor did the budget mechanism fulfil its functions. This can be explained by two factors. First, since fiscal policy presupposes the redistribution of resources between the private and public sector, it could not be realised in a country where less than 1 per cent of the GDP was derived from the private sector. Second, planning is a principally different method of resource allocation, as compared to budgeting – the basis of fiscal policy. Budgeting played a minor, secondary role in central planning. It is not surprising, therefore, that the programmes of the communist parties are silent about fiscal policy. It is also logical to assume that communists would support various quasi-fiscal, quasi-central-planning initiatives of the present Belarusian government. It is known, for instance, that in budget debates in the parliament, communists have been supporting the introduction of non-budget funds.[5]

Social democrats and the Belarusian Popular Front adopt a very similar position towards fiscal issues. Both favour significant cuts in revenue and expenditure, and both give substantial priority to social protection. In its programme, the Belarusian Popular Front is more concrete, however, in proposing measures for a thoughtful and tough customs policy, which official policy presently lacks, as well as for complex of protectionist measures to favour domestic producers.

The leaders of the United Civic Party favour stricter fiscal policy, reserving less for social security benefits and giving a concrete quantitative estimation of the maximum amount of taxes to be paid by producers – 35 per cent.[6] On the other hand, the United Civic Party advocates a substantial active role for the state, in particular support for the eight to ten large enterprises that potentially constitute the economic base of Belarus. It also advocates measures to stimulate private business and innovation, and direct subsidies and indirect measures, like preferential credits, tax exemptions, state guarantees, state purchases, and a protectionist customs policy. Quasi-fiscal elements of the present Belarusian government, like non-budget funds, social infrastructure of enterprises and forced subsidisation through the banking sector are repudiated by the United Civic Party. Finally, the Belarusian Republican Party, regardless of its active liberal position and desire for a dramatic reduction in the tax burden and simplification in the tax system, still favours measures to stimulate exports, innovation and investment activities.

Therefore, we can conclude that, except for the communist parties whose ideology has no room for fiscal policy, the rest of our sample is highly critical of the massive role of the state in reallocating resources. All the parties, though to different degrees, call for both a reduction in taxes, a simplification of the tax system, and a reduction and reallocation of subsidies. It is also noticeable that most of the parties stand for selective state support of priority industries, services and enterprises, and consider the present official policy to be *ad hoc* and ineffective.

Monetary-credit and currency policy

Official policy

In Belarus, the first years of transition were not marked by an independent monetary policy, due to the Kebich government's strong adherence to monetary unification with Russia. The Belarusian rouble circulated alongside the Soviet rouble from 1992 until 1994, after which it became the only legitimate means of payment. During the early years of transition, curbing inflation became the priority for transition states. Since excessive money supply growth was regarded as the primary cause of inflation, positive real interest rates and money emission tightening became major anchors of stabilisation policy. But Belarus differed in its credit-monetary policy, which was rather chaotic and intended to cushion the transformation shocks. On the one hand, the policy of negative real interest rates, which were maintained to support non-profitable state enterprises, prevailed over the years of transition. On the other hand, an unprecedented credit expansion policy[7] typified Belarus's transitional economy.

In 1994 Stanislau Bahdankevich, a neo-liberal economist, became chief of the National Bank of Belarus (NBB). The following year and a half was different from the rest of the transition period because of a tight monetary policy. Market credit auctions, which amounted to 80 per cent of total credits to banks, dominated the overcentralised resource allocation mechanism, and monetary emission was carried out through buying currency by the NBB. By the end of 1994 a fixed exchange rate appeared to be the instrument to control inflation. Together with a relatively restrictive credit expansion policy it resulted in curbing inflation,[8] achieving positive real interest rates and balancing the current account.[9] However, the deterioration of the real sector of the economy led the Belarusian authorities to refuse to tighten monetary policy, which resulted in soaring inflation and deterioration in foreign trade. The inability of the government to sustain its exchange rate commitments, because of an insignificant level of foreign exchange reserves, led to devaluation.

In 1996 the 'planned devaluation' system, with strict administrative control of the currency market and a state monopoly on credit allocation, was introduced. Due to the creation of a multiple exchange rate system, and widespread centralised credit resource allocation, the next couple of years bore a strong resemblance to the years of the command-administrative economy. Many prices were fixed administratively and so the price system's resource allocation functions were limited by government policy. The method of resource allocation was similar to the Soviet system, based on 'planned funding'. If in a market system, credit is designed to stimulate economic activity, in the Belarusian case its role was mostly damaging, since a soft credits policy prevailed. The banks forming the system were designed to channel directed credits at the half market interest rate to support the non-profitable sectors of the economy.

As far as multiple exchange rates are concerned, six rates existed. Belarusian exporters were obliged to surrender 30–40 per cent of their earnings at the official rate, which, in effect, amounted to an additional 15 per cent tax on exporters.[10] In addition, the multiple exchange rate system stimulated the development of the black market. With increasing inflation, economic agents switched to alternative financial mechanisms and barter. A problem with demonetisation of the economy soon became obvious. The ratio of M2 (monetary aggregate) to GDP was around 15 per cent by the end of 1998, while private holdings of US dollars were estimated at around 20 per cent of GDP.[11]

At the end of 1998 the NBB announced its intention of carrying out a tighter monetary policy, which presupposed restrictive credit expansion, positive interest rates and a convergence of exchange rates.[12] However, the main problems remained unresolved. Credit emission and inflation remained higher than planned. During 2000 positive real interest rates were achieved, but their positive values remained insignificant and they did not operate as a mechanism of efficient allocation of funds. A unified exchange rate was achieved in September 2000, but its future stability, as well as support for the 'crawling peg' regime announced in 2000–1, are questionable, because foreign currency reserves barely cover weekly imports.

The banking sector in Belarus remains dominated by state-owned banks. In 2000, there were 27 commercial banks, of which six were considered large. Four of the six are state-owned and control 80 per cent of the total assets. The banking sector is undercapitalised and the sustained policy of soft budget constraints and directed credits undermines its solvency. Severe debts have been increasing every year. Despite the implementation of banking reforms and the appearance of a two-tier banking system, the process of change seems to be cosmetic rather than real, since the state, represented by the NBB, has unlimited influence on commercial banks, depriving them of independent policy-making.

So one can conclude, first, that the credit-monetary and currency policies in Belarus have been uneven and inconsistent over the years of transformation. This led to chaotic measures in the early 1990s, a tough stance in 1994–5, a reverse move to command-administrative measures in 1996–8, and a reintroduction of stricter monetary discipline since 1998. Second, command-administrative measures have been used to resolve macroeconomic problems. Third, due to the specificity of central planning structures, the move to a market-type system, while preserving plenty of characteristics typical of the previous one, has created a situation where market instruments, such as money, exchange rates and credits fail to perform their functions.

Alternative approaches

The communist-oriented parties do not have an identifiable monetary policy programme. Because the final goal of both parties is to construct a centrally planned economic system, money is likely to play a passive role in the execution of economic activity. The programmes of other parties include similar credit-monetary policies to those of the government. All the parties advocate tightening monetary policy, beginning with the abandonment of unjustified credit emission. They all agree with restoring the independence of the National Bank, and its status as the sole body responsible for the stability of the currency. Moreover they all advocate privatising the banking system; increasing liquidity; restructuring the debts of enterprises; removing barter and monetary surrogates from settlement and payment; and assuring rigid financial discipline with efficient bankruptcy.

Their programmes are distinguished in the area of exchange rate regimes. The currency policy of the Belarusian Popular Front is rather passive, since it advocates stability by pegging to the euro, though the significant dollarisation of the Belarusian economy might suggest a peg to the dollar. The Belarusian Social-Democratic Party 'Hramada' stresses a managed floating exchange regime, while the United Civic Party (OGP) – a party of right-wing orientation – advocates a flexible exchange rate policy, aimed at supporting external competitiveness and increasing currency reserves.

Investment policy

Official policy

Economic transformation is particularly demanding of investments, since colossal economic restructuring is required. But in reality the problem is exacerbated by an extremely low level of domestic savings, which are the primary source of investment funds.

According to World Bank estimates, stable economic growth needs a domestic investment level of 20–5 per cent of GDP. At the end of 1998 the level of domestic savings in Belarus amounted to only 7–10 per cent of GDP.[13] During the 1990s the demand for savings instruments denominated in Belarusian roubles was low, because high inflation led to negative real interest rates for savers. The high share of foreign currency deposits in M3 (monetary aggregate, colloquailly known as 'broad money'), which amounted to 56 per cent and 44 per cent by the end of 1998 and 1999 respectively, indicates the declining ability of domestic currency to serve as a 'store of value'. The significant share of foreign deposits in M3 could be explained both by the rise in the value of foreign currency holdings due to the sharp devaluation of the Belarusian rouble, and by the increasing incentive to hold foreign currency as the only profitable means of savings.[14]

The significance of foreign investments lies in their ability to compensate for the insufficiency of investments from domestic sources. The main channels of foreign investments are foreign direct investments (FDIs) and credits.

In terms of foreign investment policy, Belarus stands at one extreme of the transition states' policy spectrum. The total volume of foreign investments in Belarus had reached only $237 million by the end of 1998. That is less than 0.5 per cent of the $50 billion which the government announced in 1996 as FDI needed by Belarus.[15] The plans announced by the government in mid-1999, to accelerate the sale of shares in state-owned companies by attracting foreign capital, raised doubts, since it was unlikely that the government would offer majority stakes – thus discouraging foreign investors. According to existing legislation, sales of stakes of over 50 per cent in industrial companies are forbidden, while sales of shares with a book value over US $40,000 require the approval of the President.[16] In addition to the above, the unwillingness of foreign investors to work in Belarus is influenced by the presence of various restrictions similar to those practised in the centrally planned system; by macroeconomic instability; and by the inconsistency and unpredictability of politico-economic policy.

As far as international credits are concerned, the major generator is the IMF. The IMF's relations with Belarus have been highly unstable over the years of transition. In 1993–5, when the government had a stronger neo-liberal stance, the IMF provided Special Drawing Rights (SDR) 140 million under a Systemic Transformation Facility (STF). A Stand-by Arrangement for SDR 160 million was approved in September 1995 and SDR 70 million was released in the first tranche. The second tranche was not released because a number of performance criteria had not been met, as a result of Belarus's change in economic course. Discussions between the IMF and the government resumed in November 1999. They are centred on the possibility of the Fund granting Belarus a Contingency and Compensatory Fund Facility worth US $100 million. The IMF has called for specific government action on tightening monetary policy, prices and liberalising the exchange rate, privatisation and restructuring before any new lending programme can be agreed.

As far as portfolio investments are concerned, the situation is much more complicated. After the collapse of the USSR, financial markets began to appear and were under constant development during 1992–4. A necessary base was created to build up the system of capital circulation in Belarus, involving both domestic and foreign investors. However, after 1995 further development of the capital market has slowed down, owing to the sluggish restructuring of the economy and to some degree because of a return to the command-administrative method of regulation. This meant that financial instruments[17] were unable to provide investors with an adequate return to compensate for the high risks borne by them because of contradictory legislation, low transparency of operations, high uncertainty, and inefficient control. The situation was also aggravated by a high level of inflation, continued devaluation, low or even negative interest rates, and by generally high country and liquidity risks. Therefore the capital market is unattractive to both internal and external investors due to a low risk-adjusted rate of return. It is undeveloped and its activity is reduced mostly to trade in state short-term liabilities (GKO). Eighteen banks are licensed to operate on the primary GKO market and they are obliged to purchase 1 per cent of each GKO issue.[18] Non-resident banks operating on the secondary market are mostly Russian.

The high exposure of the banks to the GKO market, the general fragility of the banking sector and its close links with Russia adversely affected the Belarusian banking sector when the Russian financial market collapsed in August 1998. Estimated losses amounted to US $70 million. Exchange rate depreciation led to a sharp fall in total share capital from US $240 million a year earlier to US $110 million by April 1999.[19] It is interesting to note that Belarus remained insulated from the chain of 1997–8 financial crises, which started in South East Asia and spread to Brazil, until Russia was affected. Insulation at first could not be explained by relative macroeconomic stability, as in the case of the Central and Eastern European countries (CEECs). It was due in part to the lack of foreign portfolio investments, which make any country more vulnerable to international financial turmoil. As discussed, the capital market is unattractive to foreign investors for many reasons, therefore one may conclude that Belarus, while closely linked to Russia economically, is not part of any global financial integration process.

Alternative approaches

Investment policy is not clearly stated in the official programmes of either party of communist orientation, as in principle it cannot develop under central planning owing to the lack of private property that dissuades foreign investors. Furthermore, domestic savings could not be considered as an important source of investment due to their extremely low level. It is therefore quite difficult to understand how the distribution of state investments between enterprises can operate and be effective in terms of the limited capital allotment, alongside the principles of central planning.[20]

Other parties are highly critical of the present official investment policy. An adequate legislative and institutional environment for stimulation of private investment activities is cited as a priority for investment policy. The Belarusian Popular Front stresses the necessity for legislative reforms, for the unimpeded delivery of land plots into the ownership of investors. Mechanisms for land selling and purchasing should be developed in advance. The United Civic Party advocates the creation of institutions for the accumulation of private savings (pension and insurance funds), which does not sound realistic in a highly inflationary environment. The Republican Party declares that investment policy should be conducted via maximum liberalisation including capital investment, regardless of its origin.

Structural policy

Official policy

Ownership reform together with pricing policy constitutes the core of the structural reform in transitional post-socialist countries. The basis for the ownership reform was set up in Belarus as early as in 1990 when the law 'On Ownership' was adopted. However, the concrete mechanisms of this process had not been elaborated by the early 1990s, which fostered the development of 'spontaneous privatisation'. As a result, the Supreme

Soviet made a decision to halt privatisation until a law on privatisation was adopted. Due to the communists' domination in the Supreme Soviet, the long-awaited law 'On Destatisation and Privatisation of State Property in the Republic of Belarus' was adopted only in January 1993. In June 1993 the Programme of Privatisation was adopted,[21] which did not come into effect immediately, however, because the law 'On Personal Privatisation Cheques', intended to go in the package, was adopted only in late 1993. By the time the basics of legislative drafting in the sphere of ownership reform had been completed, the political situation had changed, and Lukashenka halted privatisation on the grounds of corruption. In subsequent years there was little ownership reform. In 1996 and 1998[22] the state privatisation programme underwent further changes, but they did not bring serious ownership restructuring.

As for the mode of privatisation, it usually takes one of the following forms: corporatisation, sale, restitution and mass (voucher) privatisation. Owing to the limited practical significance of sale and restitution in Belarus, our main focus will be on the voucher privatisation scheme.[23] It was established in 1994 and has suffered from a number of deficiencies. First, the idea of exchanging vouchers for enterprise shares meant that enterprises did not receive any financial inflow on change of ownership. Second, there was a certain incompatibility between the speed of corporatisation and the issue of vouchers. Though the deadline for the application of vouchers was extended due to low public interest (from 1996 to 1997), the rate of corporatisation was even slower, which did not give the potential investors any adequate choice of enterprises. Moreover, those enterprises offered to voucher holders were often heavy debtors, which weakened public interest in investments. Created as alternative institutions for the public investment of vouchers, investment funds were suspended by the President in the mid-1990s. Finally, the high inflation has been depreciating the value of vouchers, which was especially important since enterprises' assets have been inflation-indexed. As a result of these and other problems, the process of voucher privatisation was very slow. Only half of the issued vouchers had been used by 2000.

Pricing policy refers to one of the most contentious legislative areas in Belarus. Over the years of transformation, pricing policy has covered various topics, such as costs of production, profit, final prices, as well as various forms like fixed, ceiling, minimum prices, price declaration and trade margin regulation.

The first shifts in terms of price liberalisation took place at the end of the 1980s and beginning of the 1990s, when certain groups of goods were gradually exposed to free price formation. From 1991 until 1995 all prices (except for some alcoholic drinks) and all price subsidies (except for some essential consumer services) were liberalised. The following years were marked by a rollback of policy, since the unprecedented inflation invoked the use of administrative control measures by the Belarusian government.

The regulation of prices over the following years was mainly centred on the regulation of prices of enterprises with dominant positions in the market, and of socially important goods. Later on, restrictive administrative measures were used for a list of products.

As far as control over dominant enterprises is concerned, the specificity of the nature of these enterprises, which grew up from the concentration of production under central planning, has caused methodological difficulties in defining the enterprises covered by pricing control. In 2000, 26 'strategically important' enterprises producing domestic supplies of fertilisers, glass and cement had their prices regulated by the state. Several changes were made in defining the list of socially important goods, which have also been eligible for price control. The number of these goods – bread, dairy products, meat and vodka – dropped from 30, to eight in 1998 and five in 2000.

The high inflation rates persisting over the years of transformation have provoked the government to introduce administrative, non-economic measures to suppress price increases: the regulation of prices by the cost of inputs,[24] the establishment of internal quotas for domestic producers,[25] and the limitation of price increases within certain ranges.

Finally, state measures to enforce the regulations have been tightened.[26] Thus, the tight price control policy of the 1980s was changed in favour of price liberalisation in the early to mid-1990s, which was then followed by the reintroduction of centrally planned instruments of price control.

Alternative approaches

All political parties opposed the spontaneous privatisation that took place in Belarus in the early 1990s, before a legal mechanism had been formulated. An extremist view was taken by the communists, who, being in principle against private property, called for the re-nationalisation of the 'plundered assets'. Private ownership, accordingly, should exist only during the transitional period to socialism and only for medium- and small-scale production, including services. Private property in land is to be forbidden and agricultural production is to be organised in collective farms.

As far as other alternative approaches are concerned, the Popular Front supported both centralised and decentralised modes of privatisation. The government seems to have come to this decision only in 1998 with the adoption of the presidential edict, discussed above. The United Civic Party has been opposed to the voucher method of privatisation, seeing it as ineffective, and instead has favoured auctions. Their position is partly incorporated into the current official government policy, since auctioning of loss-making enterprises for a minimum sum began in 1998. The Republican Party, being guided by the principles of classical liberalism, further diverges from the official position, as it calls for rapid and wholesale privatisation.

The official pricing policy before and after 1994 stood respectively further away from, and closer to, the position of the communists. This is because the considerable price liberalisation before the arrival of Lukashenka and the subsequent introduction of price control first clashed and then converged with the communists' approach to price regulation. The rest of the parties in our sample have since 1994 taken a highly critical position on such regulation. The difference between the parties is that social democrats and the Belarusian Popular Front place more weight on social protection in pricing policy, whereas the United Civic and the Republican parties call for rapid price liberalisation for all goods, except those of natural monopolies.

Conclusions

This analysis has revealed that, first, political, institutional and macroeconomic variables constitute a very interesting way of explaining the official course of fiscal, monetary-credit, investment and structural policies. Namely, the reintroduction of central planning institutions, underpinned by the political stance of Lukashenka's regime, became the means of resolving the macroeconomic crisis. Second, market instruments, being alien to central planning institutions, play a marginal role in the present economy. This preconditions their underdevelopment, which manifests itself in the very liberal character of market-type institutions in Belarus. Third, alternative positions were analysed across the spectrum, starting with the communists and finishing with the neo-liberals. It was revealed that whilst most of the parties are highly critical of the present official policy, they still support a significant role for the state in their preferred economic policies.

Notes

1 Prior to 1994, Belarus had been experiencing imbalance in its state budget, especially in 1993, when the deficit reached 5.6 per cent of GDP. With Lukashenka's accession to power, the public finances have been gradually stabilising and in 1999 the budget deficit was 2.9 per cent of GDP.

2 Indeed, until 1997 the excise tax rates in Belarus were the same for domestic and imported products. The standard VAT has undergone a number of changes (in 1991–2 it was 28 per cent, in 1993 25 per cent, and since 1994 it has dropped to 20 per cent). International Monetary Fund, *Republic of Belarus: Recent Economic Developments* (IMF: Washington DC, 1998), p. 154. VAT had certain concessions for socially important goods, state sales, collective and private farms. On the other hand, a number of exemptions were used for imported goods (items for the production of cars, buses, tractors and agricultural machinery). Customs duties, in turn, illustrate the argument more vividly. For instance, in 1996, 20 per cent of EU and Japanese, 75 per cent of Thai and all of Indian tariffs were higher than those in Belarus. In 1998, Belarus submitted a tariff proposal to the World Trade Organisation (WTO) and the tariff rates

were, again, much more liberal than in many developing, Newly Independent States (NIS) and even developed countries.

3 For instance, allocation of credit at below market interest rate, or the financing of the clearance of payments arrears, overvalued exchange rates for qualifying imports, provision of free or inexpensive lands for some activities, cheap energy and housing, and so forth. Another channel for subsidies beyond the state budget is through the so-called extra-budgetary funds, which have been growing in Belarus since 1991, and which also point to the similarity with the central planning system, since these were previously an integral part of the state budget.

4 Their economic programmes are 95 per cent identical and the difference between them is of a political nature: the Party of Communists of Belarus opposes the Belarusian President Lukashenka, whereas the Communist Party of Belarus (Chykin) does not (see party details in Chapter 5, and Appendix).

5 S. Bahdankevich, *Kak zhili? Kak zhivem? Kak budem zhit'?1994–1997* (St Petersburg: VIRD, 1998).

6 Ibid.

7 While the Central European emerging economies such as the Vyshegrad states and Slovenia tended towards decreasing the growth of domestic credit, and there was reluctance on the part of banks to engage in lending, Belarus increasingly practised a credit expansion. This rose from 1.582 per cent in 1992 to 2.03 per cent in 1994. See EBRD, *Transition Report 1999* (London: EBRD, 1999), p. 197.

8 Average annual inflation in 1995 reached 709 per cent in comparison with 2,221 per cent in 1994. EBRD, *Transition Report 1999*, p. 197.

9 This could also be explained by the floating exchange rate regime prior to the end of 1994 that increased the competitiveness of Belarusian goods in foreign markets.

10 The Belarusian exporters were obliged by law to surrender about 40 per cent of their earnings to the state, which was 60 per cent lower than the market rate. Consequently, this appeared to be an additional tax on exporters which amounted to 15 per cent (= 40 per cent × 60 per cent ÷ 160 per cent). See M. Nuti, 'Belarus: a Command Economy Without Central Planning', paper presented at the Fifth Dubrovnik Conference on Transition Economies: 'Ten Years of Transition: What have we learned and what lies ahead?', (23–5 June 1999), p. 8.

11 EBRD, *Belarus: Country Profile* (London: EBRD, 1999), p. 194.

12 Set out in 'The main Guidelines of Monetary and Credit Policy for 1999' and 'The Concept of Monetary and Exchange Rate Policy for QIV 1999 and the year 2000', in TACIS, *Belarus Economic Trends*, February–March (Minsk: TACIS, 1999).

13 V. Novik, *Gosudarstvennoe regulirovanie inostrannykh investitsii v usloviiakh perekhodnoi ekonomiki Respubliki Belarus* (Minsk: Pravo i ekonomika, 2000), pp. 61–2.

14 TACIS, *Belarus Economic Trends*.

15 M. Nuti, 'Belarus: a Command Economy'.

16 EBRD, *Belarus: Country Profile*, p. 195.

17 The securities market is mostly represented by government securities such as short-term liabilities (GKOs), which are along with credit emission one of the main methods of financing the government deficit, and are the most liquid financial instrument due to the highest nominal yield and tax exemption. Other government securities are long-term liabilities (DGOs) for up to three years, municipal bonds, used to raise funds for housing construction and corporate securities. The latter are weakly developed because of the low degree of

privatisation, the lack of transparency of company accounts and liberalisation generally.

18 TACIS, *Belarus Economic Trends.*

19 EBRD, *Belarus: Country Profile*, p. 195.

20 A centrally planned economy allocated its capital administratively, without resort to rates of return or other measures of profitability. According to Marx's labour theory of value, capital was regarded as a free factor of production and was allocated to enterprises as an interest-free grant. Only since the late 1960s an interest-like criterion for allocating investments within administrative units, which implicitly introduced rates of return and other capital profitability criteria into investment decisions, began to be used. However, investment allocation according to the principle of priority remained dominant, which made efficiency indexes insignificant in making investment decisions. Investment funds were continuously determined administratively in the investment plan, which in turn followed the output plan of the economy.

21 It centralised the process via the establishment of annual plans, and clarified the aims and objectives of privatisation, the priorities and limitations, the sources of finance for the privatisation campaign and the distribution of incomes from privatisation.

22 The law 'On the Introduction of Changes and Additions into Some Legislative Acts of the Republic of Belarus, Including Those on the Issues of Privatisation and Destatisation', 21 June 1996, included permission to decrease the price of objects for privatisation due to credit indebtedness, the level of radiation, or the lack of demand during auctioning. The presidential decree 'On Destatisation and Privatisation of State Property of the Republic of Belarus', 20 March 1998, decentralised the privatisation process. In addition a number of new measures were introduced: prohibiting the alienation of shares bought from the state on preferential conditions (20 per cent less than normal), the auctioning or sale on a competitive basis of loss-making enterprises, or the use of credits and loans for privatisation.

23 For instance, during the privatisation auctions held in 1998, less than 50 per cent of property was sold and the final selling prices were lower than the initial price by 52.6 per cent on average.

24 Apart from the justifiable cost calculations as a reason for price increases (Resolution of the Cabinet of Ministers No. 209, 'Measures to Strengthen Control over the Price Discipline', 10 February 1999), the regulation took a closer control over salaries. See Resolution of the Cabinet of Ministers No. 449, 31 March 1999. Starting from January 2000, the income grid was introduced again, which signified the serious intent of officials to return to the central planning system.

25 See, for instance, Resolution of the Council of Ministers No. 1570, 'On the Establishment of Quotas on Manufacture and Wholesale Realisation of Alcoholic and Tobacco Products', 28 November 1997; Resolution of the Council of Ministers No. 1553, 'On Import Quotas on Alcoholic Products and Spirit of Ethyl and Food Raw Materials and on Cost in 1998', 24 November 1997. Attempts to halt exports from Belarus were also made by price measures. See the Resolution of the Price Committee for the Ministry of the Economy, 12 March 1996, according to which minimum prices were set for exported alcoholic drinks.

26 In August 1997 the President issued a decree imposing penalties and even dismissals, if prices were raised beyond the monthly 2 per cent rate. The Resolution of the Cabinet of Ministers No. 209, 'Measures to Strengthen Control over Price Discipline', 10 February 1999, rules that firms are to justify their

prices by appropriate economic calculations (with an exact description of expenses). According to the Resolution, violation of this norm may result in a fine of 10 per cent sales revenue. On 9 July 1999 the Cabinet of Ministers made changes to this document and increased the fee to 30 per cent (Resolution No. 1059).

11 Russia and Belarus

The quest for the union; or who will pay for Belarus's path to recovery?*

Anastasia Nesvetailova

Introduction: why the union?

Proposals and plans to unite the two post-Soviet republics of Russia and Belarus under a common economic area and to introduce a single currency in the two states began as early as 1993, only two years after the USSR had collapsed. Yet until very recently the Russia–Belarus Union saw little progress in the way of its actual implementation. In the years that have passed since 1993, both Russia and Belarus have been facing serious economic challenges and crises, changes in domestic governments and political regimes; they have also confronted the effects of profound shifts in the international environment. Inevitably, the structural problems of politico-economic transformations in the two post-Soviet republics have been the major negative factors impeding the speed and success of the Union project. What kept the rhetoric of integration going both in Russia and in Belarus was primarily the figure of the Belarusian President Aliaksandr Lukashenka: reuniting Belarus with Russia was one of his office-winning policy proposals in the 1994 presidential campaign, and continues to provide him with massive support from the electorate.

It seems fair to acknowledge that despite all his vices, Lukashenka has proved to be a good, or at least a fast-learning, student of politics. His charisma and background have enabled him to attain the role of hero for the majority of Belarusians, namely the urban working class and the peasants. The undeniable gift of discerning and skilfully employing people's psychological sympathies and sentiments in populist propaganda has greatly assisted Lukashenka in strengthening his authoritarian rule and political regime. In the absence of any concrete measures to fight high inflation, poverty and black market activity, the slogans of 'jailing the thieves' seem to have worked quite well: public castigations of ministry officials and representatives of local governments do look picturesque and impressive in live TV reports. Amid the deepening economic degradation and political isolation, reunion with Russia is another promising idea that, it is believed, will bring Belarus into a better future. It is vitally important to recognise that the project of merger with Russia is not only an active asset in Lukashenka's political portfolio; it is also a genuine aspiration of the majority of the Belarusian population.

Belarusians' longing for reunification with Russia deserves a more detailed exploration. Belarus is perhaps the only republic of the former USSR that had no revolutionary ambitions for independence from Russia. The need to (re)institutionalise Belarus's national identity and sovereignty did not originate in civil society (as was, for example, the case in the Baltic States), but was largely imposed upon the country by the Belavezha meeting in 1991. Accordingly, the present-day Russian vector in Belarus's foreign policy is grounded first of all in people's mentality and sociocultural factors. These include the weakness of the Belarusian national idea, and uncertainty and indecisiveness in national self-identification and governmental self-determination. As one of the leading Belarusian sociologists put it, 'Belarus has Russian ideology, even everyday patriotism is essentially that of the Greater Russia. Private interests of Belarusians are in no way being transposed into the interests of Belarus as a nation or a state.'[1] The major reason for identifying Belarus with Russia is the Sovietism of the mass mentality. Ideally and psychologically, the majority of Belarusians continue to live in the USSR. Ten years after the USSR was dismantled, almost 40 per cent of Belarusians would still like the Soviet Union to be restored.[2]

Belarusians' deep distrust for the proclaimed strong causal link between a market economy, free democracy and a rise in living standards, so actively fashioned on the post-Soviet arena, is understandable. Within the USSR, Belarus's unique demographic mixture of population, lack of natural resources and geopolitical position predetermined its role as a scientific periphery for the rest of the country. The republic was known for its high-quality research institutions and personnel. Also, particularly in the late Soviet years, most of the enterprises underwent significant modernisation, were re-equipped and oriented to the production of competitive consumer products. The stable political climate and prospects of secure retirement attracted labour from other Soviet republics.[3] Today, having no tangible future to aim for, the only relief for many Belarusians is to look back to the happy times of Soviet prosperity, stability and faith. It comes as no surprise, then, that according to sociological surveys of March 2000, an absolute majority of Belarusians and Russians approve of the Union between their states. In the poll conducted by the National and International Security Foundation, 66.9 per cent of Russians and 68.2 per cent of Belarusians are positive about the benefits of the Russian–Belarusian integration.[4]

Symbolically, on 8 December 1999, exactly nine years after the Belavezha meeting,[5] Russian President Boris Yeltsin and Aliaksandr Lukashenka signed the Treaty on Unification between Russia and Belarus. Among other clauses, the document states that within the economic union, Russia and Belarus have a single currency unit. As Article 21 of the Agreement holds, the establishment of a common emission centre will be paralleled by the gradual introduction of a common currency. A year later, on 30 November 2000, Aliaksandr Lukashenka and the new Russian leader Vladimir Putin signed by far the most concrete Agreement on the economic union. As this document maintains, starting on 1 January 2005, the Russian rouble will be introduced as the currency for all transactions within Belarus in preparation for a united currency.

The major subject of the present chapter is the political economy of the emerging Russia–Belarus Monetary Union (RBMU). At the same time, it is emphasised here that the complex issue of monetary unification of the two post-Soviet republics encompasses a whole range of economic, political and social problems. Therefore this chapter will try to disclose the underlying origins and implications of the integration project as a whole. First, the chapter tries to explain why the Russian rouble was agreed on as the eventual common currency unit by the two states, and what implications this decision contains for the ultimate institutional design of the Russian–Belarusian Union. Second, the chapter looks at the central issues of the trade-off between economics and politics, which the Union implies, both to Belarus and Russia. The thrust of the argument is directed towards the historical legacies of the two post-Soviet states, their economic and political interdependence. Third, in exploring the present-day dynamics in the politico-economic systems of Russia and Belarus, it is argued that the recent changes in Russia's leadership and the country's economic progress have brought the Union project up to a more concrete and, crucially, practical stage of implementation. In 2000 the Presidents of the two states agreed to confine the integration to purely economic and monetary spheres, while rejecting speculations of a possible political merger. The present essay concludes that this line of development is likely to prove the best achievable compromise between the economics and politics of the Union, as it is potentially advantageous to both participating countries.

The rouble union: what is it all about?

Since monetary union was first mentioned in 1993, the prospective introduction of a single currency has been a popular subject of journalistic and political speculation. Two points can be made here. On the one hand, there exist serious reasons to draw on the vast economic literature on monetary unions. The theoretical microeconomic advantages of a common currency derive from the elimination of transactions and foreign exchange costs. Macroeconomic benefits of lower inflation and interest rates provide a corresponding impetus for employment and growth. The negative sides of monetary unification relate to a loss of monetary policy instruments, including the loss of exchange rate policy, which is important in the case of asymmetric shocks to member countries. Generally the net benefits from monetary unification require a prior achievement of as much economic integration as possible without a common currency; fiscal, monetary and real economic convergence and discipline by member countries; a political dialogue between the Union's new central bank and national governments; and the development of joint political institutions.[6]

On the other hand, the range of available options for the Union currency is severely restricted by the practical condition of the countries' financial systems and economic structures. For instance, the feeble state of both Russian and Belarusian finance and banking systems and the actual politico-economic arrangements in operation have made the adoption of the dollar or the euro as an anchor currency under a currency board system, or the straightforward invention of a hybrid Russian–Belarusian rouble, redundant. Hence at their November 2000 meeting Putin and Lukashenka came to the decision that in preparation for the single currency, starting in January 2005 Belarus will join the Russian rouble area. That is, the Russian rouble will be used as the denominator for all transactions within Belarus. Russia has provided the Belarusian National Bank with a loan instalment of US $30 million to stabilise the Belarusian rouble. The total Russian credit package for the purposes of the Union, aimed at facilitating structural reforms in Belarus and ultimately at creating preconditions for the currency union, is $200 million. The November 2000 Agreement sets up the Russian Central Bank as the single emission centre for the Union; the document also entails that the decision on the introduction of a hybrid Russian–Belarusian rouble will not be finalised until 2008.[7] Thus, the most significant outcome of the November 2000 Minsk meeting, and by far of the integration project generally, is the officially framed compromise between the initial ambitions of the two states regarding the Union. Minsk has secured substantial financial support from Russia; Moscow has ensured that the Russian Central Bank is the only emission centre for the Russian–Belarusian Monetary Union (RBMU).

The November 2000 Agreement is a truly significant step in the politics of integration. Instead of being just another manifesto of friendship and faith between two fraternal nations declared on paper (as most of the previous agreements have tended to be), it is effectively the first real action that Moscow and Minsk, however painfully, have agreed on and started executing. Until 2000 the central point of disagreement between Russia and Belarus has been the position and control over the money emission centre for the Union. In short, Belarus wanted two emission centres, in Minsk and in Moscow, that would provide the two participating states with the single currency, that is, the Russian rouble, while retaining Belarus's independence in economic policies. The Kremlin would not agree to that, arguing that the Monetary Union can only be implemented and function under the 'one state–one emission centre' formula.[8] Why would Minsk need control over the expansion of the Russian rouble stock? Because continual money emission, in order to subsidise governmental expenditures and finance the budget deficit, and the resulting inflation obscured by impressive official growth statistics,[9] are the key policy components of the Belarusian model of 'market socialism'. Losing the instrument of monetary emission ultimately deprives Belarus of a major policy tool, subordinating the powers of the government in Minsk to their Moscow counterparts, and thereby posing a certain threat to Belarus's sovereignty and the existing balance of political-economic forces. Therefore by complying with Moscow's choice of the Russian Central Bank as the Union emission centre, Lukashenka factually acknowledged the primacy of Belarus's current economic needs over political considerations.

Exploring the politico-economic trade-off behind the Union agreements, it is interesting to recall the most immediate historical analogue to the economic reunification of two states that were once separated: the 1991 unification of East and West Germany. In the reunited state, the West German Deutschmark was introduced as legal tender. As the German experience suggests, rapid implementation of early currency unification may precipitate a crash, producing overall economic slowdown and severe transitional difficulties in adjusting wages, employment and social systems. At the same time, German currency unification has proved the fastest way to economic and political union. By extending the circulation of the Deutschmark to the whole of Germany, economic unification quickly progressed to a degree that would have made it very difficult to prevent further political unification. In this, the leading role of West Germany as a strong economic partner, able to cushion economic and social frictions of the restructuring process, has been the key to success of the reunion.[10]

The lessons from the German experience help explain the rationale for the gradual (not until 2005) introduction of the Russian rouble, and its intended function as an intermediary currency in the Russia–Belarus Union. The interplay between economics and politics in currency unification also raises pivotal questions about the ultimate institutional and legal form the Union might take. How far is Russia willing to perform the role of a stronger economic partner, leading the economic integration? What are the real interests the two countries are pursuing by setting up the currency union? Would Minsk be willing to give up political independence and proceed to the final stage of political merger with Russia? The next part of the chapter tries to provide answers to these questions by looking at the underlying incentives for Belarus and Russia to join in the economic union. An attempt will also be made to distinguish between the economics and politics of the integration, and that requires a further clarification of the decisions taken in Minsk in November 2000.

Belarus and Russia: between economics and politics

While the collapse of state socialism has created a situation of systemic vacuum, post-Soviet trajectories are heavily dependent on the dense and complex institutional legacy, where often invisible remnants of the previous economic and political order still shape expectations and patterns of policy conduct. Transformation processes depend heavily on politico-economic structures and the constellation of social forces, and on how these factors feed into current attempts of economic, political, and social transformation.[11] In the particular case of Belarus, despite the choices opened up by the disintegration of the command system, various institutional legacies facilitated by the immediate context imposed major limits on the prospects for economic and political reform.

Due to Belarus's position within the USSR and her close yet subordinate relations with the top echelons of the ruling CPSU, there has always been a patriarchal aspect to the centre–periphery relationship between Minsk and Moscow. From the communist system, the *nomenklatura* and the technocrats inherited not only their contacts and power, but also to a significant degree their methods of rule. As it happened, these methods have appeared perfectly compatible with neo-liberal economic reforms like privatisation and liberalisation. Rather than destroying old politico-economic structures, traditional elites have played a decisive role in the formation of a new economy.[12] After 1991, Belarus's governmental elite, heavily influenced by Russia's politico-economic groups, was actively using the moment for the construction of the 'apparatus market', combining the traditional Soviet-type system of governance, state ownership and 'new market opportunities' for the higher layer of the bureaucracy. In fact, the main locus of legitimacy of the newly independent country lay in the external realm, while emerging internal forms of governance and practice added only secondary layers to Belarus's statehood.[13] In other words, authorities in post-Soviet Belarus, rather than promoting the development of national industrial, financial or banking systems, were largely reflecting the interests of Russian capital. One of the most recent and vivid examples of this would be the experience of the Ford car factory erected near Minsk in 1995–6. Despite the already tangible benefits of the direct foreign investment and new employment opportunities for the economy, Minsk was forced to shut the firm down by 1997. The pressure came from Russia, which was anxious that the Ford-Belarus venture would undermine the competitiveness of Russian-made cars. Russia also has a 77.1 per cent stake in Slavneft, a Russian–Belarusian oil company, and thus controls the Belarus-based Mozyr oil refinery. In this way, as the ex-president of the national bank Tamara Vinnikava argues, the state–crime–oligarchy nature of Russian capitalism actually created the need for Russian capital to have a monopolised, state-controlled economic model in Belarus.[14]

Objectively, though, the position and ambitions of Russian capital in Belarus can be well justified. Partly because of its inability and unwillingness to undergo fundamental structural reforms, and partly due to the inadequacies of an authoritarian political regime and the resulting isolation from international credit facilities, Belarus is heavily dependent on the Russian economy. Russia supplies Belarus with 100 per cent of oil, 100 per cent of gas, 80 per cent of energy resources, 80 per cent of coal, and 86 per cent of crude metals.[15] Belarusian foreign exchange reserves are exhausted; with the weakened national currency and colossal scale of dollarisation,[16] the country simply does not have the funds to service her foreign trade obligations, and more than half of the import payments to Russia are made in barter; besides, in only the first quarter of 2000 Belarus's indebtedness to Gazprom reached $60 million. During the whole of the integration period, the Belarusian gas and energy debt to Russia totalled approximately $250 million.[17] Moreover, Russia is the major market for Belarusian exports, most of the profits from which are skimmed off by the countries' directors and oligarchs under the shield of the customs union. The tariff-free border between Russia and Belarus is actively used by numerous dealers as a means of smuggling massive amounts of imports into Russia. With 70 per cent of the export–import flows passing through Belarus's territory, Russia's budget is annually deprived of some 11 per cent of its trade tax revenue.[18] At the same time export revenues are a critical source of Belarus's foreign exchange earnings, and so they have a significant impact on the country's economic growth. According to *The Economist*,[19] given that domestic Belarusian consumers remain too impoverished to afford higher-quality imported goods, Belarus's moderate GDP growth may continue only if demand for Belarusian exports in Russia and the rest of the CIS remains relatively buoyant. In this case, industrial output might increase by around 6 per cent in 2000 and by 4 per cent in 2001, leading to GDP growth of around 2.0–2.5 per cent in 2000 and 2 per cent in 2001 (figures remarkably at variance with the official statistics reporting a 6–7 per cent of GDP growth per annum).

Yet this optimistic forecast may be darkened by the already shaky position of Belarusian exports to the Russian market. In early 2001, Russia's domestic price for gas is $15 per 1,000 cubic meters; it goes to Belarus at $30–2, while the equivalent on the world market can go for as high as $100. For energy supplies Belarus pays 3.9 cents per kWh, Russia 1.3 cents, Belgium 2 cents. Therefore, with 90 per cent of Belarusian strategic imports coming from Russia, and with 80 per cent of Belarusian enterprises being entirely dependent on Russian supplies of raw materials and intermediary inputs, it indeed seems sensible for Belarus to obtain, via integration, these resources at Russia's domestic prices. Even with Russia subsiding the Belarusian economy by selling raw materials at prices half the world level, Belarusian goods are very likely to lose their competitiveness on the Russian market because of their high import component and cost.[20] Without the assistance of international financial resources such as IMF credit lines, adopting the Russian rouble may also be helpful in restoring the credibility of domestic currency and handling high levels of inflation in Belarus.

These calculations are, of course, only a very brief reflection of the deep-rooted deficiencies in Belarus's political economy. Domestically, there are various economic and political difficulties inherited from the 'shortage economy', such as high inflation and disguised unemployment; and political commitments to various forms of economic and social expenditure, which account for the current upheaval in the country.[21] These structural factors, including the dependence of workers on management, and the remnants of social welfare provisions and bureaucratic paternalism, are as important as the personality of the Belarusian leader in explaining the nature and consequences of the present-day crisis and the search for solutions to it via the Russia–Belarus Union project.

Russia's incentives to enter the Union tend to be more politically based, though there are certain economic considerations. The principal economic reason for Russia to join the common economic area with Belarus is the transit of gas into Europe. Oil and gas are Russia's primary export commodities and sources of hard currency, and a secure transport route to the export markets is fundamental to the country's foreign trade balance. At present, Gazprom's only pipeline to Europe goes through Ukraine, giving that country a virtual stranglehold on the company's export lifeline. In the past two years, two and a half billion cubic meters of gas have disappeared from Gazprom pipelines on Ukrainian territory. Gazprom hopes to get around this mess by building an alternative gas route, Iamal–Europe, that would extend though the territory of Belarus and Poland at the cost of $24 billion. In 1999, for instance, most of the $380 million inflow of Russian capital into Belarus went into servicing the construction of the Iamal–Europe pipeline.[22] Russia generally may achieve substantial economic benefits from easing the access to Belarus's favourable geographical position. Even despite the dire state of the Belarusian economy, for Russia economic union with its western neighbour is undoubtedly potentially lucrative, if only for the sake of easier access to European markets. An additional advantage from the currency union is that in the future, use of the Russian rouble might make it easier for Russian companies to reclaim Belarusian debts.

Still, foreign policy considerations are believed to be weightier in Moscow's decision to join the Union and provide Belarus with a $200 million credit package. The end of the Cold War, the Iraq, Kosovo and Chechnia crises have demonstrated that Russia is no longer perceived as a world superpower. In this sense, the Union with Belarus and the enlargement of the country might be a compensation for Russia's trauma of economic devastation and the loss of international status. Foreign policy and security considerations are not uncommon in western interpretations of the implications of the emerging Slavic union. Foreign media and political observers tend to regard Russian–Belarusian unification as a direct response to NATO expansion.[23] Although it is misleading to ignore the inner politico-economic reasons for the Union, it is true that Belarus's position as an official partner within the Union can indeed be a good buffer for Russia from the dangerously close NATO-befriended Poland. It is also possible that the Kremlin is generally positively in favour of

Lukashenka and would be willing to support his regime further, for under his leadership there is no possibility of Belarus joining NATO or the EU. Belarus's infrastructure does allow it to accommodate strategic nuclear warheads on her territory, and Russia's generals view it as a key base for radar and eavesdropping equipment or for placing extra troops or missiles in an effort to rattle NATO, should it expand to the Baltic States.[24] More recently, Lukashenka publicised a proposal to set up a joint border armed force on Belarusian territory,[25] which has been left unanswered by Moscow. Meanwhile it is not a secret that Lukashenka has been openly using the presence of Russian military facilities on the Belarusian territory as collateral for oil and gas loans. The 'gas for military compensations' deal between Minsk and Moscow has been a popular trick when Belarus needed Russia to write off a substantial part of Belarus's indebtedness. Besides, and perhaps even more importantly, Moscow needs Belarus in the matter of the international arms trade. If the biggest Slav brother does not wish to be seen selling arms, it is very convenient to use Belarus as a front.[26]

It is becoming apparent that setting up an economics/politics divide in the analysis of the origins and dynamics of the integration project, even if analytically feasible, is quite artificial when the issue comes to real-life events. Yet looking at the two possible levels of integration – a common Russian–Belarusian economic area, and a political merger of the two sovereign states – is necessary in light of the recent changes in Russia's domestic politics and in the progress with the Union diplomacy. According to the text of the Treaty, the Union is established between two sovereign states, while preserving their territorial integrity, national independence, statehood and constitutional structure.[27] Such phraseology indicates a very convoluted procedure for political merger or, as some have commented, is utterly absurd. When two states unite into a single state, they cannot retain their national sovereignty. If, on the other hand, they do intend to remain sovereign, then the Union becomes a kind of an interstate alliance, most likely a confederation. No clause in the Union Treaty made the ultimate legal status of the Russia–Belarus construction explicit. This vagueness in declarations, the absence of a firm political schema for the Union, has been the main obstacle to taking the integration seriously, and has led many critics both in Russia and in Belarus to regard the whole affair as nothing but political demagogy and electoral populism periodically deployed by the countries' leaders. In order to clarify this issue, it is necessary to enquire into Russia's and Belarus's preferences for the political legitimacy of the Union, and into their development.

It is generally believed that initially a Russian choice in merging with Belarus had been a classical version of confederation. Conventionally a confederation of states does not require any supranational executive bodies or powers whose decisions would be binding on the two member states. In other words, a Russian–Belarusian confederation would be very similar to the amorphous union between Russia and Belarus as it exists at present.[28]

In contrast, the Belarusian side had envisaged the Union headed by a president and vice-president. The leaders would be elected by the two peoples, and member states would not be able to veto decisions of the supranational authority. Why would Belarus risk its sovereignty and want to enter the Union on conditions so closely resembling the centre–regions hierarchy of the Russian Federation? As many analysts have pointed out, this federation-like mode of uniting the two countries would have given Lukashenka a risky, but nonetheless conceivable chance of, first, becoming an elected president of the Union while keeping his post in Belarus, and second, of getting the post of president of Russia.[29] With 70 per cent of Russians supporting the idea of the Russian–Belarusian Union, it is understandable why in the era of an impaired Yeltsin, Lukashenka – the man of 'stability and order' – appealed to many Russians and Belarusians as a potential leader for the new interstate formation. But Yeltsin's retreat from the political scene and the March 2000 presidential elections in Russia drastically changed these circumstances.

Even before coming to the Kremlin, Putin had stressed that the integration process and its outcomes should be advantageous to Russia. Unlike Yeltsin, Putin is free of the 'Belavezha complex'; he easily gained strong popularity with the Russian electorate without referring to the slogans of 'reuniting fraternal nations' and 're-establishing historical bounds'. His first actions after taking office were to reform federal governance, strengthen the country's territorial and political integrity and endorse the Russian national idea. The start of his presidency turned out to be a fortunate time for Russia's economic recovery because of the high world oil prices and the devalued rouble. With these considerations in mind it was almost certain that Russian–Belarusian integration would proceed according to Russia's preferences. Putin would never be willing to grant Belarus some special independent status under confederation, as inevitably other Russian regions like Bashkiria or Tatarstan would demand equal treatment. Lukashenka, in turn, having lost the opportunity to take the lead on the Russian political stage, would not give up Belarus's sovereignty and presidency by accepting the status of a region within the Russian Federation.

This line of logic helps explain why after their November 2000 meeting in Minsk Putin openly and firmly stated that the Russian–Belarusian integration could only proceed as an economic union; any form of political unification is not even an issue.[30] As was noted above, Moscow agreed on the Russian rouble as a common currency, plus a $200 million loan. The money, which will be doled out in tranches, comes with strings attached. These include Moscow's demands that Belarus reforms its financial system and monetary policy, reduces the budget deficit and inflation, and stabilises the economy. More specifically, by January 2005 Belarus is expected to enhance the credibility of its domestic currency, adjust foreign exchange reserve requirements to their Russian equivalents, and revise the mechanisms of the foreign exchange market operations.[31] Two hundred million dollars is a very substantial sum of money for Belarus: it is twice the size of the official stock of foreign exchange reserves, and is equivalent to 1.7 per cent of the country's GDP.[32] If used properly, the money would really help solve Belarus's problems of inflation, budget deficit, financial system and the shadow economy. But the nuance of setting up the Russian Central Bank as the single emission centre ultimately deprives Belarus of the chance of an independent monetary policy and effectively subordinates the country's economic policy to Moscow. By signing the rouble Agreement in November 2000, Lukashenka effectively acknowledged the devastating condition of the Belarusian economy and the absence of any available sources of financial aid other than Moscow. There is still a big question about whether Belarus fulfils the Russian loan conditions. Some critics have already argued that the first $30 million tranche would be used not for rebuilding Belarusian industry and the financial system, but for raising nominal wages and pensions and other populist measures in the run-up to the 2001 presidential elections. These forecasts have been justified in many ways; more-over, the Union scenario may be distorted by the unpredictability of the Belarusian leader. It is quite possible that under certain circumstances before 2005, Lukashenka might decide that it would be better for Belarus not to adopt the Russian rouble at all and instead radically change the vector of foreign policy towards the West. There is also a possibility that the Kremlin may eventually rethink its preferences in the future and support one of Lukashenka's rivals; and the Union project may eventually be altered. Or Russia, confronted by the demands of her foreign creditors, might well postpone the release of the $200 million support fund to Belarus.

The scope of the present chapter does not allow any further delving into these speculations. To resume the analysis at this stage, three points need to be made. First, Belarus's decision to establish a union with Russia comes from the personal ambitions of the Belarusian President as much as it originates in the mass consciousness of Belarusians. As the results of sociological findings indicate,[33] Belarusians tend to view their big eastern neighbour as the USSR, not a new Russia. In Belarus, the Russian Federation is still widely perceived as a giant power rich in natural resources, military potential and international weight; her current problems of economic crises, ethnic and social conflicts do not seem to affect Belarusians' desire to enter the Russian–Belarusian Union. Second, the above analysis implies that the 2000 change in Russia's political leadership and the resulting reconsideration of the Union's politico-economic framework do look promising for Belarus. With no other available sources of international financial support, Russia's conditional loan package may provide Belarus with a real chance to restore the economy and undertake serious reforms in both the financial and industrial sectors. Third, at the moment, the agreed path to economic integration and Putin's determination not to proceed to political unification with Belarus may be regarded as a guarantee that the prospect of crisp Russian banknotes does not come at the cost of Belarusian boys going to war in Chechnia.

Conclusion

At their meeting in Minsk on 30 November 2000, Aliaksandr Lukashenka and Vladimir Putin finalised the decision to proceed along the path of monetary and economic union. They agreed to adopt, starting in 2005, the Russian rouble as an intermediary currency unit for the Union. This decision was a compromise between the initial ambitions of the two countries.

Under the Agreement Belarus was promised a substantial financial support package ($200 million) from Russia for the purposes of economic Union. Belarus's main benefits from entering the Union include significant financial support from Russia, and the opportunity to receive gas and energy supplies at Russia's low domestic prices. These advantages come at the price of Belarus's discretion in monetary policy conduct, as the Russian Central Bank is designated as the only money emission centre for the Union. Russia, in turn, by entering the economic union acquires access to Belarus's advantageous geographical position as a transit route for Russian gas exports to Europe. Additionally, by effectively taking up the burden of economic adjustment in Belarus, Russia is also securing a reliable partner in terms of international security and politics. Overall, the decision to confine the integration of Russia and Belarus to monetary and economic spheres can be interpreted as an optimal compromise between economic gains and the countries' political sovereignty.

Notes

* My most sincere thanks for all kind of assistance and encouragement to the contributors of this volume, and especially to Elena Korosteleva, Colin Lawson, David Marples and Nadia Lisovskaia. My gratitude also goes to Slava Romanchuk in Minsk for providing the feedback and invaluable material for this chapter.

1 V. Karbalevich, 'Kurs na integratsiiu s Rossiei', *Belarus Monitor*, special issue (1999): 3–16.

2 *Belorusskaia delovaia gazeta*, 8 December 1999.

3 D.R. Marples, *Belarus: From Soviet Rule to Nuclear Catastrophe* (London: Macmillan, 1996), p. 134; D.R. Marples, 'The Demographic Crisis in Belarus', *Problems of Post-Communism*, January–February 2000: 16–27.

4 www.archive.deadline.ru, accessed via www.smi.ru, December 2000.

5 On 8 December 1991, the dissolution Treaty of the USSR was signed by Shushkevich, Yeltsin, and Kravchuk in Belavezhskaia Pushcha.

6 M. Nuti, 'A Russia–Belarus Monetary Union?', discussion paper (Minsk: World Bank Office, 1998), p. 3.

7 V. Sokolova, 'Belorussiia soglasna na rubl'', *Izvestiia*, 1 December 2000.

8 A. Illarionov, Interview to *Belorusskaia delovaia gazeta*, 15 April 2000, p. 12.

9 Official statistical bulletins released by the Belarusian Goskomstat report a 7–8 per cent of GDP growth per annum.
10 K. Hartwing, 'Transforming a socialist economy: currency unification, banking reform and capital markets', in P. Welfens (ed.), *Economic Aspects of German Unification* (Berlin, New York: Springer, 1992, 1996), pp. 204–5.
11 J. Hausner, B. Jessop and K. Nielsen (eds), *Strategic Choice and Path-Dependency in Post-Socialism* (Brookfield, VT: Edward Elgar, 1995), pp. 4–13.
12 B. Kagarlitsky, *New Realism, New Barbarism* (London: Pluto Press, 1999), p. 138.
13 J. Borocz, 'From comprador state to auctioneer state', in D. Smith, D. Solinger and S. Topik (eds), *States and Sovereignty in the Global Economy* (London and New York: Routledge, 1999), p. 194.
14 T. Vinnikava, 'Kukly i kuklovody', *Belorusskaia delovaia gazeta*, 25 February 2000.
15 Ia. Romanchuk, 'Ne torgovat' a voevat', mimeo (2000).
16 According to some estimates, once the restrictions on foreign exchange trading have been removed, the daily (cash) dollar purchases by commercial banks increased from $50 thousand to $1 million. See Romanchuk, 'Ne torgovat'.
17 A. Vernidub, 'Lukashenko khochet poluchit' gaz voennym putem', www.intellectualcapital.ru, 14 April 2000.
18 Goskomstat official statistics cited in Karbalevich, 'Kurs na integratsiu', p. 3.
19 *Economist Intelligence Unit* (2000), Belarus: Country Outlook, 17 October. Available at http://www.eiu.com/latest/430371.asp, accessed February 2001.
20 T. Manenock, 'V usloviiakh osazhdennoi kreposti', *Izvestiia*, 24 October 2000.
21 Hausner, Jessop and Nielsen, *Strategic Choice*, pp. 4–13.
22 www.strana.ru/print/971954008.html.
23 *Moscow News*, 22–8 November 2000.
24 Ibid.
25 Vernidub, 'Lukashenko khochet'.
26 *Moscow News,* 22–8 November 2000. Also on smi.ru/archive/printed?id=944746451.
27 *Dogovor o sozdanii Soiuznogo Gosudarstva* (proekt), October 1999.
28 The existence of the Supreme Council of the Union can be disregarded, as its decisions are taken only with the approval of the presidents of Russia and Belarus.
29 Karbalevich, 'Kurs na integratsiiu', pp. 12–15.
30 Sokolova, 'Belorussiia soglasna', p. 2.
31 Some observers noted ironically that Russian aid came with conditions as strict as the traditional structural adjustment packages of the IMF.
32 According to Belarusian periodicals, the hard currency reserves of the National Bank in 2000 totalled approximately $100 billion. The IMF estimated Belarus's GDP in 2000 at around $11.8 million (http://www.imf.org/external/pubs/ft/scr/2000/cr00153.pdf, retrieved February 2001).
33 Karbalevich, 'Kurs na integratsiiu', pp. 3–6.

12 Belarus's external relations

Denis Krivosheev

Introduction

Belarus's international standing has been the subject of fierce political debate – increasingly so at the end of the first decade of its independent existence. The Belarusian leadership's persistent intention to integrate with Russia, along with cultural, demographic and environmental factors and economic concerns, has even led to the question of whether Belarus can survive as an independent nation.[1] Authoritarian tendencies in the country and the worsening human rights record[2] have caused growing international concern, and questions have arisen about the sources of Belarus's foreign policy. Is the pursuit of integration with Russia really driven by a popular aspiration? What inhibits the development of closer and more co-operative links with other neighbours and the West? And what can international organisations do to facilitate the democratic process and economic reforms in Belarus?

In the early 1990s Belarus adopted its own traditional national symbols and elevated Belarusian to the status of an official language. It introduced moderate but promising political and market reforms and pursued an open foreign policy. By the end of the decade, however, practically every one of these achievements had been abandoned and even the national symbols had been changed back to Soviet-style ones. Common explanations given for this 'denationalized nation'[3] and its self-sacrificing policy in relation to Russia are the absence of any historical precedent for a national Belarusian state, a weak sense of national self-consciousness (or national identity), political apathy, and nostalgia for the relative prosperity of the late Soviet era among many Belarusians. Nevertheless, more needs to be said about the domestic political sources of Belarus's controversial foreign policy-making and the important external factors influencing Belarusian politics in the 1990s.

It is argued in this chapter that Belarus's strongly pro-Russian foreign policy under the administrations of Kebich and Lukashenka has been underpinned by their conflict with the nationalist-democratic opposition and their need to rely on Russian economic and political support as an additional power base at home. Continuous Russian support for the pro-Russian leadership in Belarus has never been matched by the country's prospects in Western Europe. Subsequently, the policy of disengagement pursued by the West towards Belarus in response to its worsening political record has had no positive effect on the country's transition. For the foreseeable future, the asymmetrical structure of Belarus's external relations is unlikely to alter. While any significant change in Belarus's foreign policy priorities can only occur after a significant political transformation within the country, its international environment is currently not supportive of such a development.

1990–3: independence, national statehood and political cleavages

The processes through which Belarus was asserting statehood and establishing itself internationally were uneven and often controversial. On 27 July 1990 the newly elected Supreme Soviet adopted the Declaration of State Sovereignty. Article 10 contained a clause that declared neutrality to be the ultimate aim of sovereign Belarus. This opened up prospects for the development of a sovereign national state in what was still a Soviet republic. It did not, however, amount to national independence. The declaration, among other things, asserted support for renewal of the Union (the USSR).[4] The Act of Independence was only passed on 25 August 1991 – after the abortive anti-Gorbachev coup in Moscow. However, this did not resolve the country's ambiguous international status. Full independence came only with the signing of the Belavezha accords on 8 December 1991 that formally abolished the USSR.

Belarus's external relations of 1990–1 and subsequent years reflected these controversies of state-building. They epitomised domestic political struggle, while at the same time manifesting only a vague understanding among the then political elite of what national interests were. In the situation of a newly independent state, some basic objectives of national foreign policy – such as sovereignty, international recognition, stability, prosperity – were obvious. How these could best be ensured was not. The situation was further confused by regional politics: Poland and the Baltic States were actively seeking their way 'back to Europe' while also trying to distance themselves from the 'East'; Ukraine's relations with Russia demonstrated a strong degree of tension and defiance. Belarus's independence was not a result of popular pro-western or anti-Russian mobilisation, nor did it produce conflict with any other neighbour: the country's foreign policy had no predetermined 'geopolitical' direction.

Of all parties involved in the formulation of Belarus's early foreign policy only the nationalists (first of all the Belarusian Popular Front – BNF) had a more or less clear vision of what constituted the country's long-term national interests. The BNF believed that Belarus should, like all its non-Russian neighbours, pursue its path to Europe while distancing itself from Russia as far as circumstances allowed. The latter was justified by the view that Russia had for centuries been an imperial power and that its political, military, economic and even cultural influence in the region remained too strong. The BNF was worried that economic, let alone military, reliance on Russia would be inevitably transformed into political dependency. Although no one suggested that the Belarusian economy would remain viable without retaining close economic links with Russia, the idea was actively to seek alternative sources of stability, and ultimately of security. Naturally, Western Europe and the US were favoured as new partners, but the BNF also recognised that Belarus's 'way to Europe' went through Central Europe. For the time being, the doctrine of state neutrality (non-alliance) would deter Russian geopolitical claims on Belarus and invite the West to take greater interest in its independence and stability. At the same time, Belarus had to adopt radical economic reforms and accelerate democratisation to be able to attract foreign investment and establish stable economic links with countries outside the Commonwealth of Independent States (CIS).

There were, however, problems with this vision. Belarus's future in Europe was far too distant, while western interest was scarce. Active 'Europeanisation' of foreign policy and loosening of political and economic links with Russia would cause irritation in Moscow (which the BNF's rhetoric was already doing). Belarus's recent past (with its relative prosperity and social stability) would have to be resolutely left behind. From the outset, this programme was unlikely to mobilise lasting popular support. The first economic changes, together with the disintegration of the former Soviet economic system, produced very mixed results, badly affecting most of the country's population. The BNF's argument that further, more radical reforms were needed to improve the situation was losing persuasiveness.

There were a number of influential, strongly pro-transition politicians at the centre of the Belarusian political spectrum. Shushkevich, for example, combined a more moderate nationalism and democratic reform agenda with pragmatism that envisaged the possibility of a political contract with the post-communist forces and a continuing close relationship with Russia. Thus, as the formal head of state (Chairman of the Supreme Soviet Presidium) Shushkevich actively participated in the Belavezha process, which on the one hand emphasised Belarus's independence and its recognition by Russia,[5] while on the other hand secured vital links with the other successor states. Shushkevich aspired for Belarus's wide representation in international organisations ranging from the Conference for Security and Co-operation in Europe (CSCE) to the International Monetary Fund (IMF), including a newly created forum like the NATO-sponsored North Atlantic Co-operation Council (NACC). Shushkevich also appreciated the idea of monetary union with Russia as a support to the ailing national economy. At the same time he declined joining the CIS collective security arrangements on the grounds that this would contradict the principle of state neutrality. This position appealed to many Belarusians. However, at the time of Shushkevich's presidency the Centre represented no real political force. The Speaker personally was not affiliated to any party and could only gain influence through compromise. After Shushkevich showed no support for the BNF's idea of a referendum on the new parliamentary elections and allowed the process of rapprochement with Russia to proceed, he lost the support of nationalist MPs, which led to his removal from office in January 1994.

Post-communist politicians outnumbered all other forces in parliament (about 85 per cent of deputies entered it in 1990 as Communist Party candidates). They clearly dominated the political life of Belarus in 1990–4, having their co-ordinator in Kebich's government and their support in the largely state-controlled media. The post-communist deputies were dragging their feet over anything that could advance reforms. Hence, the nationally minded parliamentary decisions of 1990–1 may seem surprising – but less so within the broader political context. Developments in Moscow and other parts of the USSR were then leading to the crumbling of communist ideology, the powers of the Kremlin were waning and profound economic and political reforms gaining pace. In response, the Belarusian communists, notoriously conservative and anti-nationalist, adopted a 'contingency plan' – they declared sovereignty.[6]

After the disbandment of the USSR in December 1991, nationalism was not embraced any further by the ruling Belarusian elite. At the same time, it became a political instrument of the opposition, albeit an instrument of limited utility in Belarusian conditions. The epicentre of political conflict in Belarus in the first years of independence shifted to questions of constitutional and economic reform. The Supreme Soviet rejected a referendum on prompt re-election advocated by the BNF, and demonstrated a strong resistance to market reforms. For the post-Soviet Belarusian elite, with its influence based on the Communist Party, heavy industry, collective farming and local administration, both prompt elections and market reforms would mean further erosion of its political base. As for foreign policy, here the post-communist strategy was taking clearer shape too. Unreformed Belarus could not count on substantial western assistance, whether economic or political. Therefore, Russia was the only viable alternative. It was also a comfortable option, since Russia had provided most of Belarus's natural resources during the Soviet period and still afforded a market for the ailing Belarusian economy. The pro-Russian orientation of Belarus's foreign policy of subsequent years took root.

The idea of Russian involvement was loathed by the BNF but was not seen as a problem by the public: an absolute majority harboured no anti-Russian feelings. For Kebich's government, a positive Russian response meant additional political leverage against the nationalist opposition.

Critical voices warned that Russia's support was being tacitly repaid by shares in the leading Belarusian enterprises (mostly oil refineries), cheap transit and an increase in the custom duties protecting Russian producers, as well as by Belarus's accession to the CIS collective military arrangements (the Tashkent Treaty). Yet these voices were far outweighed by the government-controlled media. An indirect cost of this 'Ostpolitik' was Belarus's decreasing leverage in relations with the rest of Europe, where it was increasingly perceived as a 'mere extension of Russia'.[7]

Belarus's foreign policy in 1993–4: consolidation of the pro-Russian shift

With Belarus's foreign policy increasingly formulated on the basis of domestic political struggle, polarisation between the government and the opposition on domestic issues meant further polarisation of their respective foreign policy agendas. By 1993, the cleavage was most apparent – and advances for one side inevitably meant losses for the other. What seemed to contradict national interests, let alone the constitutional principle of neutrality, was a logical continuation of the government's undertakings in its race against the nationalists and their plans for political and economic reform. From this point of view, foreign policy became instrumental and control over it – crucial.

In 1993–4, the pro-integration agenda was further accelerated by mounting economic difficulties, as it was by the approaching first presidential election. Russian support – in the form of cheap oil supplies and the promised monetary union – became a successful trump card. Two leading candidates in the election – Prime Minister Kebich and the head of the parliamentary committee on corruption, Lukashenka – were both 'Russophiles'. Kebich lost in the second run-off, haunted by allegations of dishonest enrichment and his part in the Belavezha process, and the economic deterioration of the early post-Soviet years. The winner, a vocal populist but barely known politician, promised to curb corruption and restore union with Russia. The success of the latter electoral promise owed much to Kebich's campaign waged against nationalist political forces and their 'back to Europe' rhetoric.

From Moscow's point of view, the Belarusian presidential election in May–June 1994 dispelled the worst Russian concerns about the victory of the Belarusian nationalist leader Pazniak. Nonetheless, Lukashenka's victory was not a pleasant surprise either. Populist, inexperienced, uncultured and explicitly authoritarian, he neither evoked political sympathy in Moscow nor inspired confidence in his ability to control the situation in Belarus. The initial reception of Lukashenka in the Kremlin was cold and highly distressing for him personally, since a close relationship with Russia had been his major electoral promise.[8] Furthermore, experiencing very much the same kind of pressure from the nationalist opposition as

Kebich had before him, Lukashenka needed Russian support as a means of political survival. He eventually won it – albeit with controversial consequences for the country.

External factors in the development of Belarus's foreign policy: Russia and NATO enlargement

It is by no means unusual that domestic politics – rather than abstractly understood national interests – has shaped the external relations of a newly independent state. The reverse has also been true. In particular, Russia's involvement in Belarusian politics – support for 'Russophile' politicians – was crucial to its development.

The nationalist-democratic forces in Belarus had no external support similar to that which the administrations of Kebich and Lukashenka received from Moscow, although attempts to find it had been made. The idea of a Black to Baltic Sea Union (to include the three Baltic States, Belarus and Ukraine), nurtured by the BNF and national fronts in the neighbouring countries, was one such endeavour. Although a non-starter, it had a more practical offspring – the project of a Black to Baltic Sea oil pipe, in which successive Belarusian governments refused to participate for fear of upsetting Moscow.[9] The declaration of neutrality and its associated proposals for the creation of a belt of neutral/non-nuclear states in Central and Eastern Europe were another attempt to secure transnational support for more nationalist politics. The latter, however, was not well received by Belarus's neighbours aspiring to NATO membership.

From a western perspective, Belarus represented little strategic or other interest and, naturally, western involvement was far smaller than Russian. However, this by no means meant the exclusion of Belarus from western programmes of assistance to the post-communist transition. Like other CIS states, Belarus was covered by the provisions offered by TACIS (an EU technical support project), the European Bank for Reconstruction and Development (EBRD) and the IMF, as well as by some more specific projects, such as the American Nunn-Lugar programme, for example. Belarus became a member of the NACC, was granted 'special guest' status by the Council of Europe (CoE) and was invited to participate in NATO's Partnership for Peace (PfP) initiative. All these engagements were supposed to help consolidate democratic trends in Belarus and encourage its transition to a market economy. By the same token, they meant tacit support for the Belarusian democratic forces. This support, however, did not prove sufficient. The government's policies estranged Belarus from the mainstream process of transition in the region, and in doing so directed the country's foreign policy strongly towards its eastern neighbour.

From a practical point of view, the relations between Belarus and Russia had to meet the interests of both. For Russia, it was doubtful if there were any purely economic benefits of close association with Belarus. Hence, strategic interests overruled economic reasoning on the part of the Kremlin.[10] There were significant limits to what Russia was prepared to offer in exchange for Belarus's loyalty. This was demonstrated by the fate of the Russia–Belarus monetary union, agreed upon in April 1994 but revoked by Russia soon after Lukashenka's election, on the pretext of structural differences between the two countries' economies.[11] Economic disparities, however, were coupled with political ones: Lukashenka was seen in Moscow as an awkward, if not embarrassing partner for the 'democrat' Yeltsin. Yet, with NATO enlargement into Central Europe becoming a realistic prospect, strategic factors outweighed all other Russian considerations.

NATO 'helped' Lukashenka to win recognition in Moscow by making its enlargement plans fully explicit in 1995: his offer of union became irresistible for the Kremlin as a means of rebutting the expansion of the western alliance. The moves towards Belarusian–Russian integration have produced fewer practical outcomes than the grandiose titles of the signed documents suggest. This was no coincidence: the Russians each time curtailed the number of draft provisions suggested by the Belarusian side – much to Lukashenka's displeasure.[12] Moscow's tactics consisted in minimising its commitment to Belarus in political and especially economic terms – which unambiguously suggests that expectations of a Russia–Belarus unification are unrealistic. Nonetheless, Russia's involvement in Belarusian affairs is deeper than seems on the surface. Putin, Yeltsin's successor as Russian President, is generally perceived to be less compromising on the issue of integration with Belarus.[13] Nonetheless, he and his government – like any future government in Russia – have to face the same geopolitical pressures as his predecessor: Russia's declining international influence and the encroachment of NATO. Russian strategists are also concerned about stability in the 'near abroad' – the possibility of political calamities and nationalist upheavals.[14] As far as Belarus is concerned, there is currently little chance for a peaceful democratic transfer of power from the current leadership: any prospect of change contains seeds of instability. Besides, any successor to Lukashenka is likely to be more 'nationally conscious', which creates a further predicament for Russia. In other words, from the Russian point of view 'regional stability' is best served by preserving the status quo in Belarus for as long as possible.

Belarus's relations with its non-Russian neighbours and the West

Belarus's relations with its other neighbours are constantly running into inevitable difficulties. As far as Poland, Lithuania and Latvia are concerned, Minsk never appreciated their aspiration to join NATO. Reciprocally, they never responded positively to Belarus's initiative for a nuclear weapon-free zone in the region. The three are negotiating their future membership of the EU (in which connection Poland has already put more restrictions on cross-border visits from Belarus). For the government in Minsk, the gradually approaching EU with its manifest ideology of liberal democracy and market economy is a constant source of discomfort. Continuing cross-border and long-distance travel, the influence of the foreign media, humanitarian contacts facilitated by western NGOs and access to the Internet all further stir critical moods in Belarus. At the same time, Poland and Lithuania are conscious of their informal 'democratising role' for Belarus. Since the BNF's founding congress in Vilnius in June 1989, Lithuania has been a window of opportunity for the Belarusian opposition – whether this concerned printing facilities, access to the television, or asylum for exiled Belarusian politicians. Poland has played a similar role by, among other things, promoting democratic opportunities among the Belarusian minority on its territory. 'Setting a good example' is a conscious strategy adopted by both countries.

Ukraine has less to offer through example, although it is certainly more successful than Belarus in its European policy. The two are strongly linked in many ways: historically, politically (through membership of the CIS), economically, culturally and personally – when it comes to people. Both pragmatically appreciate this and are cautious about the existing political and economic divisions (for example, Belarus's union-making with Russia puts pressure on Ukraine where some political forces would like to follow suit; Ukraine's close partnership with NATO has a similar effect on Belarus). Although criticism is regularly heard and reciprocated in Minsk and Kyiv, both prefer to avoid friction and focus on the economic aspects of bilateral cooperation. Overall, the Belarus–Ukraine relationship remains close but ambiguous.[15]

Belarus's relationship with the West has never been especially fruitful or easy, and for most of the time has been mediated by international institutions. From the early days of its independence Belarus 'lacked the international attention and appeal of Russia or Ukraine'.[16] Populated by just over ten million people and short of natural resources, it was neither a potentially significant market nor a supplier of strategic goods. Belarus stood out among its neighbours mainly in two respects: by quickly renouncing control of the former Soviet nuclear weapons on its territory, and by being placid and 'Russophile'. Leaving behind the controversial legacy of Stalin's territorial arrangements, Belarus settled the issue of borders with its neighbours quickly and effectively and, prior to Lukashenka's election, was never perceived internationally as a potential trouble spot. Consequently, the amount of international attention that the country received was often minimal.

There was, however, one important advantage for Belarus in its relations with the West and the rest of Europe – its relative geographic proximity. Immediately after gaining independence, Belarusian diplomacy rapidly developed a European dimension. Striving for recognition and international support, Belarus was establishing bilateral diplomatic relations with other countries; it signed the CSCE documents in winter–spring 1992, established diplomatic relations with the EC (EU) in August 1992 and, after having been granted special guest status in the Council of Europe in September 1992, applied for full membership in March of the following year. In March 1995 Belarus and the EU signed a Partnership and Co-operation Agreement, which, pending ratification by all EU members, was followed by an Interim Agreement. Benefits of the European 'vector' of Belarus's external relations were beyond dispute, and although it could not overshadow the importance of co-operation along post-Soviet lines,[17] Belarus did not see its future outside the broader European context (curiously enough, membership of the EU was officially announced as Belarus's distant foreign policy goal). The country was more cautious in its relations with NATO but nonetheless accepted PfP and other 'Atlantic' initiatives (NACC, EAPC). And, in the early independent years, Belarus's value as an international partner was demonstrated through notable diplomatic initiatives. The operation of the CIS co-ordinating centre in Minsk, the willingness to co-operate on arms control in Europe (START, CFE) and Belarus's initiative of hosting the CSCE group on Nagorno-Karabakh all helped to mark its presence in European politics.

However, difficulties in Belarus's relations with countries lying west of its borders quickly surfaced. They were exacerbated by its floundering transition and further affected by disagreements between Russia and NATO over their respective places in the new European security order. Belarus's opposition to NATO enlargement developed on political as well as psychological grounds: the country found itself at the centre of geopolitical clashes. NATO's military campaign over Kosovo increased concern, prompting rumours that Belarus might be 'next': President Lukashenka himself indicated the possibility of NATO strikes against Belarus.[18]

Even before the Kosovo campaign (during which Belarus followed the Russian line and suspended its contacts with NATO), the country's relationship with the alliance had been modest and uneasy at best. Belarus had never contemplated membership of the alliance, while constitutional provisions precluded it from 'co-operating on the ground' – sending troops in support of the UN- and NATO-led peacekeeping operations in the Balkans which all of its neighbours did. Slow and unenthusiastic, Belarus was the last to sign the PfP framework (January 1995) and did not present an individual programme of partnership until May 1997. The latter was quickly approved by NATO at its Madrid summit – at which the decision to enlarge was taken and Russia and Ukraine obtained special agreements with the alliance. Subsequently, Minsk asked for a similar privilege – a request incompatible with its own hostile rhetoric and dubious diplomacy.[19] In May 1999 the North Atlantic Standing Committee adopted a declaration in which Belarus was criticised over the situation regarding the observance of human rights and freedom of the mass media, and which refused to recognise President Lukashenka as a democratically elected head of state after his initial term expired on 20 July 1999.[20]

Similarly, little room is left for dialogue with other international institutions. The results of the referendum of November 1996, which extended President Lukashenka's term in office by two years, gave him extraordinary powers over the legislature and the Constitutional Court and replaced the Supreme Soviet with the People's Assembly of 110 handpicked deputies, were not recognised by any international organisation that was concerned with upholding democratic values. Thus, it became a common view that the Belarusian legislature cannot claim democratic legitimacy after November 1996. The former was enough for the CoE to suspend Belarus's application for full membership together with its special guest status. The OSCE Parliamentary Assembly refused to recognise the delegation of Lukashenka's appointees – an example followed by the North Atlantic Assembly. The EU suspended ratification of its agreement with Belarus in 1997 and froze the Interim provisions. The crisis which arose when Lukashenka tried to evict foreign diplomats from their compounds in Drazdy, a suburb of Minsk, in the summer of 1998, prompted the EU to freeze its TACIS Civil Society Development Programme – the last remaining major EU commitment to Belarus. Later, some rapprochement with the EU was achieved, but a milder moratorium on official contacts continues. The latest parliamentary elections in Belarus in October 2000 have been widely criticised as undemocratic and non-transparent and have led to continuing non-recognition of Belarus's main legislative body.

The OSCE has had a difficult time with Belarus as it has attempted to strike a compromise between the issues of legitimacy and official representation. Within this forum, only Russia has demonstrated full diplomatic support to official Minsk. Unlike most other international organisations, which simply reduced their contacts with Belarus, the OSCE preferred to be actively involved 'on the ground'. It opened an Advisory and Monitoring Group (AMG) in Minsk and attempted to initiate a dialogue between the authorities and the opposition (first of all the dissolved thirteenth Supreme Soviet whose legitimacy rests with the constitution of 1994). The OSCE's mediation resulted in some preliminary agreements concerning the opposition's limited access to the media and further negotiations, which, however, the Lukashenka administration soon rejected. The democratic-nationalist opposition was unhappy too because of the OSCE's recognition of the political status quo. Subsequently, many of the opposition leaders voiced despair at the OSCE's decision to send a limited observer mission to the October 2000 elections that they and their supporters were widely boycotting as undemocratic and unfair.

Since July 1999, the American and other individual western governments have been refusing to recognise the legitimacy of the current Belarusian government and have continued official relations with Minsk on only a *de facto* basis. Naturally, these individual and collective initiatives, the constant political pressure coming from Europe and the US to restore the democratic process and economic reforms in Belarus – a precondition for an improved relationship – continue to antagonise the Belarusian leadership, contribute to the fear of 'external enemies' and provoke warnings against interference with Belarus's 'internal affairs'. Meanwhile, Minsk continues to rely extensively on the political and economic support coming from Russia. It is also looking for new foreign policy opportunities. In summer 1999 President Lukashenka spoke strongly in favour of a 'multi-vector' foreign policy. This was commonly interpreted as a sign of Lukashenka's frustration about the slow progress with the Russia–Belarus Union, and left commentators wondering where Minsk could possibly find new partners when its relations with the US, Western and Central European capitals were at an all-time low. A year on, some new 'vectors' in Belarus's foreign policy came to light: Minsk has actively engaged in diplomatic exchange with Iraq, Cuba and Libya, while also intensifying its contacts with China.

Engaging with new partners: pragmatism or opportunism?

Minsk prides itself on its good relations with China, a distant but significant partner. During a visit by two high-level Chinese delegations to Belarus in July and September 2000, both sides repeatedly stressed their good relations and mutual interest in expanding trade, investment, technological, scientific and cultural co-operation. President Lukashenka called China Belarus's strategic partner and even suggested that his country was 'always ready to share with China whatever we have that is valuable, and we are even ready to launch joint projects in military research'.[21] How far this promise can be taken is difficult to say (not least because Russia would hardly remain neutral towards such potentially sensitive co-operation). The two countries also stress a wide commonality of political interests. In practical terms, however, this mainly amounts to hostility towards NATO, opposition to the proposed American National Missile Defence System, and the affirmation of each other's right to interpret freely international standards relating to human rights and political process and to dismiss western criticism on this issue.

Belarus's interest in developing economic links with China and other distant countries is understandable and fully justified. There is, however, also an obvious (and somewhat inevitable) tendency to look for prospective partners among the countries which find themselves in a similarly awkward international situation. It suffices to mention the festive inauguration of the Belarusian embassy in Baghdad attended by Deputy Prime Minister Zamiatalin, the warm reception of an official Iranian delegation, President Lukashenka's own visit to Cuba and Libya (all in August–September 2000) and the planned opening of the Belarusian embassy in Tripoli. The opening of permanent representations in Iraq and Libya in particular (at a time when there is no Belarusian consulate in Spain, a country that takes thousands of Belarusian children with Chernobyl-related health problems each summer for recuperative holidays) raises inevitable questions about political opportunism. This, however, is by no means only a recent impression. Perhaps the most eccentric diplomatic gesture was President Lukashenka's visit to Belgrade during the bombing campaign launched against Yugoslavia by NATO in 1999. The purpose of the visit remained somewhat unclear, but it clearly contained a message of support to the Yugoslav leadership (there was also discussion in Belarus at the time of whether Yugoslavia could join the Russia–Belarus union).

How significant is this trend on the part of Belarus to seek co-operation with countries, some of which are known as the 'rogue states', and to make provocative foreign policy gestures? Internationally this makes little real difference. From Belarus's point of view it only further limits its foreign policy options.

Looking to the future

Belarus's foreign policy will continue periodically to run into difficulties. For as long as the Belarusian government is unwilling to engage in an open dialogue with the western governments and with the democratic opposition at home (and it has insufficient motivation to do so), the West will not be interested in a higher-key co-operation. Western aid at present is scarce and mainly targets non-governmental sectors in an effort to bolster civil society. At the same time, the country's economic future is very uncertain and recovery is unthinkable without genuine western involvement.

For the foreseeable future, Russia remains central to Belarus's external relations. There is a slight prospect of change in this relationship. On the one hand, trust in Lukashenka is constantly becoming eroded among the Russian elite. On the other hand, the centre of gravity of political opposition in Belarus is gradually moving from the vocal nationalists to the politicians and parties of the more moderate Centre whom Russia may potentially be interested in supporting. However, the broader international context of Russia–NATO 'geopolitics' will remain very significant for the development of the Belarusian politics and may effectively preclude such 'realliance'.

On the whole the factors, both domestic and external, that have shaped Belarus's foreign policy in the past decade will continue to operate, keeping Belarus in the coming years what it is today – a country with a one-sided foreign policy. Speaking in terms of 'next generation politics', Belarus is likely to demonstrate a much greater degree of nationalism and national cohesion, with its foreign policy becoming more balanced or strongly pro-western. Young Belarusians are less nostalgic about the comfortable Soviet past and more nationally conscious, and those with stronger nationalist sentiments are often also more motivated to get involved with politics. Thus, slow evolution is more likely than a sudden radical change.

Conclusion

Belarus's experience of the past decade suggests that inasmuch as its external relations have been significant for the process of transition, they have generally not been supportive of the country's democratic prospects. While the West has been increasingly disengaging from Belarus, Russia has been and will remain its key partner. Belarus's strategic interest in Russia is underpinned by the logic of political struggle between the current Belarusian leadership and the nationalist-democratic opposition. Consequently, significant changes in Belarus's foreign policy remain as distant as the prospect of major political change within the country.

Notes

1 See 'Preface' to D. Marples, *Belarus: a denationalized nation* (Amsterdam: Harwood, 1999).
2 AI (Amnesty International), *Belarus: Dissent and Impunity*, report published 21 June 2000.
3 Marples, *Belarus: a denationalized nation.*
4 J. Zaprudnik, *Belarus at the Crossroads of History* (Oxford: Westview, 1993).
5 Marples, *Belarus: a denationalized nation*, p. 61.
6 K. Mihalisko, 'Belarus: Retreat to Authoritarianism', in K. Dawisha and B. Parrott (eds), *Democratic Changes and Authoritarian Reactions in Russia, Belarus, and Moldova* (Cambridge: Cambridge University Press, 1997), pp. 240–2.
7 P. Szyszlo, 'Post-Soviet Orphan: Central European security issues through the Belarusian prism', *Central Europe Review*, Vol. 1, No. 9 (23 August 1999).
8 Marples, *Belarus: a denationalized nation*, p. 110.
9 See Zaprudnik, *Belarus at the Crossroads of History*, p. 219; V. Kremen, 'The East Slav Triangle', in V. Baranovsky (ed.), *Russia and Europe: The emerging security agenda* (Oxford: Oxford University Press for SIPRI, 1997), p. 296.
10 A. Rozanov, 'Vneshniaia politika Belorussii: predstavleniia i real'nosti', *Pro et Contra*, Vol. 3 (1998), No. 2: 68–80.
11 Marples, *Belarus: a denationalized nation*, p. 110.
12 'Lukashenka Says Russia–Belarus Union Treaty Draft Is "Laughing Stock"', *RFE/RL* (*Radio Free Europe/Radio Liberty*) *Newsline*, 10 October 1999, http://www.rferl.org.
13 'Belarusian Official Says Putin Strengthening Union Opponents', *RFE/RL Newsline*, http://www.rferl.org.
14 See 'Kontseptsiia natsional'noi bezopasnosti Rossiiskoi Federatsii', approved by President Yeltsin on 17 December 1997, text published in *Rossiiskaia gazeta*, 26 December 1997.
15 'Ukraine Dismisses Lukashenka Criticism', *RFE/RL Newsline*, 29 October 1999, http://www.rferl.org; 'Ukrainian Communists Want Russia–Belarus Union Expanded', *RFE/RL Newsline*, 10 December 1999, http://www.rferl.org.
16 Marples, *Belarus: a denationalized nation*, p. 35.

17 See Kremen, 'The East Slav Triangle', p. 296; Rozanov, 'Vneshniaia politika Belorussii', p. 71.
18 Szyszlo, 'Post-Soviet Orphan'.
19 Rozanov, 'Vneshniaia politika Belorussii', p. 76.
20 'NATO Assembly Session In Warsaw Adopts Declarations On Kosovo, Belarus', *RFE/RL Newsline*, 1 June 1999, http://www.rferl.org, retrieved January 2000.
21 Reuters, 7 September 2000.

13 Belarus's relations with the European Union

A western perspective

*Teresa Dumasy**

Introduction

Hopes for the development of democracy, an open society and a working market economy in Belarus, which were entertained in Western Europe in 1991, have been disappointed over the last few years. Initial engagement with the European Union (EU) has fallen away under the presidency of Aliaksandr Lukashenka and Belarus has focused its foreign policy on reintegration with Russia. The level of co-operation between Belarus and the EU is now minimal and dialogue is difficult.

This chapter will take a look back at the relations between the EU and Belarus over the last ten years of Belarusian independence. It will examine the motives behind the EU's policy towards Belarus and explore why the European Union remains committed to engagement with Belarus despite setbacks in the relationship in more recent years. In addition, it will explore some of the challenges that western governments face, working on policy towards Belarus, and will look ahead at some of the factors for change in the future.

EU–Belarus relations since 1991

In 1991 the West initially gave a cautious welcome to the declarations of independence in Belarus, Ukraine and other former Soviet republics. This wary reaction stemmed from difficulty in coming to terms with the break-up of the Soviet Union and a fear that nationalist aspirations for independence would threaten the status of national minorities in these countries, none of which were homogeneous. The danger that this might lead to instability in the region was of particular concern given the presence of strategic nuclear weapons based on the territory of Ukraine and Belarus. However, fears of conflict and instability quickly receded as Ukraine and Belarus successfully managed the peaceful transition to independence. Soon western leaderships came to realise that national aspirations were in fact a positive force, which could assist the development of democracy in the former communist bloc. The European Community (EC)[1] hoped that, with newfound independence and western assistance, countries like Belarus within a number of years would successfully manage their transition to democracy and a working market economy.

In its first few years of independence, prospects for relations between Belarus and the European Community appeared to be good. Under the leadership of Stanislau Shushkevich, Chairman of the Belarusian Supreme Soviet, Belarus set out to co-operate with Europe and swiftly began to establish relations with key western European institutions. In February 1992, for example, Belarus acceded to the Conference on Security and Co-operation in Europe (CSCE)[2] and in August diplomatic relations were established with the European Community. In September Belarus gained 'special guest' status in the Council of Europe and in the course of the year became a member of the International Monetary Fund (IMF), the European Bank for Reconstruction and Development (EBRD) and the World Bank. Direct co-operation with the EC was envisaged through the signing of the Partnership and Co-operation Agreement (PCA) in 1994 and an Interim agreement on trade issues.

At the same time, Belarus played a central role in the creation of the Commonwealth of Independent States (CIS). On 8 December 1991, Shushkevich, along with the future President of Ukraine, Leonid Kravchuk and head of the Russian Federation Boris Yeltsin, signed the Belavezha accords, establishing the Commonwealth of Independent States (CIS) and effectively ending the Soviet Union. Subsequently the CIS Secretariat was set up in Minsk. At the outset, however, the efforts to retain links with Russia and Ukraine were not seen to contradict Belarus's European orientation. Good relations with Russia were, and still remain, a political and strategic necessity. Moreover, rather than ensuring the continuation of the USSR, for Belarus and other CIS states, the Commonwealth has primarily been a forum for discussion and a means for economic co-operation.

The West was reassured by the declaration of non-nuclear status made by Belarus in 1992 and by the speed with which Belarus relinquished its strategic nuclear weapons inherited after the collapse of the Soviet Union. Belarus's decision to remove all nuclear weapons from its territory was welcomed as contributing to stability and security in Europe and the country began to benefit from substantial US and European financial and technical assistance. Since Belarus had borne the brunt of the Chernobyl disaster, particular international effort was devoted to drawing attention to the extensive environmental, economic and social consequences of the accident for the country.

Owing to its co-operative attitude over the nuclear issue, Belarus did not attract the same degree of attention, albeit negative, in its early years of independence as Ukraine. Ukraine adopted a far more belligerent stance over relinquishing its stocks of nuclear weapons, and its demands for adequate compensation and western assistance in return earned it the image of a 'problem country' in the eyes of the West. Instead Belarus's compliance over nuclear disarmament and willingness to co-operate with Europe presented a false impression to western policy-makers of the true strength of commitment to a Europe-oriented foreign policy. Indeed, contrary to appearances, in Belarus there was weak public understanding of the foreign policy agenda, and remote elite interest in pro-European policy-making in particular. Unlike other western republics in the former Soviet Union, during the Gorbachev era Belarus's elites had not actively sought independence from Moscow. Moreover, the key issues championed in the campaign of the nationalist opposition movement, the Belarusian Popular Front (BNF), were those of Chernobyl and the perceived neglect of Belarus by Moscow. This has consequently resulted in the nationalists' manifesto of national sovereignty and European foreign policy, which, however, did not find much support amongst the general population. To this day, opinions vary as to the strength of popular feeling on Belarusian independence, as well as to the strength of opposition to the Belarus–Russia Union.

Belarus was also hampered in its development of a pro-European foreign policy by a number of other factors. Economic ties with Russia were extremely important to Belarus particularly given trade barriers with Western Europe and Belarus's energy dependence on Russia. Closer relations with Russia and the CIS countries remained vital to Belarus as governments of CIS countries began to seek ways of reducing trade barriers between these countries and increasing economic co-operation. Practical problems also hindered Belarus in the field of diplomacy and policy-making. On gaining independence, Belarus lacked both the financial means and the trained and experienced personnel capable of formulating and conducting an independent foreign policy. Under the Soviet Union, the Belarusian Foreign Ministry had played a symbolic role, and officials merely followed foreign policy directives received from Moscow. The country was therefore ill-prepared for its sudden entry on to the international stage.

Internal political developments also played a central role in the republic's external relations. While the centrist politician Shushkevich was receptive to the West's drive to establish relations with Belarus, as a head of the legislature he did not wield sufficient authority to impose his will on foreign policy. In the course of 1993 Shushkevich was increasingly sidelined by Prime Minister Kebich, who controlled the government and was supported by the largest, conservative faction in parliament. In contrast to Shushkevich, Kebich advocated closer relations with Russia, including the establishment of monetary union and participation in the CIS Collective Security Pact. In January 1994 Shushkevich was removed by a majority parliamentary vote and replaced by the Chairman of the National Security Council, Miacheslau Hryb. Even as Belarus signed a Partnership and Co-operation Agreement with the EU later that year, the period of balance in Belarus's foreign policy between Europe and Russia appeared in doubt.

The consequent deterioration of Belarus's relations with the EU coincided with the election in July 1994 of President Aliaksandr Lukashenka, who chose to pursue a more radical foreign policy goal than Kebich of 'unification' with Russia. In itself, the shift towards Russia was not the trigger to this downturn in relations, rather the internal anti-democratic developments within Belarus, criticised by the West, and the distinctly anti-western character of Lukashenka's foreign policy. Lukashenka is suspicious of western financial institutions and resents what he perceives as western 'interference' in Belarus's internal affairs. Such views appear to resonate with a large section of Belarusian society. Consequently, however, areas of common ground and attitude have diminished as Belarus rejected the ideas and principles of liberal democracy and a market economy espoused by western European countries and institutions.

Co-operation between the EU and Belarus first began to falter in 1995 over Belarus's application for full membership of the Council of Europe. Negotiations over its accession were delayed following concerns over the conduct of the parliamentary elections that year. Finally, in January 1997, following the referendum on changes to the Constitution and the extension of Lukashenka's term in office by two years, declared unconstitutional by the Belarusian Constitutional Court and deemed illegitimate and undemocratic by the European Union and the US, Belarus's 'special guest' status in the Council of Europe was suspended.

Opposition to the changes under the referendum amongst EU countries, as well as concerns over lack of democratisation and over human rights violations, have had a knock-on effect for most areas of co-operation with Belarus since 1996. In reaction to the developments, on 15 September 1997 the EU General Affairs Council (GAC) adopted a number of conclusions, which form the basis of EU policy towards Belarus today. In its conclusions, the Council affirmed its support for efforts towards democratisation, including attempts to set up an OSCE Advisory and Monitoring Group in Belarus,[3] but criticised the lack of progress on political and economic reform and expressed its concern at the political and constitutional situation, as well as violations of human rights. The text read:

> The Council deplores the lack of progress in recent months on the plans for political and economic reform. It continues to be especially concerned by the political and constitutional situation and by the recurrent violations of human rights and fundamental freedoms, in particular the freedom of the media.

It also criticised the 'non-constructive, indeed obstructive, attitude to its relations with the European Union'.[4]

Under the GAC conclusions a number of policy measures were adopted in an effort to push Belarus towards democratisation and economic reform: bilateral ministerial contacts were, in principle, to be established solely through the EU Troika; technical assistance programmes, other than humanitarian or regional projects or those which directly support the democratisation process, were cancelled; conclusion of the Partnership and Co-operation Agreement and the Interim agreement was halted; and member states agreed not to support Belarus's accession to the Council of Europe.

However, the increased pressure on Belarus from the EU measures failed to have their desired effect, and, bolstered by support from within Russia and Belarus, Lukashenka refused to back down. Relations with the EU hit their lowest ebb in 1998 over the 'Drazdy affair' when EU ambassadors were withdrawn after a number of ambassadors, including those from France, Germany and Italy, were forced to leave their diplomatic residences, located close to Lukashenka's own presidential residence.[5] By the end of 1998 an agreement was reached for their return, but progress in building bridges since that time has been painstakingly slow. During the early months of 1999 the EU grew increasingly concerned by the growing polarisation between the government and the opposition, led by the former members of the thirteenth Supreme Soviet. There were concerns that the internal political situation would be aggravated by the opposition's plans to stage unofficial presidential elections in May, according to the timetable in the 1994. As a result, in an effort to inject some movement into the dialogue between the EU and Belarus and to revive co-operation in the field of democratisation and economic reform, in the spring the EU decided to try to encourage progress by adopting a policy of 'benchmarks'. This ties specific actions by the Belarusian government on constitutional and human rights issues to specific responses by the EU, which would be of benefit to Belarus. However, so far these new proposals have produced little consistent progress.

Yet while the level of co-operation between the EU and Belarus has been reduced to a minimum over the last few years, there is no sign that the EU is about to abandon its interest in Belarus or its efforts, however limited, to encourage democratisation and market reform. Five EU member countries maintain embassies in Minsk despite the Drazdy incident,[6] and this has been reinforced by regular visits by senior officials from the wider EU, sometimes in the Troika format. The adoption of the 'benchmarks' policy illustrates the EU's commitment to encouraging peaceful opposition and a regard for human rights in the country. This commitment is clearly based on the hope that, in the short or long term, healthy, working relations might be established between Belarus and the EU.

Behind the EU policy towards Belarus

Given the poor record of relations between the EU and Belarus, it is worth examining the motives behind the EU's policy towards the country. First, interest in Belarus stems from a basic acceptance by the EU of

Belarus's strategic position in the region. This is particularly important given the prospect of EU enlargement. Three states sharing a common border with Belarus (Poland, Lithuania and Latvia) have been invited to begin the accession process to the EU. Poland hopes to achieve full membership within the next few years. The process of enlargement raises a number of concerns for the EU and for the accession countries, including questions of border security and visa regimes, problems of illegal migration, cross-border smuggling and crime. Poland, in particular, is concerned by the 'civilisational' as well as the economic divide which is developing on its eastern border with Belarus and Ukraine, and fears that, unless addressed properly and urgently, EU enlargement will only serve to widen this gap.

The EU is currently examining these issues as far as they concern Ukraine, Russia and Moldova, through PCA processes, for example, but poor dialogue and co-operation with Belarus hinders efforts to examine the potential problems. Currently no forum exists where such issues might be discussed. Lukashenka himself has tended to focus on the perceived security threat to Belarus from the expansion of NATO, particularly following the conflict in Kosovo. Hopes for the country's economic recovery have been pinned on the potential of the Belarus–Russia Union, and this, combined with a generally low level of understanding of the EU and of the implications of expansion, have meant that the EU has been perceived by Lukashenka as a lesser threat. Yet for associate and full members, the question of the EU's eastern border is of great importance.

Economic reform in Belarus is also seen as vital to stability in the region as a whole. In Ukraine and Russia, political forces, nostalgic for the relative economic security of the Soviet Union, often appeal for a return to economic policies of the past. Such ideas have wide appeal amongst those with poor living standards, appalled by high levels of corruption and disaffected with what they see as 'capitalism'. There is a concern that Belarus, by clinging to many aspects of the Soviet system, may drag back other societies trying to move towards some form of democratic society and market economy. While economic performance in Belarus has appeared more respectable than in some other CIS countries, living standards have deteriorated steadily over the last few years and, as is widely acknowledged in the West, the current economic policies pursued by the Lukashenka government are not sustainable in the long term and are unlikely to ensure Belarus's economic recovery. The danger of social unrest through economic decline and poor living standards therefore raises concerns for stability in the region.

Moreover, Belarus represents a potential market for European companies interested in trade and investment. Western companies recognise the attractions in Belarus, not least a highly skilled and low-cost workforce. Yet current conditions for foreign firms wishing to operate in Belarus deter many from launching or developing operations there, thus depriving Belarus of much-needed investment and foreign currency. Compared to its neighbours Poland and Lithuania, Belarus's level of trade with the United Kingdom alone is extremely low. In 1999 the value of UK exports to Belarus amounted to around £27 million, whereas exports to Poland were over £1 billion and to Lithuania £95 million. Import figures reveal a similar pattern. Last year imports to the UK from Belarus amounted to only £21 million, yet the same figure for Poland was almost £693 million and for Lithuania £163 million.[7] Trade figures with Germany are somewhat higher, but the majority of Belarusian goods continue to go to the poorer countries of the CIS, and in particular Russia. In 1998 Belarusian exports to CIS countries represented 73.7 per cent of the overall figure for exports, of which 65 per cent went to Russia.[8] Furthermore, rather than seeing the potential benefits of foreign investment for the economy, Lukashenka has regarded western businessmen and investors with suspicion. Little has been done to create a favourable economic and legal environment for foreign companies, which in turn has meant that Belarus has lost opportunities to other developing economies.

As regards Belarus's relations with Russia, while the EU continues to take an interest in the development of the Belarus–Russia Union and Lukashenka's aspiration to integrate the two countries' economies, the EU position on the Union itself has been neutral. Many of the provisions of the Union Treaty mirror those in the EU itself, providing, for example, for a single market, customs union and a common currency. In addition, polls on public support for some degree of unification (rarely defined) present an unclear picture to the West of the strength of Belarusian national identity and of popular commitment to independence. Yet, while all states are free to make alliances, it is clearly important for Belarus that any decision on a union be democratically endorsed and there are concerns that the necessary conditions for this do not currently exist.

Looking ahead

There is clearly a danger, present in the minds of western policy-makers as Belarus's western neighbours gradually align their domestic policies and institutions with the EU's Copenhagen criteria for EU accession, that Belarus will become increasingly isolated. Relations between Belarus and Ukraine are not close, and have been coloured by Kuchma's insistence on Ukraine's European path and rejection of any suggestion of membership of the Belarus–Russia Union. Beyond its ties with Russia, which dominate political and economic foreign relations, Belarus has nurtured relations with countries in the Middle East and Asia in order to secure vital revenue from commercial contracts, including in the field of defence. Belarus has few other strong bilateral relations or allies. The EU therefore faces the challenge of delivering a policy which will both keep open channels of communication and convey a strong message of the need for democratisation and economic reform.

Over the last few years, the lack of significant economic and commercial interest in Belarus from Western Europe has allowed the EU to pursue a consistently tough line on democracy and human rights. However, beyond sporadic periods of dialogue and optimism, this has produced little consistent improvement in relations or in the level of democracy in Belarus. In 1999 hopes for progress were raised when Lukashenka, frustrated by Russia's foot-dragging over the Union, indicated that he wished to improve relations with the West. Rather than heralding a shift in policy, however, it soon became clear that this was intended to push Russia into speeding up the process of integration. There was also optimism last September when the Belarusian government agreed to begin preliminary round-table talks with the opposition and non-governmental organisations, mediated by the OSCE. Lukashenka appointed Mikhail Sazonau as his official representative to the talks, which were aimed to establish agreement on the conditions and procedures for free and fair parliamentary elections in October 2000, including a revised electoral code and the opposition's rights of access to the state media and to determine the functions of the future parliament. While a set of arrangements was accepted for opposition access to the media on 5 November, before the end of the month they were rejected by Lukashenka and on 7 December, the day before the signing of the Union Treaty with Russia, Sazonau was dismissed. Lukashenka subsequently abandoned OSCE-mediated talks, and proceeded with direct dialogue between government and representatives of civil society. However, the majority of opposition parties refused to participate directly.

Such false moves and about-turns by Lukashenka have instilled scepticism amongst some in the West towards the sincerity of any expression by Belarus of desire for rapprochement with the EU. In the eyes of some western commentators, Lukashenka is both unwilling and unable to change. He has identified himself so closely with unification with Russia, and harbours such deep mistrust of the West, that it is impossible for him to redress the balance in foreign policy and to permit a move domestically towards a policy based on western values. Clearly, however, such an attitude leaves little room for dialogue or movement in relations and dictates a passive policy based on hope for a future, more democratic leader, more amenable to the West.

Equally, one might see in Lukashenka's unpredictability, opportunities for initiatives in relations with Belarus. Both internal and external pressures on Belarus could conceivably produce a change in foreign policy towards greater co-operation with Europe. One of the strongest internal pressures would come from the economy. While the population has continued to receive wages and pensions on time over the last few years, there has been a significant deterioration in living standards, a surge in inflation and an increase in shortages of consumer goods. This is particularly significant in a country which enjoyed a higher standard of living under the Soviet Union, and where Lukashenka has made promises of economic prosperity part of his campaign rhetoric. Discontent amongst the population with the prevailing economic situation, expressed in public protest or strikes, might therefore increase pressure for co-operation with the richer economies of Western Europe. In the course of 1999 there were signs of mounting popular discontent, with increasing independent trade union protest and organised strikes against the decline in living standards and restrictions on private economic activity. Independent trade unions have taken up the fundamental economic concerns of the population which have been neglected by political parties and in so doing they have attracted significant popular support. In addition, the strength of public protests against the internal political situation, in particular against violations of human rights, as well as the planned union with Russia, has also been growing over the past year, and the combination of discontent with both the economic and political situation could represent a powerful force for change.

At present, popular opinion about the internal situation and the way forward is not accurately reflected in the national parliament by elected representatives. Flaws in the electoral process continue to discriminate against the more critical voices in society. In 2000 the international community, and in particular the OSCE Advisory and Monitoring Group in Belarus, focused its efforts on attempts to work with the Belarusian authorities, opposition parties, and civil society to correct these deficiencies. However, little concrete progress was made. On the basis of a decision by the OSCE/Office for Democratic Institutions and Human Rights (ODIHR) Technical Conference in Vienna on 30 August, a Technical Assessment Mission conducted a four-week assessment visit to Belarus prior to the legislative elections on 15 October.[9] The Mission's Statement of Preliminary Findings and Conclusions was issued by the OSCE/ODIHR on 16 October and criticised in particular: fundamental deficiencies in the electoral legislation; the executive's excessive control over electoral commissions; candidate registration procedures, which were abused to prevent 'undesirable' candidates from participating; the authorities' monopoly over the media; and the excessive use of the early voting procedure. The overall conclusion, supported by the US and the EU, was that the elections failed to meet the minimum international standards for holding 'free, fair, equal, accountable, and transparent elections'.

However, despite the significant shortcomings of the elections, the OSCE recognised that measures had been taken by the Belarusian authorities, and that they represented limited progress towards greater transparency in the electoral process. In particular, a registration appeals process, open to public scrutiny, had been established. There were more opportunities for observation by domestic observers, and some opposition figures had been allowed on to election commissions as observers. Some leading opposition figures had been allowed to advocate a boycott without being subject to prosecution, or to stand for election without hindrance. Such measures have given the EU cause for optimism and have reinforced arguments to remain engaged in dialogue with Belarus. In a statement on 17 October, OSCE Chairperson-in-Office, Ferrero-Waldner, outlined the four substantive criteria, agreed by European institutions for free and democratic elections, which would serve as the basis for further democratic reforms leading to the presidential elections in 2001: greater transparency of the election process; a climate of confidence and trust; regular access to state-controlled electronic mass media for opposition parties; and, above all, the strengthening of the functions of the parliament. While progress will undoubtedly be slow, the EU and European institutions have resolved to encourage and work with the Belarusian authorities to address these key aspects of the electoral process.

In contrast to the European community, Russia gave unequivocal support to Belarus at the time of the legislative elections, refuting claims that they had been undemocratic. Russia's role in influencing the direction of Belarus's foreign policy is pivotal, and it may be that the key external pressure for a shift in foreign policy towards Europe will come from Russia. In the absence of its own energy sources, the Belarusian economy remains wholly dependent on Russian supplies. So far Russia has been willing to continue the cheap supply of gas to Belarus. In practice, much of this has been free of charge, since Belarus struggles to meet its energy debts and repayment, if made at all, has often been in the form of barter arrangements. The continuation of such support is currently vital to the Belarusian economy. Given Russia's dependence on Belarus as a transit route for gas to Western Europe and Belarus's strategic importance to Russia, it is unlikely that, under President Putin, the terms for energy supply will alter dramatically. Yet should, at some point, Putin's Russia choose to pursue a more pragmatic policy in the interests of its own ailing economy, demanding, for instance, from Belarus, Ukraine and Moldova, cash payments for gas supplies and clearance of debts, this may act as a force for change in economic and also foreign policy in Belarus.

Equally, the formation of the Belarus–Russia Union is unlikely to proceed as quickly as hoped and tensions over the shape of the Union between the two sides might affect Belarus's attitude towards the West. Already President Lukashenka's purported ambitions to head a Belarusian–Russian state, and even to run for the Russian presidency have been disappointed. Furthermore the Union Treaty was based on Russia's own preferences and makes no provision for either the unification of two sovereign states, or for the post of a president of the Union with executive powers over and above the heads of the participating states. While the Treaty is far-reaching in its vision of economic integration, to date the two sides have been slow to implement existing agreements on economic co-operation, and measures such as monetary union will require significant economic and legislative changes, particularly on the part of Belarus, in order to align the two economies in readiness for its introduction. As mentioned earlier, Russia's foot-dragging over the Treaty and the implementation of existing agreements has frustrated Lukashenka and on occasions led him to threaten to redirect foreign policy towards the West. While there is scepticism in the EU as to the sincerity of such threats, the combination of other internal and international pressures might converge to incite real change at a time of difficulty in relations between Russia and Belarus.

Conclusion

Clearly the EU has a genuine interest in maintaining and developing relations with Belarus as the enlargement process goes ahead. To date, the policy of restricted relations over the last three years in protest against the lack of democratisation and economic reform in Belarus has not produced the serious moves towards reform and co-operation desired by the EU. Rather it has coincided with a period of determined rapprochement with Russia. The West's strong criticism of the political developments in Belarus since 1996 and the consequent restrictions on co-operation and diplomatic relations have reinforced Lukashenka's anti-western attitudes and he has remained largely impervious to EU pressure. Rather than recognising, even indirectly, any justification for EU criticism, Lukashenka has denounced the EU's lack of understanding of and interference in Belarusian internal affairs. The EU's concerted policy towards Belarus has also helped Lukashenka to strengthen his image, popular amongst some Belarusians and in some Russian regions, as a stalwart of the 'brotherhood of Slavic nations' and as a defender against creeping western influence. The economic benefits to Belarus of developing trade links with the western European countries and encouraging inward investment remain distant prospects, rather than existing channels via which to engage both the Belarusian and EU governments.

The emphasis of the European conditions for re-establishing relations with Belarus has been on political and constitutional factors, and it is obviously these elements that are the most unpalatable for President Lukashenka. For besides criticising the overall deterioration in democratic standards over the last few years, the EU has disputed the legitimacy of Lukashenka's position by recognising only the 1994 Belarusian Constitution and not the amendments to it by referendum in 1996, and by accepting the thirteenth Supreme Soviet, disbanded in 1996, as the sole legitimate parliament. This, the EU's refusal to entertain high-level bilateral visits and, in particular, the encouragement of peaceful opposition activity have been taken as a personal affront by Lukashenka, and even as a threat to his position. It is little wonder, therefore, that Russia represents a far more agreeable partner for Lukashenka in foreign relations. In 1996, and again in 1999, at the time of the 'alternative' presidential election organised by the opposition in Belarus in line with the election timetable of 1994, and more recently in October 2000, Russia has given its support to Lukashenka. On these occasions and others, and over issues such as human rights, Russia has acted as an important counterweight to western criticism. However, alliance with Russia has brought little improvement in the economic situation and merely allowed Belarus to subsist. In the longer term, the decline in the economy and living standards may act as a driving force for co-operation with Europe from within Belarus.

The EU's relations with Belarus are in direct contrast to those with Belarus's southern neighbours, Ukraine and Moldova, whose leaderships have made certain efforts to prioritise pro-EU foreign policy, with the aim of joining it as full members sometime in the future. Membership of European institutions, such as the Council of Europe, has been seen, at least in leadership circles, as the key to adapting to western European standards of democracy and to acceptance as a European state, as well as to opening doors to assistance from international financial institutions. While relations between Ukraine and the EU are not always smooth, as a result of its clear pro-European stance Ukraine has benefited from substantial economic and technical assistance and political support. Discussion and co-operation on the impact of EU enlargement between EU full and prospective member states and Ukraine has also begun. Yet Ukraine's pro-European orientation has not precluded collaboration with Russia, with whom Ukraine has been careful to cultivate friendly and co-operative relations. Membership of any union with Belarus and Russia has been ruled out for the time being, however, and for the current leadership, co-operation and eventual integration with the EU is perceived to be in Ukraine's long-term strategic and economic interests.

For various historical, political and economic reasons, some of which have been highlighted here, Belarus has not chosen such a path, although Ukraine's example shows that engagement with Europe depends largely on the political will of the leadership. Indeed, a future change in the Belarusian leadership might well alter the direction of the country's foreign policy. For Belarus, however, alliance with Russia may always remain a greater priority than for Ukraine, given the differences in the strength of the national consciousness between the two, and other strategic and economic factors. While defending internationally accepted norms of democracy and human rights, EU policy must be sensitive to such national differences and the scale of difficulties facing Belarus and other fledgling democracies. It must take into account the fact that, as young states, Belarus and other former Soviet republics are poorly equipped to cope with massive internal problems, the majority of which were inherited from the Soviet period and which would test any established democracy in Western Europe. Recognising these difficulties, expectations entertained ten years ago within the EU for the pace of reforms have now become more realistic, and the EU has chosen to tailor its policy towards Belarus to avoid rigid formulae and to encourage change. Despite Lukashenka's apparent lack of interest, the European community recognises the need to keep open channels of communication.

This is in contrast to the United States, which has adopted a more condemnatory line towards Belarus than the EU over the last few years. Most recently the USA refused, for example, to arrange any form of election monitoring for the 2000 legislative elections, judging that this would only have lent legitimacy to a flawed election process. Consequently, contact and dialogue between the Belarusian and US authorities have been reduced to a minimum with little prospect of movement on either side. For the European community, however, relations with Belarus are a European issue of immediate relevance. The EU will therefore continue to seek the normalisation of relations with Belarus, and seize opportunities for co-operation as they arise.

As a final point, it is worth noting that the EU itself is an organisation in transformation. The prospective accession of Poland, Hungary, the Czech Republic and the Baltic States to the EU poses a host of practical challenges and the latest wave of invitations to other states to begin accession negotiations raises broader questions of the direction, scope and structure of the organisation over the next few decades. In this respect, Belarus's future place in a wider Europe will fit into a more general debate on the vision for the future of the EU. It falls also to Belarusian policymakers to decide whether Belarus should seek its place in this new European landscape and reap the benefits of normalisation in relations with European institutions.

Notes

* Dr Teresa Dumasy was formerly Senior Research Officer for Ukraine, Belarus, and Moldova at the Foreign and Commonwealth Office, London. The views expressed here are personal and should not be taken to represent government policy.

1 As of 1993, the European Union (EU).

2 As of 1995, the Organisation for Security and Co-operation in Europe (OSCE).

3 The OSCE AMG began work in Minsk in February 1998.

4 *General Affairs Council Conclusions* (Brussels), 15 September 1997.

5 Other embassy residences were also affected by the move, including those of the US, Japanese, Polish, Russian and Lithuanian ambassadors. The US and Japanese ambassadors were withdrawn and the Lithuanian and Polish ambassadors were recalled temporarily for 'consultations'.

6 France, Germany, Italy, Greece and the UK.

7 Figures produced by the East European Trade Council.

8 Figures from the Economist Intelligence Unit, *Belarus Country Report* (First Quarter, 2000).

9 The OSCE/ODIHR Technical Conference of 30 August 2000 decided that no observers were to be deployed on election day. They assessed that provisions

for early voting, mobile ballot boxes, the vote count and aggregation of results fell 'far short of minimum transparency requirements for independent verification', and that 'even in the best of circumstances, election day proceedings could not remedy these fundamental shortcomings'. OSCE/ODIHR Technical Assessment Mission, *Statement of Preliminary Findings and Conclusions* (15 October 2000).

Afterword

The presidential election of September 2001

Official Results of the Presidential Election in Belarus, 9 September 2001:

Aliaksandr Lukashenka: 75.6 per cent
Uladzimir Hancharyk: 15.4 per cent
Siargey Haidukevich: 2.5 per cent
Turnout: 83.9 per cent.[1]

On 9 September 2001 Belarus witnessed the second presidential election since independence. As shown above, this resulted in the re-election of Aliaksandr Lukashenka as President of Belarus for a second five-year term, with a massive majority. Before the election, western commentators had trusted that the election would be democratic, free and fair, and many people in Belarus had hoped that the result would reverse the trend towards dictatorship. This, nevertheless, did not occur, and realistically never could have occurred in a country where authoritarian structures are so robust. 'This was a brilliant, elegant, and persuasive victory', Lukashenka commented one hour *before* the closure of polling stations, and when no official election results had yet been released.[2] Since, as this book demonstrates, in pre-election polls Lukashenka had the the support of between 40 and 50 per cent of the electorate, the additional 25 per cent which he claimed to have won was highly questionable and vulnerable to allegations of fraud. The high turnout of 83.9 per cent was reportedly achieved by ordering students and civil servants to cast a vote, and by the selective manipulation of elderly rural voters by election officials.[3]

The OSCE's preliminary conclusions suggest that there were fundamental flaws in the electoral process, of which many were *specific* to the political situation in Belarus.[4] These included:

- A political regime that is not accustomed to opposition and does everything in its power to block it;
- Executive structures with extensive powers, including rule by presidential decree, that are not balanced with commensurate legislative controls, and that allow the electoral environment to be arbitrarily changed;

- A legislative framework that still fails to ensure the independence of election administration bodies, the integrity of the voting results tabulation process, and free and fair campaign conditions, and imposes excessive restrictions on campaigning and observers;
- Legal provisions for early voting which do not guarantee the proper control and counting of early votes;
- An election administration system that is overly dependent on the executive branch of government from the national to the local community levels, and is partisan;[5]
- A campaign environment seriously to the disadvantage of the opposition candidates;
- A campaign of intimidation directed against opposition activists, domestic observation organisations, opposition and independent media, and a smear campaign against international observers; and
- Highly biased state-controlled media and censorship of the independent print media.

So, what was 'specific' about the political situation in Belarus? We hope that this book will leave the reader with some definite answers. We also hope to demonstrate that Belarus's situation is highly complex and needs sophisticated explanations to account for its 'double standards' – namely, a seemingly stable economy which is nevertheless on the brink of collapse; a 'democratically' elected, though authoritarian leadership; the ostensible espousal of human rights by the government in the shadow of allegations about regime death squads abducting and assassinating political opponents; and full dependence on Russia through political and economic union.

White House press secretary Ari Fleischer, in his judgement of the Belarusian election, noted that 'Not only did Aliaksandr Lukashenka, Europe's last dictator, [steal] the elections from the Belarusian people . . . for the moment, he also stole their opportunity to return to a path towards democracy and a free-market economy.'[6]

This, however, is a misleading statement, which overlooks the fact that elections in Belarus took place *freely*, but under *unfair* circumstances. On 9 September 2001 the Belarusian people were given the opportunity to *ratify* the institutional, structural and cultural circumstances dictated to them – not to elect an alternative. Ironically, however, despite allegations of election rigging, it was highly likely that Lukashenka would have won the election in any case because of his popularity, especially among the poor, the old and the rural population. As this book demonstrates, there was no obvious single opposition leader in Belarus comparable to Kostunica in Serbia capable of challenging President Lukashenka, and although the fragmented opposition finally agreed to support Uladzimir Hancharyk, a relatively conservative trade union leader who is not affiliated to any political party, this belated consensus was reportedly only achieved under considerable pressure from the US government.[7] Overall, the USA provided aid of about $50 million to various opposition organisations, including the student leader Aleksei Shidlovsky, whose 'Zubr' ('Bison') movement was modelled on the Serb student organisation 'Otpor'. However, at least in the short term, Lukashenka's undoubted popularity, the efficiency of his secret police who instantly tore down opposition posters, along with the divisions of the opposition, all combined to prevent US intervention from creating similar conditions to those which helped the Serbian opposition to overthrow Miloševich. Nevertheless, Lukashenka himself indirectly acknowledged that the situation may change in the future: a day after his claimed victory he stated that the revolution against him had collapsed, 'or at least been postponed'.[8]

Sincc the elections, hundreds of Belarusians have demonstrated in Minsk, answering a call from Uladzimir Hancharyk to protest against the result. The conclusions which Lukashenka will draw from such continuing democratic opposition and the choices the future holds for the Belarusian people are as yet unknown, but it is possible that the next free election or referendum in Belarus may lead to the installation of Lukashenka as the 'President for life' of this small but strategically important Eastern European country.

Notes

1 http://www.rec.gov.by/index.php.
2 P. Cockburn, 'Belarus re-elects president amid vote-rigging row', *Independent*, 11 September 2001.
3 *RFE/RL Newsline*, Vol. 5, No. 171, Part II, 10 September 2001.
4 OSCE Statement of Preliminary Findings and Conclusions, http://www.osce.org/Belarus, retrieved 15 September 2001.
5 Cockburn, 'Belarus re-elects president', cites Lidia Ermoshina, the head of the commission which organised the elections, as saying that she would 'consider it a personal tragedy' if President Lukashenka were not returned.
6 *RFE/RL Newsline*, Vol. 5, No. 177, Part II, 18 September 2001.
7 See I. Traynor, 'Belarussian foils dictator-buster ... for now', *Guardian*, 14 September 2001, on the alleged activities of the US ambassador to Belarus, Michael Kozak.
8 Ibid.

Index

For Product Safety Concerns and Information please contact our EU representative GPSR@taylorandfrancis.com
Taylor & Francis Verlag GmbH, Kaufingerstraße 24, 80331 München, Germany

www.ingramcontent.com/pod-product-compliance
Ingram Content Group UK Ltd.
Pitfield, Milton Keynes, MK11 3LW, UK
UKHW021720240926
475702UK00029BA/1705
* 9 7 8 0 3 6 7 0 2 6 8 9 9 *